*How to Put Together
a Real Estate Syndicate
or Joint Venture*

How to Put Together a Real Estate Syndicate or Joint Venture

DANIEL S. BERMAN

Prentice-Hall, Inc.
Englewood Cliffs, N.J.

Prentice-Hall International, Inc., *London*
Prentice-Hall of Australia, Pty. Ltd., *Sydney*
Prentice-Hall Canada, Inc., *Toronto*
Prentice-Hall of India Private Ltd., *New Delhi*
Prentice-Hall of Japan, Inc., *Tokyo*
Prentice-Hall of Southeast Asia Pte. Ltd., *Singapore*
Whitehall Books, Ltd., Wellington, *New Zealand*
Editora Prentice-Hall do Brasil Ltda., *Rio de Janeiro*

Copyright © 1984,
by Daniel S. Berman

All rights reserved. No part of this
book may be reproduced in any form or
by any means, without permission in
writing from the publisher.

Library of Congress Cataloging in Publication Data

Berman, Daniel S.
  How to put together a real estate syndicate or joint venture.

  Includes index.
  1 Real estate investment—Syndication. 2. Joint ventures. I. Title.
HD1382.55.B47 1984   332.63'247   84–3324

ISBN 0-13-430653-8

Printed in the United States of America

Dedication

To my wife, Evelyn, who urged me to update
this book and encouraged me all the way.

Acknowledgments

No creative work is the effort of one person. I would like to acknowledge the able assistance of Arthur G. Jakoby, who spent many hours reviewing my earlier works on syndication and joint ventures and came up with many valuable suggestions, as well as doing much of the underlying research work necessary to bring the book up to date. His clear thinking and help were indispensable.

Also, my secretary and assistant for many years, Carol Flowers, was of great assistance in managing to squeeze out this manuscript on top of all of her other duties.

About the Author

Daniel S. Berman is a New York attorney, author, and lecturer on various aspects of real estate, building, and tax law. For more than 30 years he has consulted on, taught, and organized real estate syndications involving hundreds of millions of dollars. Mr. Berman has seen, commented on, and helped solve the technical real estate and financial problems of real estate syndications that have varied during the past four decades The syndications of the 1950s, 1960s, 1970s, and 1980s are all different. Mr. Berman believes that the basics have remained the same and the decades of perspective are most helpful.

More than 4000 real estate owners, brokers, and builders and their tax, accounting, and legal advisors have spent literally millions of dollars to travel to New York, Chicago, Houston, and other financial centers to hear Mr. Berman's lectures on real estate syndication and to have him explain how to put together a syndicate, step by step.

Mr. Berman is a member of the firm of Fink, Weinberger, Fredman, Berman, and Lowell, with offices in New York City and White Plains, New York. There he practices what he preaches. As an attorney for syndicators, builders, and real estate people, and as cocounsel to other lawyers, tax advisors, and accountants, he helps solve the real estate tax and financing problems involved in getting syndication concepts off the ground and into good working order. In addition, during his four decades of practical experience in the field, he has done battle with the Internal Revenue Service over the tax consequences of real estate syndication, and when hard times have come and particular deals have become "ill," he has worked to put them back on track. With pride, Mr. Berman states that none of his clients ever had a net out-of-pocket loss in a real estate syndication and that, in the real estate field, working out mistakes is more important than sales hype. Besides, you learn more from your mistakes than from your triumphs.

This is Mr. Berman's sixth book for Prentice-Hall. His five other books deal with various practical and legal topics in the real estate, securities, and tax law fields, and he has appeared, lectured, and consulted with such professional groups as the National Association of Home Builders, the National Association of Real Estate Boards, and the Mortgage Bankers Association. He has taught all of those topics at New York University's Real Estate Institute.

Introduction: What This Book Can Do for You

This book has evolved from a workshop I first conducted more than 30 years ago, dealing with how to put together real estate syndications and joint ventures.

In the past 30 years, we have seen joint ventures and syndications change somewhat—but only superficially. In this book, the subject of syndicates involves putting together a group that consists of an expert plus a group of investors. The expert may be a builder, a lawyer, a real estate broker or manager, an accountant, a Wall Street securities firm, or a financial consultant–insurance advisor.

The investors may include as few as three or four individuals who personally know the syndicator and have confidence in his or her ability to put together a deal that will be profitable to them. Or, it may be a large public syndication that may be sold all across the country in hundreds of stock brokerage houses to thousands of people. Yet, as I have said before and as I will repeat throughout this book, the same basic principles apply to the small deals as to the large ones.

We will deal mainly with the large syndications and joint ventures here, because they are more spectacular and because, since large syndicators are able to afford better legal and accounting counsel, their deals are more creative and imaginative. You can benefit by thinking through these larger formats and asking yourself, "Can I apply that to my deal even though it is a smaller one?"

JOINT VENTURES

When I discuss joint ventures, I am not dealing with a group of passive investors (as in the syndication field) but with a venture or transaction among equals, as when builders or developers put together a shopping center or office building deal that is too large for them to handle themselves; they take in, as partners, large national insurance companies, real estate investment trusts or banks.

In these joint ventures between equals in bargaining strength and sophistication, there will be no more than two or three parties. They will all be able to take care of themselves and will exercise equal leverage against one another, so that they are equals at the bargaining table. What welds them together is a community of interest and the understanding on the part of each venturer that the other parties have something to offer.

Thus, an insurance company may turn over decision-making control of substantial funds to a developer in a particular job because it recognizes that the developer has found a fine site and has local expertise. The developer will take in the insurance company as a partner not because he or she wants to give up half of the profits but because he or she just cannot find another way of tapping the large amount of front money to do the particular deal. To the developer, half of three deals is better than 100 percent of no deal.

No matter how you look at it, then, this book deals with the various ways of raising equity funds to put together real estate deals, whether by syndication to the many or joint ventures among the few.

WHY DO IT?

Why syndication or joint venture? The answer is simple: In no other way can an expert assemble sums as large and control deals as large as through the use of the real estate syndicate or joint venture. It is possible (and you will see samples in this book) for relatively young people with know-how to put together real estate syndicates involving more than $1 millon in equity, risking as little as $25,000 or $30,000 of their own cash. When the deal was finished, not only could they get their $25,000 or $30,000 back, but they could have a profit in their pockets, too. For young people in a hurry, syndication or joint venturing is the only route.

Introduction

HOW TO DO IT

The syndicate and the joint venture are both relatively simple devices. In this book, you will see how they grew to the position where they now dominate the real estate and building industry.

You will see what attracts investors to syndicates and joint ventures and what you must do if you want to attract syndicate or joint venture partners to your deals.

You will be shown how to do it, what the first steps are in tying up the real estate, how to merchandise or market the concept to the investors, and what kind of format or formula you should put together to leave yourself in control of the property while you assure your investors of their preferential position regarding cash flow, tax benefits, or both.

WHICH TECHNIQUE IS FOR YOU?

You will see why some syndicators prefer to use a leasing technique, why others use the piece-of-the-deal technique, and why others prefer a wraparound mortgage. You will learn how to decide what to take for yourself, if you are the syndicate manager or developer, and what to give the investors.

You will be taken through such technical problems as the use of the corporate dummy, the effect of inflation, the profit-sharing opportunities for the investors, and repurchase options, and you will be told how money is raised from the public and how to decide how much to raise. You will find a frank discussion of what should be revealed to the investors and what, if anything, should not. And you will be told the risks involved in sweeping things under the rug and hiding facts.

ACTUAL DEALS TAKEN APART

A number of actual deals will be taken apart for you, piece by piece and step by step, so that you can see the risk involved at the syndicator's level and how to hedge it. You will be given rough timetables and will be shown how to maximize your flexibility so that you do not get yourself into a trap.

The use of options will be discussed, as well as some of the more troublesome spots in SEC regulations, local blue-sky laws, and the use of salespeople and broker–dealers.

TAX BONANZAS AND TRAPS

There will be a discussion of the important tax problems of syndicators and how they avoid paying an ordinary income tax on the free piece or free lease they may take for themselves. As mentioned above, you will be shown how to apply the syndication techniques used on jumbo deals to the smaller, local deals.

Then we will go over the tax aspects of syndication, and you will learn something about the tax treatment of real estate in general. You will see why you must avoid being taxed as a corporation and how to choose the best form of depreciation for your deal. There will be a fairly detailed discussion of the use of corporations and limited partnerships and safe-harbor rules, real estate trusts, and many other types of vehicles being used to chop up large real estate equities into small, retail-sized bites.

SIMPLIFYING THE FORMS MAZE

You will be taken through a number of legal forms, and there will be a discussion of the more important clauses to be included, both from the syndicator's viewpoint and that of the investor. I will take you through some of the trouble spots and pass along the experience not only of myself, my law partners, and my clients, but also those of other syndicators and real estate investors. The forms and experiences discussed here have been accumulating in my files for more than 30 years, with constant revision and updating to today's market and tax needs.

LEARNING FROM THE MISTAKES OF OTHERS

I believe you learn more from your mistakes than from your successes because the pain and anguish sticks with you longer and because you become self-critical about your mistakes, while successes only go to your head. I will try to point out to you the disasters that overtook the real estate syndication industry in the 1960s and 1970s. We will also point up the successes, so that you will be able to contrast the successes and the disasters and learn from the troubles of others.

Introduction

You will see when to use the limited partnership and when to use the general partnership, and why both are preferable to the simple trust, the tenancy in common, the thin corporation, the tax-sheltered corporation, and, in many cases, the real estate investment trust. You will be shown what the real estate investment trust can do and what it cannot do, and you will get a look at some of the other syndication and joint venture vehicles.

THE SECURITIES LAWS

We will also discuss the SEC and state blue-sky (securities) laws (securities laws), you will be shown how private offerings are simpler to handle than public offerings, and you will be shown why the distinction is so uncertain.

In the field of public offerings, you will be told something about the expense, the inconvenience, and the time required. Registered deals will be contrasted with exempt deals, and you will be shown the traps awaiting the unwary in both the private and the public offering fields. You will be given a number of practical tips to enable you to avoid grief.

RAISING MONEY FROM THE PUBLIC

There is a brief discussion of going public (using a common stock, limited partnership, or real estate investment trust offering) as a way of raising money from the public, and you will be shown the pros and cons of using that technique.

You will be taken through a number of successful and unsuccessful syndications. You will see how the syndicate business is changing, how customer and mailing lists are compiled, what it costs to put together a syndicate, and how to recoup those costs. You will see what kind of returns those investors are looking for and how much profit a syndicator can make.

FINDING YOUR OWN MARKET

You will be shown how to select your own best market and how to decide whether to make a broad public offering or to attempt a private offering. The subject of when cash returns to investors should commence is discussed; the advantages of local syndication versus national syndication are dealt with; and there is a discussion of how to sell your units, how to package a number of deals, the strengths and weaknesses of diversification, the advantages and disadvantages of having investors get involved early, the utilization of early tax losses, the kind of properties that are being syndicated, and the kind that cannot be syndicated.

ACTUAL PROSPECTUSES AND FORMS

Finally, a separate section presents a number of syndication forms and prospectuses covering dozens of different ideas and paragraphs. They should help you get your own syndicate or joint venture off the ground by saving you months of tedious research. Each form has been taken from an actual syndicate, trust, or joint venture. Some involve small deals (less than $250,000), while others involve offerings in excess of $25 million.

One word of warning: This is an idea and source book. It is *not* a how-to kit for the self-made lawyer. Get the best real estate, tax, and securities lawyers you can find, and translate this book into a money-maker instead of a litigation trap. If you cannot find the talent you need locally, go to New York, Los Angeles, or Chicago, where there are experts who will work with your local lawyer and accountant.

No book is a substitute for legal advice. For a lay person or even a lawyer to slavishly copy any of the forms in this book could be a disaster. In many cases, single paragraphs have been used out of context to illustrate a point, or only one of several agreements has been reproduced because there was a good idea in it. This idea may be illegal or disastrous in your state, or it may be ineffective without utilizing the rest of the techniques or papers involved.

APPLYING THE KNOW-HOW

Syndication is a complicated business; it involves real estate law, tax law, securities law, partnership and corporate law, and lots of real estate know-how and common sense. Even in cases where I have been called in to do legal work for syndicators in various states throughout the country, I have never done so without working in conjunction with the client's local lawyers. There is no such thing as a set of papers that is good in all 50 states, and, as a matter of fact, the set of papers

Introduction

applicable to one part of the state may be useless in another.

Therefore, I repeat my warning: This is an idea book—a workshop—it is not a substitute for competent local legal and tax advice. If you keep in mind its limitations, you will find it an invaluable source of material in a field on which too little has been written and in which too many mistakes have been made.

At the same time, bear in mind that sensible application of syndication techniques has enabled successful real estate people to build fortunes running into the millions in a relatively short period of time. Many of these young people started out with only two nickels of their own, but they all had solid real estate or financial know-how, and they assembled the best backup team they could find to add prestige and know-how to their efforts.

Enough theory! Let's get to work. Let's roll up our sleeves and see how to go about forming your own real estate syndicate or joint venture, step by step.

Daniel S. Berman

Table of Contents

About the Author   vii

Introduction: What This Book Can Do for You   ix

Part 1   Putting Together a Syndicate or Venture   1

Chapter 1   Getting Started in Real Estate Syndication or Venturing   3

Staying in Your Field of Expertise	3
The $250,000 Equity Deal	4
Putting Up the Contract Money	4
Don't Be an Amateur	5
The Two Major Techniques of Syndicating or Venturing	5
Who Gets the Refinancing under a Lease?	10
Buying Out the Lease	10
The Importance of Refinancing	11
When Does Rent Start in a Leasehold Deal?	11
Delaying Rent	12
Leasehold Options to Purchase	12
The Repurchase Option As a Sales Tool	13
With the Sale Leaseback Technique, Should You Put a Dollar Value on the Lease?	13
How Much Money Should You Raise from the Public?	14
Pocketing a Profit out of Investor Sales	14
Foregoing the Profit As a Sales Tool	15

	Contents
Shall the Syndicator Also Be an Investor?	16
The Size of the Syndicator's Investment	16
A Free Piece of the Deal	16
Some Differences Between the Lease and the Piece	18
Subordination	18
The Wraparound Mortgage As a Free Piece	19
The Syndicate from Beginning to End	21
Taking Apart Some Actual Deals	22
Public and Private Offerings	22
What Kind of Real Estate Will You Syndicate?	23
How to Sell Your Units	24

Chapter 2 How to Structure the Syndicate to Avoid the Corporate Tax **27**

Saving the Corporate Tax	27
How to Handle a Loss Deal	28
Business Musts and the Syndicate Format	28
Corporate Differences	29
Solving the Association Problem	29
A Closer Look at the Corporation-Partnership Problem	30
Two Practical Syndicate Forms	32

Chapter 3 Joint Ventures, Trusts, and other Types of Syndicate Vehicles **43**

Trusts, Tenancies in Common, and Joint Ventures	43
The Simple Trust	44
Thin and Tax-Sheltered Corporations	44
The Real Estate Investment Trust	49
Summary	53

Chapter 4 Calculating Returns on Investment **55**

The Computer Is No More Reliable Than the Assumer	56
Computer Disasters	56
Measuring the Time Value of Money	57
The Effect of Less Up-Front Cash on Returns	57
Some Definitions and Concepts	59
Computing Internal Rate of Return or Discounted Cash Flow	61
Non-Real-Estate Yields for Comparison Purposes	62
Using the Computer to Compare Real Estate Deals	62

Chapter 5 Tax Angles of Syndication and Joint Ventures **63**

The Value of Tax Shelter to the Investor	64
Tax Know-How Makes Sick Deals Saleable	65

Contents

    Depreciation and Leverage   65
    Spreading Out Your Payments   67
    More Building, Less Land   68
    More Interest, Less Amortization   68
    The Wraparound Mortgage   69
    The Wraparound Mortgage Loan and Syndication   70
    How to Use the Accrual Method to Get More Partnership Deductions   71
    Cash or Accrual Method of Accounting   73
    Tax Structuring Your Deal   75
    Beware of the Mortgage Basis Trap   76
    The Tax Basis Problem for Investors   77
    Practical Tips on Tax Basis   77
    Partnership Liabilities and Traps   78
    Section 754 Election   78
    Sale of More Than a 50 Percent Interest in a Partnership   79
    Traps in Adding New Partners   79
    Depreciation Rules Since the Economic Recovery Tax Act of 1981   80
    The Investment Interest Trap   83
    Construction Period Taxes and Interest   83
    The Net Lease Trap   85
    Impact of TEFRA on Syndications   86

Chapter 6 What Goes into the Joint Venture   *89*

    Venture Prospects   89
    Why the Venture?   90
    Short-Form Ventures   90
    Some Tax Problems   91
    Avoiding Tax on Organizing the Venture   91
    Accounting Reporting Problems for Sellers   92
    Purpose and Term of Agreement   92
    Disclosing the Facts   93
    Contributions by General Partner and Withdrawals by Limited Partners   93
    Cash Distribution Problems   94
    Rights and Powers of the General Partner   94
    Other Management Problems   95
    Change in Partnership Personnel   95

Ratification by Limited Partners	96
Delineating Sales Program	97

Chapter 7   The Securities Laws and Syndication 99

Importance of Disclosure	99
No SEC Jurisdiction in Intrastate Matters	100
All Tests Must Be Passed	100
The Number of Offerees	101
Exemptions for Private Placement	101
Financial Sophistication	102
Tests of the Private Offering	102
SEC's Current Guidelines on Private Offerings	103
Some Other Limitations of Regulation D	104
Your Prospectus	105

Part 2   Encyclopedia of Syndication and Joint Venture Forms and Checklists   **107**

Checklist for Syndicators	109
Subscription Agreement	112
Subscription Agreement-Limited Partnership Interests	113
Prospective Offeree Questionnaire	125
Purchaser Representative Questionnaire	132
Investor Suitability Standards	137
Broker-Dealer Sell Sheet	140
Limited Partnership Agreement	167
General Partnership Agreement	186
Guide 5—SEC Regulations	190
Regulation D Private Offering Sample Table of Contents	223
Joint Venture Checklist	229
Joint Venture Agreements	233

Index   283

PART I

Putting Together a Syndication or Venture

CHAPTER 1

Getting Started in Real Estate Syndication or Venturing

To become a real estate syndicator or venturer, you first have to have a piece of real estate—any kind of real estate. I have seen successful real estate syndication and venturing in vacant land, office buildings already constructed or to be built, shopping centers, apartment houses, motels, hotels, garages, nursing homes, resorts, golf courses, condominiums, ski slopes, and vineyards.

Obviously, if you are going to become a syndicator you should syndicate the kind of real estate you or your associates know best. Since the prime requisite of syndicators is that they or their associates have real estate expertise, you should pick the kind of real estate with which you are most familiar.

STAYING IN YOUR FIELD OF EXPERTISE

Having chosen the kind of real estate you want to syndicate, you will next select as your first deal a transaction that is the right size for you and your prospective investment group. If there were no other factors at work, I would urge you to take the smallest deal you can handle as your first deal. Be sure to sell out the first time around; don't start out with a failure.

On the other hand, we are all victims of inflationary economics, and the smallest deals somehow don't seem to be able to support themselves, let alone throw off enough money to attract investors to a new syndicator.

Still, you should make your first deal the smallest one that makes sense; if economics force you into taking on a larger deal, take in a partner who will help you syndicate by raising some of the money in return for a piece of the profit.

Since the legal and tax work alone, without things like printing bills, will probably run at the very minimum $7500 to $10,000, and on an average for the larger deals at the very minimum more than $25,000, you obviously cannot do nickel-and-dime deals.

THE $250,000 EQUITY DEAL

In today's market, I have not seen many deals in which the equity sought to be raised is much less than $250,000. I would think that $500,000 would be a better size, but I have known of informal syndicates being put together with a half-dozen people in which the amount put up by each was as little as $5000 or $10,000 and the paperwork was kept very simple because of the private nature of the offering, so that a very small deal was possible. However, these are exceptional.

Once you have decided the size of the equity you intend to raise, the next step is to go to contract to buy the property or to have an exclusive option to buy it.

It is essential that you have a contract in your own name (or in the name of a nominee or dummy of yours) if you are ever to do any real estate syndication.

PUTTING UP THE CONTRACT MONEY

In most cases, you have to put up some kind of a deposit for the contract or the option. If you don't have the money, borrow it, but you cannot escape the fact that you must have the property under option or contract before you can syndicate it. There are two important reasons for this. The first is an income tax reason; the second is a business reason.

I will not discuss the income tax reason in this chapter. But, without having the property under option or contract, you face a potential ordinary income tax if you become a successful syndicator—a tax that you can hope to avoid if you follow the instructions in this book. However, such avoidance is possible only if you have the property under option or contract.

What business reason is there for you to have the property under contract? Suppose you find a nice piece of real estate that meets your criteria, and you attempt to syndicate it without tying it up under option or contract. Suppose you put together all of the information on the project and go to your investors. Unless the property is under contract, any one of the investors might go and buy the property by himself or herself.

Or, worse yet, as you visit a half-dozen or a dozen people and speak to them about the property, it might get back to the seller, who finds out how interested you are and raises the price.

DON'T BE AN AMATEUR

After you visit all of your pet investors, the people upon whom you hope to base your successful syndication career, and after you have sold all of them and they are all eager to put their money into the deal, you discover that the seller has changed his or her mind, has changed the price, or has sold the property to someone else. What would you tell your pet investors?

They would never speak to you again, because you would have demonstrated to them that you tried to sell something you did not own and wasted their time. You would look foolish if you could not deliver the product you had sold.

Let me repeat: Without putting up a deposit and binding yourself to a deal—regardless of how small or how large the deposit is—unless you are able to get an option or a contract without putting up any money, you cannot syndicate. There must be a binding contract or option to buy the property that you, as a syndicator, own or control. There is just no other way to do it.

In the almost 40 years that I have been in private law practice, I have never seen a successful syndication that violated this rule. Tie up the property under option or contract, and you are ready to move on to the next step.

THE TWO MAJOR TECHNIQUES OF SYNDICATING OR VENTURING

You have decided to become a syndicator, you have selected the kind of real estate you think should be syndicated, you have picked out a particular parcel for which you think you will be able to raise money from a group of investors, and you have put down a deposit and have contracted to buy the parcel or have it under option.

Now, before going to your investors, you have to decide on the technique you will use to handle their money when you get it, so that you can explain to them exactly what they will be buying and how their return will work out.

The two basic techniques of syndication involve either the free lease or the free piece.

Assume that you have selected a piece of real estate to syndicate which requires raising $500,000 of investor cash. The property you plan to buy throws off a 10 percent cash return on equity, so that the $500,000 produces a $50,000 bottom line in terms of cash flow.

In other words, a $500,000 equity investment produces $50,000 of cash flow a year. Cash flow, as you know, is the actual cash left in pocket after paying all of the expenses of running the property, including amortization of debt service as if it were an expense, and without taking into consideration income taxes on the individual investors or such book entries as depreciation.

If your investors will put in $500,000 to get $50,000 in cash flow, how shall it be divided between the investors and the syndicator? Assume that the investors are willing to take an 8 percent return on their investment, so that if they put up $500,000 they would be satisfied to make $40,000 a year. That leaves $10,000 for the syndicator. As I mentioned above, there are two ways to get the extra $10,000 to the syndicator, as his or her share of the profit.

The Free Lease

Let us look at the lease first. What happens there is that the syndicator gets the investors to use the $500,000 to buy the real estate in their name (or, rather, in the name of a partnership in which they are partners). The partnership, in which the investors have ownership, leases the property on a long-term net lease basis to the syndicator. Since the investor partners are looking for an 8 percent return, the syndicator prepares the lease so as to pay them a net rent of $40,000 a year (8 percent on $500,000).

The syndicator sublets the premises and collects the differential of $10,000 from the subtenant. Thus, the investors have invested $500,000 for a $40,000-a-year net return, and the syndicator has invested nothing for a $10,000-a-year return.

What happens if rents go up? Suppose the syndicator, through careful management, increases the bottom profit line to $60,000 a year. Assuming a fixed net rent to the investors, they still get $40,000 a year or 8 percent on their $500,000 investment. The syndicator, with

Getting Started in Real Estate Syndication or Venturing

no money and a hugely leveraged position, would make $20,000 on no investment.

Of course, the leverage works both ways. Suppose rents go down, so that the syndicator, instead of collecting $50,000 or $60,000 a year from the subtenant, begins to collect $30,000 a year. The syndicator is bound nonetheless to pay the investor-owned fee partnership $40,000, so that the syndicator is out of pocket $10,000 a year.

Return to the investors. Use of the free lease or sale leaseback position with the investors owning a partnership interest in the fee and the syndicator owning the operating position in the lease offers the investors a predetermined return, which does not have to be a fixed return.

In some cases, the net lease between the investors and the syndicator may provide that the investors get $40,000 a year net income from the lease and, in the event that gross rents exceed a certain amount, the overage will be split between the syndicator and the investors, 50–50 or 80–20. The purpose of such a share to the investors in the overages is to give them an inflationary kicker and to permit them to share in the prosperity that ensues as a result of skillful management on the part of the syndicator.

In addition, with the investors in the fee-owning partnership position, they are able to get allocated to themselves the depreciation generated from the building, while the syndicator merely collects operating income dollars that are not tax sheltered unless there is some lease acquisition cost or some leasehold improvements on the part of the syndicator.

The syndicate manager's liability on the lease. The sale leaseback or free lease technique gives rise to a number of interesting questions. To begin with, it is important to note that the leasing technique permits the syndicator to assure the investors of return in excess of the return the property is making. In a way, it involves (to the investors) the risk that the syndicator is using their own money to give them a nonexistent return until such time as the property falls flat on its face and the investors lose everything.

On the other hand, I know of quite a number of transactions where the syndicator entered into a net lease transaction and paid to the investors a return in excess of what the property was throwing off, because the syndicator knew he or she could not sell the package to the investors without assuring them of a certain definite return to tempt their money into the project.

However, the syndicator's deal was well conceived, and the syndicator hoped (correctly) that he or she would turn the property around, make it generate the return that had been promised the investors, and still make a nice profit on the project for himself or herself.

How it's done. What the syndicator did in that case was to buy a property that was either underrented or overexpensed, use the investors' money to acquire the property, enter into a net lease transaction assuring the investors of the return necessary to tempt their money out of the piggy bank, finance the deficit himself or herself during the early years while turning the project around, turn the project into one profitable enough to pay the investors the fixed return they had expected and to make a huge bottom line for himself or herself in later years.

The lease technique to turn around an underrented or overexpensed property has been used successfully for many years by such first-generation syndicators as Larry Wien in his famous Garment Center Capitol Buildings Syndication. Intelligent use of the net lease can be a boon to both syndicator and investor.

On the other hand, misuse of the net lease to offer to the investors a return that is not there and never will be is tantamount to a fraud.

Thus, in the first syndication boom in the 1950s, many syndicators bought buildings with the investors' money, overcapitalized the buildings so that there would be extra funds in the deal which the syndicator either put into his or her pocket or kept in reserve for bad years, and paid to the investors a return under a net lease position that was unwarranted. It was like telling someone you would pay 20 percent interest if he or she would lend you $5, and then turning around and using the $5, at the rate of $1 per year, to pay back the interest.

Syndication frauds. Since there were no earnings to support the interest, the only way to keep going was by continuing to borrow more money from more and more people—a plan originally made famous by the infamous Charles Ponzi in the 1900s.

The sale leaseback or free lease is no stronger than the credit line of the syndicator or the strength of the underlying property. The strongest syndicator can go broke or die and, ultimately, the only security the investor has in a net lease position is based on the strength of the underlying property.

If the property is profitable and makes more money than the rent paid to the investors, the investors need not worry. If the contrary is true, they must examine carefully both the credit strength of the syndicator and the strength of the property, if their equity is to be safe.

If there is to be a net lease to the syndicator, what is the syndicator's ability to pay the rent thereunder? If you are a syndicator and the property is net leased to you and you sign as the net operating tenant,

Getting Started in Real Estate Syndication or Venturing

the first question that comes up is what happens if the property turns around and starts to lose money? Are you personally obligated to pay? If so, for how long? Can you be obligated to pay the investors a return forever on a building that is losing money?

Escape clauses for the syndicator. Unless there are some personal escape clauses for you, if you sign personally, it is obvious that, as tenant, you will be liable for the rent for as long as the lease goes on. A 99-year lease is a substantial albatross to hang around your neck. There are very few syndicators who would not go broke if they were personally responsible for 99 years on 99-year net leases with their investors if the real estate starts losing money.

There are usually two escape routes: Either the syndicator is personally liable on the lease for only a limited period of time or the syndicator does not sign personally but puts a nominee corporation on the lease so that he or she can walk away from the deal whenever he or she wants to, leaving the nominee holding the bag—or, rather, leaving the investors holding the bag.

So, if a syndicator buys a property for $500,000 of the investors' money, and if the syndicator is going to enter into a net operating lease promising to give them $40,000 a year plus paying all the expenses of operating the building, he or she can do one of two things. The syndicator could provide in that lease (if personally liable) that, after two, three, four, or five years or some specific period, he or she can abandon the lease or transfer it to someone else and not be personally liable thereunder. That is one way to get out. Lawyers call it an exculpatory or escape clause. If such a clause is used, the investors need to look at it carefully to determine just how long it will be until the syndicator has the right to walk away from the deal.

If this occurs in a short period of time (too short for the investors to recapture their entire investment), they must ask the syndicator such hard-nosed questions as, are you sure, Syndicator that the deal can be turned around in that time? What happens if it isn't? How can we be sure? Is our money safe in this deal as contrasted with other deals available to us? How much of your own money will be at risk, and how secure is your commitment?

The other alternative for the syndicator is never to be personally liable on the lease. John Doe, syndicator, may put the John Doe Corporation on the lease, and the John Doe Corporation may have as its assets 22 cents in cash plus the leasehold itself—which means that the most that the corporation could ever be called upon to pay is the 22 cents invested in it. That is what I mean when I say that syndicators, in some cases, use nominees or dummies to avoid personal liability.

If a nominee or dummy is on the lease instead of the syndicator personally, it is most important for the investors to examine what assets the nominee has and how long they will last in case of bad times.

Finally, the investors in a nominee deal must look very carefully at the real estate to see if it can support the lease.

WHO GETS THE REFINANCING UNDER A LEASE?

This is a sophisticated question not always understood by investors who purchase an interest in the fee ownership of real estate. They may, if they are reasonably alert, understand that the syndicator is going to make his or her profit out of operating a lease. A more sophisticated investor with a higher order of real estate expertise would ask about what happens to the syndicator's lease on a sale or refinancing. The question is important for both the syndicator and the investors.

Bear in mind that the investors own the fee (the underlying real estate). If the fee is sold, or if it is refinanced, either the buyer (in the case of a sale) or the mortgage lender (in the case of a refinancing) will probably want release of the long-term tenant's (syndicator's) position. A long-term lease encumbers the real estate, and a new buyer can collect no rent other than the rent the syndicate investors were collecting.

BUYING OUT THE LEASE

No one would want to buy the real estate encumbered by the syndicator's lease. Similarly, unless the lease or the existing mortgage provides otherwise, any future mortgage financing or refinancing would be behind the leasehold position, which means that the mortgage lender would want a release from the syndicator, which means that the syndicator would probably want to be paid for the release.

In other words, while the investors may not realize it, a syndicator who owns a long-term lease on the investors' real estate has an opportunity to share in any sale or refinancing proceeds. Unless this is spelled out specifically in the lease or the fee-owning partnership agreement, the investors could be at the mercy of the syndicator, who theoretically could ask for all or most of the sales proceeds or mortgage refinancing proceeds.

Similarly, if there is a condemnation or a fire loss, the syndicator is in a position to ask for his or her piece of the proceeds. This is not an uncommon question, nor is it a hypothetical discussion.

With many pieces of real estate, the syndicator feels that the sole reason for purchasing the real estate is that the mortgage can be refinanced. The role of the syndicator and the lease then becomes of utmost importance.

THE IMPORTANCE OF REFINANCING

In other words, if a mortgage refinancing is imminent, or if the present mortgage has a very high rate of interest and amortization and can be refinanced with another mortgage requiring a smaller cash input, or if the present mortgage is too low, so that the syndicator could get the mortgage substantially increased, how sales or refinancing proceeds will be divided becomes a key to the deal between the investors and their syndicator.

This now becomes a question of bargaining and lease draftsmanship. In some cases, the syndicator will feel that his or her position should get half of the refinancing or half of the sales proceeds. In other cases, the syndicator will keep as little as 5 or 10 percent. Whatever the percentage to be split, it should be thought through by the syndicator as early as possible and inserted unequivocally into the lease and any prospectus material distributed to the investors, so that the investors will understand it and there will be no dispute later, when the subject comes up and checks have to be written.

WHEN DOES RENT START IN A LEASEHOLD DEAL?

By adjusting when rent starts under the lease, the syndicator can lighten his or her burden or make it heavier, and the return to the investors will then commence earlier or later.

In some cases, the answer is obvious. Suppose a syndicator takes a long-term net lease on a "to be built" property in which construction will not start until after the investors come in. While the property is being built, the syndicator is collecting no rent and has no way of paying any net rent to the investors. If the deal does offer net rent during the construction period or before the deal fully rents up, it is apparent that the syndicator is subsidizing the net rents to the tenants either from his or her pocket or by overcapitalizing the deal (selling it for too high a price) to raise enough money to pay the investors a return out of their own pockets.

Whatever the case may be, it is best, particularly in the construction or vacant land field, for investors not to be paid any return until there is sufficient money generated by the project itself to cover all of the cash payments to the investors. Anything else is a delusion.

DELAYING RENT

It is also possible for the syndicator to start net rent to the investors several months after the project is completed, even though it may not be fully rented up. By waiting several months before starting rent, the syndicator is getting the breathing spell necessary to do the rent-ups.

Setting up the lease so that the investors do not get any return until the project is fully rented means that the syndicator is throwing the full rent-up risk upon the investors.

LEASEHOLD OPTIONS TO PURCHASE

In some cases, the syndicator's lease position will contain an option to the leasehold owner (the syndicator) to buy the underlying real estate from the investor partnership (the fee) at a price fixed in the lease. This is a useful gimmick for the syndicate manager, although many investors, when they find out about it, are very unhappy.

From the investor's viewpoint, an option to the syndicator makes the syndication a one-way street. They say to the syndicator, "If you have an option to repurchase the property from us, and if all goes well and the deal turns out to be a bonanza, you will exercise your option and cancel our lease. If the deal turns out badly, you will keep the lease, and you will have bought the property with our money, so that, if the deal goes sour, you will not exercise the option to repurchase, and we will be in trouble."

On the other hand, some syndicators have turned the option into a plus. "What," the syndicators ask, "is the disadvantage to you, particularly if we have a sliding scale, at a higher price, on such repurchase or redemption?"

The syndicator is saying, "It is true that I have an option to repurchase, and it is true that an option is a one-way street, but, by the same token, it offers you a substantial bonus by getting your money out safely and quickly, and it offers us an incentive to buy you out, which we might not do otherwise."

Getting Started in Real Estate Syndication or Venturing

THE REPURCHASE OPTION AS A SALES TOOL

In order to make a useful sales tool out of the option, syndicators may put an incentive sliding scale option price into the lease. Such an incentive option price might provide that if the syndicator is to repurchase the property, he or she must pay a bonus of, say, 5 percent, if the repurchase takes place during the first two or three years, a 10 percent bonus if it takes place in the next two or three years, a 15 percent bonus if it takes place, say, from the seventh to the tenth year, and so on.

"You see," says the syndicator, "we have an incentive to turn the property around as quickly as possible, and you get all your money back plus the return that was paid during the period you held the property, plus a time-related bonus on top of it.

"So," says the syndicator, "suppose you put $10,000 into the deal; suppose it pays you, as a member of the fee-owning partnership, 10 percent; and suppose there is a 5 percent bonus if we buy you out during the first three years. You will all get your money back if we buy you out in the second year. In other words, you would get back your original $10,000, plus $1000 a year net rent (10 percent), plus a 5 percent bonus (or $500), so that you would make $12,500 on your investment in two years, or approximately 25 percent for a short risk period."

Looking at it from the syndicate manager's viewpoint, if the syndicate manager can refinance the property or increase the return to pay the investors out in full, and own the property without having them share in the profits from then on, the syndicator has a good deal, even if he or she has to pay 25 percent to the investors. Without the investors, there might not have been any deal at all.

WITH THE SALE LEASEBACK TECHNIQUE, SHOULD YOU PUT A DOLLAR VALUE ON THE LEASE?

Once in a while, you will see a set of papers in which the syndicator has said, "The lease I take back shall have an agreed value of $10,000," or some other sum. Unless the syndicate manager actually invests some money to procure the lease—in which case the value of the lease will be the exact amount of the purchase—it is inadvisable to put a hypothetical dollar value on the lease just to beef up the picture.

If you arbitrarily assign a dollar value to the lease but do not actually pay for it, you may wind up with an income tax on your hypothetical dollar value that would be particularly irritating since you cut the value up out of whole cloth and have no cash with which to pay the tax. Only if you sell a lease can you assign a true value to it, and only if there is a real sale will you have any money with which to pay a tax on the lease's value.

HOW MUCH MONEY SHOULD YOU RAISE FROM THE PUBLIC?

We have been assuming all along that if a piece of real estate costs $500,000, you will raise $500,000 from the public and own your lease free. There are all kinds of other possibilities.

One possibility is that you would raise less than $500,000 from the investors so that the lease would have an actual cost to you. Thus, you might raise $400,000 from the investors and put up the other $100,000 yourself. That is unusual but possible.

The other possibility is, although the real estate costs $500,000, the syndicate manager might raise $600,000 from the investors, who will then own the fee. What does the syndicator do with the extra $100,000 over and above the actual cost of the deal? The answer is relatively simple: The syndicator pockets it or uses it to defray syndication costs. Is there anything morally wrong with that? Would the syndicator making a profit on selling the property to the investors be wrong?

I do not pass on the morality of it; that is between you and your conscience. However, if you do intend to make such a profit, you had better be certain that all of your papers reveal to the investors that you are putting a portion of their proceeds into your pocket, so that the investors cannot claim later that it was concealed from them and sue you for fraud or for rescission.

For your own protection, your papers or prospectus should warn the investors about all hidden profits, risks, and so on, and the investors should sign a receipt for the prospectus or disclosure documents, to avoid having them sue you later because they did not understand or were not told the facts.

POCKETING A PROFIT OUT OF INVESTOR SALES

The syndicate manager often raises more money from the public than the actual cost of the real estate because the extra dollars are

Getting Started in Real Estate Syndication or Venturing

needed to defray such items as legal expenses, registration expenses, and closing costs. In other cases, as mentioned, the syndicate manager raises an excess price and pockets it.

The defense of such a bonus charge is that the property is worth the price at which it is being sold to the investors. The syndicate manager is saying something like, "I happened to find a bargain. I found it because of my real estate expertise. This property is clearly worth $600,000. Any real estate appraiser or investor would tell you that; but, because I was such a good negotiator and worked hard to find the property, I was able to buy it for $500,000. I don't see any reason to let you, as investors, into the project for less than its true value—$600,000. I could sell the property to a complete stranger by turning the contract over at a $100,000 profit, and he or she would pay $500,000 to buy it directly from the owner, so that his or her cost would be $600,000. Why should your cost be less? How do I, as a syndicator, owe you, as a potential investor, the duty to give up a $100,000 profit I could make by selling the contract to a stranger?" That, at least, is the argument.

FOREGOING THE PROFIT AS A SALES TOOL

Wiser syndicators often forego making the $100,000 profit for two reasons: If the deal goes sour, the investors will never believe they have not been swindled; and, even if the deal goes well, they may resent the syndicate manager's making a $100,000 profit on them—his or her partners.

Perhaps the better way to handle the situation might be for the syndicate manager to take a bigger piece of the rental, leaving a smaller return for the investors. The argument might be that the return is ironclad and that the syndicator is getting some kind of return on the $100,000 that the investors did not have to put into the job, which acts as a cushion for them and a testing or sounding board for the syndicator.

"After all," says the syndicator, "if I did catch a bargain purchase, it will show up in rents in excess of what one might have expected for the cash invested by the investors. Therefore, I will not sell the property to them at a profit, but, by keeping 50 percent of the rents or by taking all of the rents above a certain amount, I will be giving my position a premium value and putting my money where my mouth is. If I don't collect excess rents, I will not get the extra bonus of the overage."

SHALL THE SYNDICATOR ALSO BE AN INVESTOR?

Sometimes the syndicate manager becomes an investor because he or she is not able to sell all the units to outside investors. Such a syndicator is an "involuntary" investor.

Occasionally, however, you will examine a syndicate and discover that the syndicate manager is a voluntary investor, who has voluntarily put some of his or her own money into the deal.

In some cases, the syndicator may do so just because he or she cannot find another outlet for the funds. In other cases, the syndicator may invest a sum of money merely to show the potential investors that the syndicator has enough confidence in the deal to put some money into it.

If the syndicate manager is investing purely as window dressing, the sum of money he or she invests will be small in relation to the total amount of money raised, though it may be large compared to the average investor.

THE SIZE OF THE SYNDICATOR'S INVESTMENT

Some syndicate managers invest as little as $5000 to $50,000 in a deal in which $1 million of equity was to be invested, but $50,000 was the largest single investment in the deal, since most investors put up $25,000 or less. Under such circumstances, while the syndicate manager had as little as 2½ to 5 percent invested in a $1 million deal, he or she was truthfully able to tell the investors, "I have invested more in this deal than you have, because you, as an individual investor, are putting in less than the $50,000 I have invested."

Unless the syndicate manager has a substantial amount of money invested in the deal—substantial in proportion to the total amount raised from all of the investors—a small investment by the syndicator cannot be considered as anything but window dressing. It seems that the real estate should stand on its own two feet. If it is a good deal, an investment of several thousand dollars by the syndicator will not make it a better deal, and if it is a bad deal the syndicator should invest nothing in it.

A FREE PIECE OF THE DEAL

When the syndicator takes profit out of the deal by taking back a lease on the premises without cost to himself or herself, the lease is

Getting Started in Real Estate Syndication or Venturing

the equivalent of taking back the common stock in a corporate financing, giving the preferred stock to the investors.

However, there is the other possibility that both the investors and the syndicator may participate at the same level, all getting common stock but the syndicator acquiring his or her share without cost to himself or herself (or at a lesser cost than that offered to the investors). In stock issues, the concept is called investor dilution.

I call this the free piece of the deal. As an example, let's take the same figures we worked with before, the transaction that required $500,000 to purchase, for which $500,000 was raised entirely from investors, and in which the real estate threw off $500,000 a year or a 10 percent cash return.

In the lease deal, the syndicate manager raised the whole $500,000 from investors, took no share in the equity itself, and retained only his or her leasehold position out of which he or she hoped to make income if all went well.

However, in the free piece of the deal, the same $500,000 will be raised from the investors, but $500,000 will get the investors only an 80 percent interest in the deal, with the syndicate manager owning a 20 percent interest. The syndicate manager will pay nothing for his or her position.

In other words, the investors will put up all the money, but the deal will be watered down for them so that they will only be buying an 80 percent interest for 100 percent of the cash.

Now, if the deal still earns the same $50,000 illustrated before, the syndicator is in the same position as if he or she had a free lease, because the syndicator will get 20 percent of the $50,000 bottom line and the investors will get 80 percent, so that the investors will get $40,000 and the syndicate manager will get $10,000.

Economically, the free piece works out to be the same as the free lease.

If all else remains the same, if the syndicate manager is going to participate by getting a free piece, there is no need for a leasehold entity. The syndicator will get a 20 percent interest in the partnership that owns the underlying property. If nothing else was said, this would give the syndicator a 20 percent interest in the depreciation also, and he or she would get some tax shelter on the free piece. This is contrasted with the leasehold position, which offers no tax shelter unless something more is done in the documents.

Of course, there is nothing to prevent the syndicate manager from taking both a lease and a piece. Thus, the syndicate manager may own a 10 or 20 percent interest in the underlying fee-owning partnership without cost to himself or herself and still own 100 percent of the leasehold position.

The syndicate manager may raise money for both the leasehold and the fee positions and get free pieces of both, sometimes even involving two separate investment groups. One group is interested in getting a large cash return; the other group is interested more in tax shelter. One group might have a more speculative return; the other group might have a more conservative return.

SOME DIFFERENCES BETWEEN THE LEASE AND THE PIECE

The free piece is a simpler transaction in terms of legal paperwork. It requires no complicated leasehold—just a partnership agreement.

The leasehold is a more complicated document. I discussed earlier how the leasehold had to cover the problems of sale, refinancing, personal liability on the lease, and so on. If the syndicate manager owns a free piece, he or she is assumed to have the same rights as the other investors, limited, of course, to his or her pro rata piece thereof. In the leasehold, everything has to be spelled out.

The leasehold—on paper at least—offers investors in the fee a fixed return, regardless of whether or not the property earns anything. The fixed return comes out of the syndicate manager's pocket, as the long-term leasehold tenant. Of course, if the leasehold earns money from subletting the space to subtenants, the leasehold should be an asset to the owner of the lease—the syndicator—and not a liability.

Obviously, some deals, because they offer no current income, are not susceptible of leasehold treatment. Thus, a vacant land deal involving a leasehold that begins to pay rent when the land is yielding nothing is an oddball deal that requires substantial explanation to the investors, since it would appear that the syndicate manager is doing deficit financing that must lead to ruin, unless there is an explanation for it that the investors can understand.

SUBORDINATION

The free piece does give rise, however, to at least one complicating problem, which can be turned into an advantage. It is the problem of subordinating the syndicate manager's free piece to the investors' return on their cash contributions.

Getting Started in Real Estate Syndication or Venturing

Let us go back to our hypothetical set of figures. The investors put up $500,000; the investors own 80 percent of the deal. Suppose the deal is resold at its actual cost two days after it is bought. Suppose it is sold for exactly $500,000. If nothing else was said, the syndicate manager would be entitled to 20 percent of the sales proceeds and the investors entitled to 80 percent.

Two days after the deal is bought for $500,000, the syndicate manager winds up with a $100,000 profit on his or her 20 percent, and the investors have a $100,000 loss on their 80 percent. That is why I call the free piece dilution.

Actually, there has been neither a profit nor a loss to the entity as such, since the property was sold for exactly its purchase price. If such a deal were really transacted, the syndicate manager would certainly not transact any more of them; he or she would probably have to run out of town.

Obviously, it is not the intention of either the syndicate manager or the investors that this immediate dilution should occur; therefore, the partnership agreement between the syndicate manager and the investors can provide that the syndicate manager's equity will be subordinated to the investors' capital contributions, so that the syndicate manager will get nothing for the 20 percent until the investors recapture their entire $500,000.

The syndicate manager is thus subordinating his or her 20 percent to the first $500,000 of sales price, which will go to the investors for their 80 percent.

Subordination may be not only regarding capital contributions but also regarding income distributions. Thus, the syndicate manager could conceivably subordinate the 20 percent in distributions so that the investors would get the first $40,000 of cash flow. The syndicate manager would be subordinating the 20 percent to provide that the first 8 percent on the investors' $500,000 would go to them.

It is possible to subordinate regarding capital or cash flow or both, and the subordination percentages and amounts might be different for each. The effect of this subordination is, once again, to give investors a position in the real estate deal similar to a preferred stock.

THE WRAPAROUND MORTGAGE AS A FREE PIECE

When the wraparound mortgage became popular in the mid-1970s, another technique of giving the syndicator a free piece became available.

A more detailed discussion of the wraparound mortgage is provided in Chapter 5, but at this point I would like to illustrate how the wraparound mortgage is used to give the syndicator a free piece.

The wraparound mortgage is a mortgage that wraps around an existing, assumable first mortgage and thus is, essentially, a second lien.

So, in our standard $500,000 example, let us assume that the syndicator decided to buy the property for $500,000 over and above an existing $250,000 lien, which would make the total purchase price $750,000. But let us assume that the syndicator further decided to mark up the property by $100,000. The syndicator could, as discussed before, raise $600,000 in cash and put $100,000 in his or her pocket.

However, suppose that does not make sense in the deal the syndicator has in mind. He or she might prefer a free piece instead of a cash mark-up. That piece could be taken by having the syndicator agree to take a wraparound mortgage of $100,000. That would leave the property with $500,000 in cash over and above a $350,000 mortgage. The syndicator, by wrapping around the existing first mortgage, would agree to make payments on the $250,000 underlying loan, and whatever payments went to the $100,000 top piece the syndicator would be keeping.

Similarly, if the property were resold or refinanced at a later date, the proceeds would have to go to the $350,000 wraparound mortgage, so the syndicator would be carving out a potential $100,000 profit on resale or refinancing, as well as a share of the cash flow that might be allocable to debt service or the upper portion ($100,000) of the $350,000 wraparound mortgage.

Similarly, the syndicator could structure the wraparound mortgage either to subordinate his or her return to the investor return or to give himself or herself some kind of preference. Obviously, the wraparound mortgage would have to be structured as a mortgage if it is to stand up tax-wise. That means that the wraparound mortgage must call for interest payments.

However, let us assume that the underlying mortgage called for annual payments of $35,000 a year on the $250,000 underlying mortgage. The wraparound mortgage could also call for $35,000-a-year payments, so that the syndicator would be pocketing nothing on his or her position, unless and until there was a resale or refinancing, when he or she would get $100,000 of principal if the $350,000 wraparound mortgage were paid off.

By putting nothing into his or her pocket out of the operating cash flow, the syndicator would actually be subordinating the wraparound mortgage to the investors' cash flow, in the same way he or she might subordinate the free piece of the equity.

Similarly, the syndicator might subordinate his or her $100,000 portion of the wraparound mortgage by agreeing not to sell the property for less than $500,000 cash above the wraparound mortgage of $350,000, which would secure return of their capital contributions to the investors.

THE SYNDICATE FROM BEGINNING TO END

Stripping down the typical real estate syndicate to its skeleton, we discover that almost every real estate syndication involves either a leasehold to the syndicate promoter (on which he or she pays the investors a prefixed return, either with or without an opportunity for investors to participate in an override) or in a free piece—or a combination of both.

Making an analogy of this kind of real estate financing to the corporate stock and bond market, we might say that the leasing transactions are similar to giving the investors mortgage bonds, with the syndicate manager retaining the common stock.

The free piece of the deal (if there is no subordination) is similar to a pure common stock deal with investor dilution, with the syndicate manager getting his or her common stock free. The wraparound mortgage is a variation of the free piece.

If the free piece deal involves subordination, the transaction could be equated to capitalizing an entity in which the investors get preferred stock and the syndicate manager gets common stock.

As in the corporate financing field, combination packages can be arrived at in which the syndicate manager participates at both levels—free lease and free piece—and in which equity kickers are given to the investors in both deals so that, in the leasehold, they may participate in rent increases. Subordination clauses in the free piece deal can be adjusted to give the investors higher returns in the case of an early redemption or greater shares of the profit, if they stay in the deal longer, and so on.

Raising real estate equity by syndication is limited only by the imagination of the syndicator and his or her advisors. As in the corporate finance field, real estate deals can be evaluated by the strength of their management and the strength of their assets. Ideally, the perfect real estate deal has strong assets (sound real estate values) and capable, aggressive management (a good syndicator).

The deal should be structured to give the investors some good tax shelter, to minimize their investment risk and give them a crack at growth, and to avoid the wasting effects of inflation.

TAKING APART SOME ACTUAL DEALS

Real estate syndications all involve marketing pieces of real estate deals to a group of investors.

The investors are motivated by sharing in one or more of the following benefits: current income streams, income tax benefits, future potential appreciation.

If you want to become a syndicator, you should study your competitors' products. If you want to become a syndicate investor, you certainly would want to sample the current marketplace.

Therefore, whether you are a syndicate investor or a potential syndicator, you will want to look at as many current offerings as possible.

Perhaps the best way to see what the marketplace is showing is to contact various kinds of professional advisors. Accountants and attorneys are constantly being offered real estate syndications of various types. Local stock brokers and many life insurance people sell syndications to supplement their other products.

Financial publications, such as the *Wall Street Journal, Barron's, The New York Times* financial section, and other periodicals, constantly advertise syndication offerings. There are a number of professional newsletters in the field, among them *Questor Real Estate Letter* (115 Sansome Street, San Francisco, California 94104), *Tax Shelter Insider* (10076 Boca Entrada Boulevard, Boca Raton, Florida 33433), *The Stanger Report* (20 Bingham Avenue, Rumson, New Jersey 07760), and many others.

PUBLIC AND PRIVATE OFFERINGS

As mentioned elsewhere in the book, there are two kinds of real estate partnerships—public and private. The public real estate partnerships register with the SEC; the private ones usually put together prospectuses under Regulation D. While the contents of both disclosure documents may be similar (both usually track the requirements of Guide 5 found in Part 2), the public limited partnerships file with the SEC and, therefore, are more readily available to the public, while the private limited partnerships are usually distributed to a limited number of investors and are not readily obtainable unless you happen to be on someone's mailing list.

Large sums of money are involved. Professionals estimate that three or four times as much money is raised by Regulation D private offerings as by the publicly registered SEC ones.

In 1982, public real estate limited partnerships were estimated to have raised $1¼ billion. If the private partnerships raised three or four times as much, we are talking about a $5 billion industry.

Some public real estate limited partnerships that are constantly engaged in raising money include Balcor Partners (10024 Skokie Boulevard, Skokie, Illinois 60077), American Property Investors (affiliated with Integrated Resources, 666 Third Avenue, New York, New York 10017), JMB Realty Corporation (Chicago, Illinois 60611), Consolidated Capital Management Company (1900 Powell Street, Emeryville, California 94608), E. F. Hutton Real Estate Services (One Boston Place, Boston, Massachusetts 02108), Robert A. McNeil Corporation (San Mateo, California 94403), and many others.

More updated and detailed descriptions of current public offerings may be obtained by subscribing to the *Questor Real Estate Letter*.

WHAT KIND OF REAL ESTATE WILL YOU SYNDICATE?

If you are going to become a syndicator, you should syndicate the kind of real estate you understand best or aim at the market where you have the most contacts.

If you are looking for deep tax shelters (real estate that shows substantial enough losses so that the property operates at a tax loss each year that can be used to offset other income of the investor), you will want highly leveraged properties, properties with large mortgages requiring small cash down payments, or the government-subsidized housing programs or historical rehab parcels. Syndication of these kinds of properties offers maximum tax deduction for each dollar invested.

If you are looking for substantial economic deals, you will have to decide whether you and your investors would rather have current income streams or long-term appreciation. Long-term appreciation usually does not have current cash flow; that is why you are buying the property cheaply so that it can appreciate over the long term.

Thus, an office building or apartment house may show little current cash flow, but its prospects may be good because the rents are under market or the cash flow can be improved by refinancing the existing mortgage on a more favorable basis.

If you tap the sources we have suggested above—the accountants and attorneys, the stock brokerage houses, the financial periodical advertisements—if you subscribe to one or more of the tax shelter newsletters, and if you speak to knowledgeable real estate brokers in your community, you will find out what the competition is doing.

By taking apart their prospectuses and examining what is being offered, you will soon learn how to tailor your own deals.

Once you have picked your field of syndication, whether it is economics or tax shelter, get the best professional tax and legal advice you can from professionals who have engaged in many transactions before. You do not want to reinvent the wheel. You want to tap somebody else's know-how and constructive thinking so that your deal can be a couple of points better than the competition—so that your deal will sell faster, be more secure, and give you something to build on for next year's marketplace.

HOW TO SELL YOUR UNITS

Most syndicators sell their first deals to close acquaintances. They may be relatives or long-time personal friends. If you are a real estate broker, they will be some of your better brokerage clients. If you are a lawyer, again, they will comprise some of your best clients. Similarly, insurance people, accountants, stock brokers, real estate owners, and other entrepreneurs have discovered that getting the first deal off the ground is difficult, and their best potential investors are people who have known them all their lives and who have confidence in them.

As you get ready for your first syndication, prepare a list of those people from your phone or address book, and try to make the list as long as possible. Make sure to see them all personally; don't just mail batches of papers.

A certain number of these people will buy anything you have to sell, because they rely on you as a human being and have confidence in your intelligence and ability. Others will want hard questions answered, but it is from this initial nucleus that you will get started.

Most syndicators discover that after they have transacted a deal or two they have exhausted their personal contacts. At that time, you might ask each of your investors whether he or she has some friends who would be interested. If they have been in on a couple of deals and have had good tax write-offs or some dividend distributions, they will add to your customer list.

Once you have exhausted that expanded customer group, you will probably have to go outside to get your syndications sold. Again, your fellow professionals may be interested in making sales for you. Accountants, lawyers, stock brokers, real estate brokers, financial advisors, and insurance people are often willing to make such sales among their own clientele. Of course, discounts or commissions will have to be offered

Getting Started in Real Estate Syndication or Venturing 25

to these people to help you make the sales, and, depending on the various professional groups you are dealing with, conflicts of interest and ethical problems must be overcome. Attorneys will have difficulty accepting commissions from you, as the seller, if they represent the purchaser. Similarly, certified public accountants have ethical constraints governing who may pay them and for what. However, on occasions where payment gives rise to an ethical problem, a discount may be given to an offeree representative who may pass it along to his or her client, on a fully disclosed basis, and the offeree representative may bill the client by the hour or charge the usual fee.

To summarize, your sales program will begin with your own acquaintances. You will broaden the base by asking them for recommendations as you move into additional deals. Finally, you will sell through other professionals, either by offering commissions or discounts or simply by offering good deals.

CHAPTER 2

How to Structure the Syndicate to Avoid the Corporate Tax

Before you get ready to sell your units, you have to make up your mind about what kind of vehicle you are going to take title in, what kind of an entity this syndicate is going to be when you have it all set up. Is it going to be a corporation? A partnership? A trust? How will you choose from among these particular entities? What are the advantages of each from the syndicate manager's viewpoint and from the investor's viewpoint?

SAVING THE CORPORATE TAX

One thing you want to do, if you are a syndicate manager, is save the corporate income tax, which in recent years has hovered at around 40 to 50 percent on income over $25,000. Let's assume that a deal throws off $100,000 and that this represents a 10 percent return on the equity money that has to be raised. If the deal, on a before-tax basis, paid 10 percent, and if you had to pay a 50 percent corporate income tax, all you would have left for your investors would be 50 percent. You would only have $50,000 left out of $100,000 for you and the investors.

You would have given $50,000 to your other partner, the U.S. government. You must eliminate the corporate income tax because otherwise you will not be able to show an acceptable return to your investors. In today's market, no deal can pay a 40 to 50 percent tax and survive.

To put it in reverse, merely by eliminating the corporate income tax you will be doubling the investment return.

The first objective, then, is to make sure you don't have a corporate tax to pay. Of course, all of the investors still have their own taxes to pay. They will have a tax on their own income tax returns, whatever their brackets, but at least they won't be stuck with a second tax at the corporate level.

HOW TO HANDLE A LOSS DEAL

The next problem for the syndicate manager is, "If I am to use a corporation here, what do I do if the deal actually shows a tax loss (a loss that comes out of a very good depreciation deduction)?"

If the deal actually shows a tax loss, you won't want a corporate vehicle, because the corporation will be entitled to the loss and your investors won't be able to use that loss on their personal income tax returns. If you had no corporation, you would be able to deduct the loss from the personal tax returns of each of the investors, while, in the corporation, that loss is useless.

So, if you have a deal that has income, you don't want a corporate tax. If you have a deal that shows loss, you don't want a corporation between your investors and the tax deduction. Either way, the corporation is no good.

BUSINESS MUSTS AND THE SYNDICATE FORMAT

The problem, at a practical level, is how to avoid the corporate income tax but keep the corporate advantages. For example, you want your syndicate to be continuous (the way a corporation is). In other words, if one of the investors dies, you certainly don't want the syndicate terminated (as a plain partnership would terminate on the death of a partner).

You don't want a legal dissolution on death. If you have 1200 investors in the deal and if the syndicate terminated because of the death of one of them, you would have to read the obituary notices every day to see when you would have to sell off the building.

You want continuity, which is a major advantage of the corporate vehicle. You also want transferability. That is, you want your investors, if they become unhappy with their investment or if they need the money, to be able to sell the piece of paper you gave them. You want

How to Structure the Syndicate to Avoid the Corporate Tax

centralized management, too, which is another corporate feature. You don't want 1200 investors to run the building; you want to be able to run it yourself, as the syndicate manager.

Aside from your own selfish interest in running the building, your investors don't want to run that building. They may not be capable of running that building, they may not be interested in running the building, and they want you to do it.

CORPORATE DIFFERENCES

You know that, in a publicly held corporation, the most the stockholders are called on to do is come together once a year to elect directors. The directors select the officers, and the officers run the building. Corporate management is not by the stockholders; it is centralized in the director-elected officers.

You want limited liability in your syndicate—another corporate attribute. You do not want to be personally responsible for the actions of any one of the other 1200 investors.

If you are an investor, for example, and if the syndicate manager does something unorthodox (suppose he or she personally signs an agreement to be responsible for the mortgage), in a true partnership instead of a corporation you would not have limited liability, and the partners might subject you to personal liability. Without limited liability, a mistake of a general partner might subject the investor to many hundreds of thousands of dollars of liability. But you want limited liability, and you want it badly.

If you get controlled management plus limited liability plus transferability plus continuity, you will have a sound syndicate; but you will also be taxed as a corporation. As you will see, your effort will be to get as many corporate attributes as possible and still not be taxed as a corporation.

SOLVING THE ASSOCIATION PROBLEM

The whole effort of the syndicate manager is to get as many of these corporate advantages into the deal as possible, get as much business protection as possible, and still get taxed as a partnership. Ideally, the syndicator would like to get all four corporate advantages, still be taxed as a partnership, and avoid the corporate income tax. At the present time, no one has been successful in getting all four of these advantages—

continuity, transferability, central management, and limited liability—while still being taxed as a partnership.

The legal juggling that goes on in syndication is an effort to eliminate one or two of these corporate attributes, so you can say, "Well, we won't have more than two corporate attributes and so we will be a partnership; we won't be a corporation."

All of the subtle ramifications that come into play result from the balancing each syndicate manager goes through in making a format that gives him or her the necessary control and the necessary continuity, and yet does not subject the deal to the corporate income tax.

Once again, remember that the techniques we are discussing, although they have been used in deals of $16 million and $20 million, can be used for the smaller deal just as well. In essence, they are very simple.

A CLOSER LOOK AT THE CORPORATION–PARTNERSHIP PROBLEM

Now, let's take another look at this problem. Bear in mind that if you get too many corporate attributes into your picture you are sure to be taxed as a corporation. Let's compare a pure partnership with a pure corporation (in which you have not drawn an agreement that will change the responsibility between the investors and the manager). Let's first contrast the partnership with the corporation, and then we will show you how we balance these attributes in typical deals.

There is practically no such thing as a pure partnership. Whenever three people get together and enter into a partnership, they draw up a partnership agreement. That agreement takes away some of these true partnership attributes and changes them. This doesn't alter the fact that they still have a partnership. But when you go too far in changing the partnership, by agreement, you may wind up with a corporate tax.

Transferability

A true partnership does not have transferability of interests. If you and I and a friend enter into a partnership agreement, then it is not possible for you to sell your interest to somebody else, because we are entering into a highly personal relationship in a partnership, and we don't want strangers forced on us.

In a pure corporation, there is absolute transferability of interests. If you buy a share in a company in the open market, you don't have

How to Structure the Syndicate to Avoid the Corporate Tax

to call up the corporation and ask permission if you want to sell your stock. In fact, you don't even have to buy the stock in your own name. It can be held in a "street name" by your broker.

Continuity

Suppose someone died. A corporation exists without taking cognizance of the death of any of the stockholders, while a partnership (in the absence of an agreement to the contrary) stops at the moment of the death of one of the partners. Again, because the pure partnership is a highly personal relationship, it stops at death. The partnership is legally obligated (in most states) to wind up its business, to sell off the assets, to pay off the surviving partners and the heirs, and to fold up. Obviously, you couldn't permit that in any real estate deal, but in a pure partnership you would have no continuity past the death of a partner.

Centralization of Management

In a pure partnership you have no delegation or centralization of management. Each partner has an equal voice in the business and expresses it directly. There is no intervening group of directors or stockholders. Partners participate directly. A partner can bind the entire partnership group merely by going out and signing an agreement.

In a corporation, you have full delegation of management. If you are a stockholder, you have no management rights at all except to vote for directors. The directors manage the business.

Limited Liability

In a pure corporation, you have limited liability. The company can lose $200 million; the maximum loss a shareholder would have would be the purchase price paid for the stock (except in certain banking corporations).

In a partnership, however, if one of three partners goes out and signs an agreement to buy $4 million worth of cans, each partner would be personally responsible for all of the $4 million (if the other partners had no money and if the partnership had none).

The pure partnership has none of these attributes. It has unlimited liability, no central management, no continuity, and no transferability. The pure corporation has all of those advantages. Now, let's start balancing them to put together a workable syndicate that will avoid corporate tax.

U.S. Treasury Regulation §301.7701–2 provides a simple test that can be used to determine whether the IRS will classify an association as a corporation or as a partnership. All you need to do is look at the four corporate attributes. If your association possesses three or all four of them, it will be taxed as a corporation. If, however, your association possesses only one or two of the corporate attributes, then you will be taxed as a partnership. Two is the magic number.

Regulation §301.7701–2 was cited in the case of *Philip G. Larson*, 66 T.C. 159 (1976), in which the court applied the four attributes test and held that the association would be taxed as a partnership because it possessed only two of the four corporate attributes.

If the IRS ever successfully challenged a syndicate manager's classification of an association as a partnership, the result could spell disaster for the investors. Virtually all of the tax losses the investors were counting on would be wiped out, and the investors might be forced to pay taxes for past deductions that were now disallowed. If this were to happen, your reputation as a reliable syndicator would be finished.

One way in which the syndicate manager reassures investors that the association will be taxed as a partnership is by obtaining an opinion of tax counsel, after reviewing all of the documents of the offering, that the association will be treated as a partnership and not as a corporation for federal income tax purposes.

Each syndicate manager selects a format that gives him or her the necessary control and the necessary continuity, and yet does not subject the deal to the corporate income tax.

TWO PRACTICAL SYNDICATE FORMS

There are other syndication vehicles, but the two most common are the limited partnership and the general partnership. We will try to change the pure partnership elements enough so that we will still have a workable business vehicle and yet not be so close to the corporation that we will be liable for a corporate tax. The mere fact that you call your group a partnership under state law will not protect you (if the IRS is able to demonstrate that you have three corporate attributes so that you are, in fact, a corporation for income tax purposes).

It is only by testing out these elements, no matter what you call your entity under state law, that you can be sure to escape the corporate tax. Let us examine the two most commonly used devices.

How to Structure the Syndicate to Avoid the Corporate Tax

Limited versus General Partnerships

Let us examine the difference between a limited and a general partnership. The general partnership is a common device. Suppose three people enter into a partnership, each with equal voice in the management and each personally responsible for the partnership debts. That is the common garden variety of partnership.

But for many years now there has been a device that is useful in bringing in silent partners or money investors—a limited partnership. The advantage is that the silent or limited partners may participate in a partnership by putting their money in, and their maximum risk is loss of that investment. In other words, they are very similar to corporate stockholders. They cannot lose more than their investment, as long as they remain limited partners.

The disadvantage is that the investors must remain silent partners. If they seek to participate in the management, they then become personally liable for the debts of the partnership. A limited partner who attempts to run the deal is subjecting himself or herself to personal liability.

Something amusing happened to one of my clients. He had a limited partnership set up in which he was a general partner and a whole group of investors were limited partners. In every syndicate, there is one investor who, in spite of the fact that his or her maximum investment is $750, feels that the building cannot be run without his or her advice.

My client would constantly get calls from this one limited partner, who would say, "Listen, I was in the building yesterday and I noticed the roof is leaking." Now, while it is nice for investors to have pride in the building, it also becomes a nuisance after a while. Since my client knew the legal differences between limited and general partners, one day when this fellow called and told him that there was a vacant office on an upstairs floor still not rented out, my client asked in annoyance, "Tell me, do you know the legal difference between a limited partner and a general partner?" The investor said, "No, I don't." "Well," my client said, "one difference between a limited partner and a general partner is that a general partner is personally responsible for all of the debts of the partnership, and this could be several million dollars."

The investor said, "That's very interesting." The general partner continued, "Wait. I want to tell you how the theory applies to you. Under state law, any limited partner who takes part in the management of the partnership becomes liable as a general partner. Now, if you keep calling me, you are going to become personally responsible if anything happens to the building." He never got another phone call.

The story illustrates that limited partners have no voice in the management. The limited partnership, then, is a perfect vehicle for syndication because it starts out giving you two of the important attributes you must try to achieve. You have centralization of management in the general partners. Only the syndicate managers become the general partners. Only they run the building. You have delegation of management and limited liability.

Well, the limited partnership solved two out of our four problems. Still open: How do you get a limited partnership with continuity (in case one of the partners dies), and how do you get a limited partnership in which the interests are fully transferable (so that the interests can be sold)?

Since you have two of the four business attributes you need by law, you may want to try for the next two by an agreement between the parties. Don't do it. If you get all four attributes, even though under state law you will be a limited partnership, once you add full transferability and absolute continuity to centralized management and limited liability, no matter what the state law says, you will certainly have a corporation for tax purposes.

The Limited Partnership Agreement

If you look at the sample limited partnership agreement (on pages 167 and 180), you will see how it worked on transferability and continuity. In a limited partnership you have limited liability and delegation of management. The only advantages you now have to worry about are how to restrict the transferability and how to make the partnership survive death. If you go too far, though, you are going to have all four corporate attributes and you will surely have a corporation. Here is how the problems were resolved in the sample agreement.

Continuity. There is no continuity in the sample agreement, because, if one of the general partners dies, the partnership terminates. You may think that means you might as well take out life insurance on the general partner's life, because, if he dies, the building will have to be sold. Actually, if one of the partners dies, the general partners may elect to set up a new partnership. (Note that I did not say "continue the old partnership" but "set up a new partnership." The semantics are legally very important here.)

The surviving general partners may elect to set up a new partnership; in that case, all of the limited partners must come along and enter it. The sample agreement is not only a partnership agreement, but it also constitutes a power of attorney whereby the limited partners au-

How to Structure the Syndicate to Avoid the Corporate Tax 35

thorize the general partners to act on their behalf to set up the new partnership.

So, technically speaking, you do not have genuine continuity. You are able to go to the IRS and say, "In the first place, there is no guarantee that the surviving general partners will elect to continue the partnership. In the second place, the old partnership will cease and a new one will have to be set up."

You are able to go to the IRS and say that the partnership is not really continuous in the same sense that a corporation is continuous. It could terminate when one of the general partners dies, particularly if the other partners do not feel like continuing the business and if they fail to set up a new one.

A variation on continuity. Perhaps a safer device covering continuity is this: Your agreement might say that the limited partnership terminates at the death of one of the general partners. The surviving partners may elect to set up a new partnership, but any one of the limited partners who refuse to come into the new venture has a right to demand purchase of his or her shares.

Though you won't find a buy-out of the objecting limited partners in the sample agreement, it would probably be safer to have one. Some newer agreements have provided for this right of the limited partners not to continue with the new group. Your effort in the tax field is always to conduct a safer tax deal than your competitor.

Please do not copy any of the agreements in the forms section of this book just because they were safe for someone else. You will run into trouble, because no two deals are the same and because the tax trends change. The forms are only a guide and must be adapted to your deal.

Transferability. In the sample agreement we did not want the partnership interests to be fully transferable, as corporate stock certificates would be transferable. In essence, we said, "We are going to restrict the transferability somewhat." You cannot transfer a certificate in this limited partnership without the consent of the general partners.

I have not attempted to find out if there is any instance where the general partners did not consent, but theoretically you have to get the general partners' consent before you can transfer your interest.

In other words, in order to have a limited partnership certificate different from a corporate stock certificate, it is usual to provide that you can't just transfer your certificate. You have to ask the general partners, and if they refuse you cannot make your transfer. It is theoretically possible for transfer of a certificate to be refused.

To make this palatable to the investors, the agreement goes on to say that if transfer of the actual limited partnership interest is refused, future monetary distributions will nevertheless go to anyone who is designated as substitute limited partner.

In other words, while the partnership may refuse to recognize the new limited partner on the books, he or she will nevertheless get the monthly checks. Although the assignee will have the right to get checks, the old limited partner will still be the record owner of the interest.

While other solutions to problems like this have been developed, agreements like the sample are being used all the time.

The General Partnership Agreement

Let's look at the sample agreement for a general partnership on page 186.

The general partnership is almost always coupled with a lease from the investors back to the general partners and an agency agreement. This serves a very useful purpose.

To be safe, you must avoid having all four of the corporate attributes. You must set up your deal so that the investors have personal liability, they lack continuity, there is no centralized management, or the certificates are not transferable. The limited partnership agreement reviewed above worked on continuity and transferability. The general partnership works on personal liability and centralization of management.

Centralized management and the general partnership. If you are going to have a general partnership with 1200 or 1300 people, the first thing that worries you is how to manage this deal. If everybody had an equal voice in the management, who would run the building?

Certainly, if you were going to syndicate a building with thousands of investors, it would not be practical to require their consent on every management decision. In a general partnership in which your investors have a voice in management, you need a leaseback to you, as the syndicate manager, so that you, as tenant, can make the day-to-day management decisions.

In the first place, by the leaseback you are practically eliminating the subject of management altogether. Realistically, if all the investors are going to get is a monthly rent check, what is there for the investors to manage?

Since the entire management of the building will be left to the syndicate manager (as tenant), managerial decisions have been removed from the hands of the investors as a practical matter (as long as there

How to Structure the Syndicate to Avoid the Corporate Tax

is no default on the lease). The investors have leased the building to the general partner syndicate manager for 99 years or for 70 or 30 years.

You accomplished two things with the lease to yourself: In the first place, the lease gives you a chance to keep all or part of the build-up in income from rent increases; in the second place, the lease takes away from the investing group any management problems at all. The investors now manage only one thing: they manage to get their rent checks each month.

Mortgage refinancing. Now, of course, since the investors own the underlying real estate itself, you might have to come to them once or twice for some management decisions. What do you do if you have a mortgage refinancing? The investment partnership has some management decisions to make on refinancing.

Most syndicate managers who use the general partnership technique say, "We will go back to the investors and ask them if we can sell the building or if we can refinance the mortgage."

If you think about these two rights (investor consent on sales and on refinancings), you should not worry too much. You would probably want to get their consent anyway, because you certainly don't want to be in the position where you, as syndicate manager, could sell the building out from under the investors without their consent after they have put up all or most of the equity funds.

Voting on sales and refinancing. So, under the general partnership coupled with a leaseback to the syndicator, you leave the investor group certain veto powers, such as on the mortgage or sale, but all day-to-day management decisions on renting, building maintenance, and hiring and firing lie with the leasehold group, and that leasehold group consists of the syndicate manager and insiders and needs no representation from the investing group as such.

The basic difference between the limited and the general partnership is that the limited partnership automatically has a key management group (the general partner) and doesn't need the leasehold. In the limited partnership, if there is a leasehold, it will not be a tax device exclusively. It will be a profit-sharing device to keep the build-up of rents in the syndicate manager's hands. But the general partnership needs the leasehold for management. Without a lease, the whole general partnership agreement will fall apart at the practical level. You can't have 1200 investors each participating in day-to-day decisions.

Mortgage and sale problems in the general partnership. If you examine the sample general partnership agreement, you will see that the key partners have retained the power (as syndicate managers) to sign mortgages, deeds, and so on, and, in so doing, to bind the investing partners. (See paragraph 3 of the agreement.) Note that in paragraph 4 a technique has been evolved to buy out dissenting investors.

Liability problems. The general partnership agreement solves the problem of delegating management to the inner group with a lease from the investors to the syndicate managers. If you examine the general partnership sample carefully, you will see that there was an actual general partnership. This means, on paper at least, that every one of the investors was personally responsible for the partnership debts and that managers, as general partners, are also personally responsible for the partnership debts. This is technically true, but that liability is largely theoretical.

The investors are not general partners in the lease; they are general partners only in the group that owns the underlying real estate (subject to the net lease given to the managers). What kind of liability could property owners be subjected to, since all management, operation, and subleasing are in the hands of the tenant managers?

What if there were a major catastrophe and somebody were killed and there was no insurance; or, suppose the building fell over. Casualty liability is almost 100 percent protectable by insurance.

There also could be liability in case one of the general partners signed the bond and mortgage and bound the partnership for a deficiency judgment. Under the agreement, the general partners agree that they will not enter into a mortgage transaction without getting the consents of the investor partners (see paragraph 4). In addition, it is unlikely that people of the financial stature of most general partners would sign a bond and mortgage with personal liability just to see what effect it would have on the investor partners.

Theoretically, then, there is a general partnership among all of the partners; practically, there is almost no risk of liability because of the leaseback plus the usual lack of personal liability on mortgages. There is, however, unlimited liability in the general partnership even though that liability is theoretical.

That unlimited liability is what the general partnership type of agreement hangs its hat on. You are able to tell the IRS, "Look, you have a large group together here. They are actually, each of them, personally responsible for the partnership indebtedness."

Management problems of the general partnership. In the sample type of general partnership (with a leaseback), there is no delegation of management to the managers. The agreement requires the managing partner to go to the investors to get their consent in the only two management acts the ownership group might want to exercise: mortgages

How to Structure the Syndicate to Avoid the Corporate Tax

and sales. All other management functions are in the hands of the separate leasehold group. But, if the building is sold or if it is refinanced, 100 percent of the general partners, including the investors, must consent.

Buy-out of dissenters. You may ask, "How could I possibly enter into a deal like this?" What would happen if one of these small investors were to come to the closing and say he or she did not want to sell? Can this investor hold you up?

The answer is that while this agreement requires 100 percent consent, the agreement further states (paragraph 4) that in the event that 90 percent of the general partners consent to any particular course of action, then the dissenting general partners give an option to the remaining partners to buy them out at a specific price, in accordance with the formula set forth (paragraph 4). So, 90 percent is all that is required, and, while the agreement states that unanimous consent of all partners is necessary, 90 percent is actually all that is necessary, because of the option to buy back.

Because it would be cumbersome to require the investors to sign all documents, each of the three master partners of the inner syndicator group signs an agency agreement with his or her group of investors.

Summary of the general partnership. You have a partnership that should not be taxed as a corporation. This is sound because there is no delegation of management. There is nothing to manage here. On the two acts that need management, 100 percent consent is required (with a right to buy out dissenters). You also have unlimited liability, at least on paper. Now, because these two noncorporate attributes appear, the general partnership agreement should escape the corporate tax. As a result, you are able to make your certificates readily transferable (paragraphs 7 and 8) and are able to make the agreement continuous beyond the death of any one partner (paragraph 8).

The general versus the limited partnership. The limited partnership automatically has to delegate management to the inner group, because that is how a limited partnership works. The limited partnership must have limited liability to start with. The only things that a limited partnership can work with are restrictions on continuity and restrictions on transferability (see paragraphs 12 and 14, respectively, in the sample agreement).

The safe harbor rules. Suppose your general partner will be a corporation. Under the Uniform Partnership Law of most states, there is nothing that compels the general partner to be an individual. There are some special rules you have to follow if the general partner is a corporation.

The IRS has established certain criteria that it wants to see the general partner pass, if the IRS is to issue a favorable ruling that the partnership will be taxed as a partnership and not as a corporation, in the case of a limited partnership.

The first thing to note is that the IRS procedure involved in getting the ruling is merely the IRS's price for exacting a ruling. There is nothing that compels the IRS to tell you in advance that your partnership will be taxed as a partnership as distinguished from a corporation.

If you want a ruling—if you want the IRS to go out on a limb for you in advance—you must comply with its rather stringent rules. It is important to note that many taxpayers do not believe that the IRS has a right to exact compliance with this particular procedure as a price for having an entity taxed as a partnership. If you are content to take a chance, and if your investors will take a chance on whether you are right or not under the law, you may decide to go ahead with the partnership and use a corporation without complying with the IRS procedure (which lawyers call the safe harbor rules).

However, since many syndicators will be reluctant to fly in the face of an IRS policy, let us assume that you will want to comply with these so-called safe harbor rules. What do they require you to do?

The ruling branch of the IRS has stated that, in addition to meeting the general requirements of the law and the regulations, if you want to have a corporation as the sole general partner, you will have to meet the following additional tests:

1. The corporate general partner must have a fair market value net worth (without considering its interest in the partnership as part of its net worth) in an amount equal to the lesser of $250,000 or 15 percent of the amount invested by the limited partners, if the amount invested by the limited partners is $2½ million or less; or, if the amount invested by the limited partners exceeds $2½ million, the net worth of the corporate general partner must be 10 percent of the amount invested by the limited partners.

2. The limited partners, as a group, cannot own, directly or indirectly, 20 percent or more of the corporate general partner or of any corporation affiliated with it.

Please note a number of factors:

1. The safe harbor rules are applicable only to corporate general partners. If an individual is a general partner, he or she need

How to Structure the Syndicate to Avoid the Corporate Tax

only have a substantial net worth. No one knows exactly what that means, but he or she has to be somewhat better than judgment-proof and should not be a nominee.

2. In addition, if there is an individual general partner as well as a corporate general partner, presumably the stringent tests of the safe harbor rules need not apply.
3. There appears to be no statutory or regulatory basis for the prohibition against the limited partners owning as much as a 20 percent interest in the corporate general partner. Therefore, if it is important to your deal to have the limited partners own an interest in the corporate general partner that exceeds 20 percent, you should consider two alternative routes:
    a. Going ahead without a ruling and taking your chances on litigation on the theory that the IRS is wrong.
    b. Making sure there is an individual limited partner, thus avoiding the safe harbor rules.

Finally, if you don't want to take the time to get a ruling (or fear that it may open a hornet's nest of other issues), you may seek the opinion of counsel that the partnership will be so taxed.

CHAPTER 3

Joint Ventures, Trusts, and Other Types of Syndicate Vehicles

---

The limited and general partnership syndicates are not the only types being used. In this chapter, we shall discuss some of the other vehicles.

TRUSTS, TENANCIES IN COMMON, AND JOINT VENTURES

In the early days of syndication, syndicate managers began looking around for a vehicle that would give them the tax results they wanted plus the business protection they needed. One of the devices that was used was the tenancy in common. Some groups were set up as tenancies in common, with each investor's name on the deed. It was felt that each of the investors would like to see his or her name on the deed.

If you have a deed on a deal in which there are 100 tenants in common, you must realize the problems that will occur if and when that building is ever resold. Suppose 15 years elapse; to trace out heirships and prove that the estate taxes have been paid for so many people would make title almost unmarketable.

Let us examine a couple of other devices sometimes used. The problem with the true joint venture is that it is very difficult to predict its full legal ramifications. A joint venture has some elements of a partnership, but it is put together to cover one specific deal only. There is not nearly as much clear law on the subject as exists on general and limited partnerships.

If you have a general or a limited partnership and a client asks you what the law is in a particular instance, you are usually able to answer with a fair degree of certainty. When it comes to a joint tenancy, you have to pull down all the law books going back to Henry I in the 1500s. In the partnership, the legal research is clear and complete, but this is not so in the joint venture field, because joint ventures are a less common vehicle. The joint venture has the same tax problems and pitfalls as the general or limited partnership, but it lacks their certainty.

THE SIMPLE TRUST

The common business trust is undesirable because of a case called *Morrissey* (296 U.S. 344) that went up through the courts almost 50 years ago. A lot of language in that case says that if a trust is set up for the purpose of actively engaging in a business, if you have a delegation of management to the trustee, if you make the trust certificate transferable, and if the trust survives the death of one of the investors, you will have to pay the corporate tax.

Because of the *Morrissey* case, the business trust is to be avoided. A number of effective trust agreements have been transacted in the syndication field, but they involve unusual deals, with passive management. If you want to use the trust, get an IRS ruling in advance to make sure you are safe. In addition, in New York, there is another problem. In order to avoid the corporate tax, the trust must be passive. But, if your trust is passive, trust and real estate law may nullify your vehicle.

THIN AND TAX-SHELTERED CORPORATIONS

It is possible to have a corporation as a vehicle for a syndicate. You need either a thin corporation or a tax-sheltered corporation (whose depreciation reserve wipes out its taxable income). Such corporations may escape tax as long as the money they pay out to their investors is not essentially equivalent to a dividend. For the money to be a dividend under the tax laws, the corporation must have earnings or profits.

If the corporation gives money to its stockholders and there are no taxable earnings or profits, then the stockholders will not be subject to the ordinary income tax on dividends. There will be no problem of

Joint Ventures, Trusts, and Other Types of Syndicate Vehicles 45

a double tax, because the corporation won't be taxed, since it has no earnings or profits, and the stockholders won't be taxed, because what they are getting is return of capital. The stockholders may be taxed at capital gains rates.

The key test is whether you can put together a corporation that will have no taxable earnings or profits. You may be able to do this if you can use depreciation to wipe out the taxable income. To the extent that depreciation wipes out only part of the taxable income, you will have a partially tax-free distribution to the stockholders.

The Corporate Earnings Trap

Bear in mind that, beginning with January 1, 1972, corporate earnings for tax-free dividend purposes can be sheltered only by straight-line depreciation; accelerated methods of depreciation cannot be used to wipe out profits for the purpose of computing a tax-free dividend.

If you have a loss as a result of depreciation, you probably won't want the corporate vehicle anyhow. You will go back to one of these partnership deals because, if you get a loss in a partnership, then each of the partners can deduct his or her piece of the loss on his or her tax return. If you have a loss on a real estate renting corporation, it stays in the corporation.

So, if you can tax shelter and wipe out the corporate earnings of your syndicate by depreciation, you are in good shape, because then the money that comes to the corporation or to the stockholder cannot be taxed at ordinary income rates.

The Thin Corporation

Everyone in the real estate business is probably familiar with the thin corporation and the repayment of a loan concept. For years now, real estate corporations were set up with lots of loans and little stock investment. Say you are setting up a corporation. You have a choice. Suppose you need to raise $1001 to buy this building, You could put $1 of your investment in as stock and invest $1000 as a loan from the stockholders or as a second mortgage to the stockholders. Or, you could have $1000 worth of stock and a $1 loan.

Almost every real estate person would prefer all loans and no stock. He or she would like to be thin on equity and fat on loan. If the corporation earns $1000 in the first year of its existence, it can give that $1000 to the stockholders and have them pay no tax. Repayment of a loan made to the corporation is tax-free. Nobody pays tax on money he or she lends to somebody else when he or she gets it back, if it is really a loan.

But, if the corporation has $1000 of stock instead of a loan, what are the stockholders getting when the corporation sends them a check? It can't be $1000 of loan, because there is no loan. Where there is no loan and the corporation has earnings, the money is a dividend and will be taxed as a dividend at ordinary income rates.

Everybody in the real estate business sets up as much loan and as little stock as possible. In some deals, years ago, the ratio has been nearly 1000 to 1.

Thin corporation safe harbor rules. If you plan to issue debt to stockholders, you must comply with Section 385 of the Internal Revenue Code and its regulations. Among other things, the IRS will look at the debt-to-equity ratio of a corporation and the interest rate charged in determining whether the debt issued is really debt or preferred stock.

A corporation's debt will not be considered excessive if the corporation's financial situation would be satisfactory to a bank that makes ordinary corporate loans. The Internal Revenue Code has provided a safe harbor standard within which corporate debt will not be considered excessive. Debt is not excessive if the corporation's outside debt-to-equity ratio does not exceed 10 to 1 and if its inside debt-to-equity ratio does not exceed 3 to 1. The outside debt-to-equity ratio is the ratio that the corporation's total liabilities bear to stockholders' equity. The inside debt-to-equity ratio is determined in the same way, excluding liabilities to independent third-party creditors.

The annual rate of interest on an instrument issued by a corporation is reasonable if it is within the normal range of rates paid to independent creditors on similar investments of similarly situated corporations.

To avoid a challenge by the IRS regarding the validity of the debt issued, be careful to stay within the safe harbor rules of Section 385 of the Internal Revenue Code. Make sure that the corporation meets the debt-to-equity ratios test and that its interest rate is reasonable (comparable to rates a bank would charge). If the IRS is successful in an attack, disaster will follow, corporate deductions for interest payments on the debt will be disallowed, and tax-free repayment of principal loaned will be considered to be taxable stock redemptions or dividends.

Subchapter S Elections (Pseudo-Corporations)

Subchapter S (Sections 1371 through 1378 of the Internal Revenue Code) allows a corporation to elect to be taxed as a partnership. If

Joint Ventures, Trusts, and Other Types of Syndicate Vehicles 47

this election is to be utilized, reference should be made to the transaction in the syndication agreement. It is true that the S corporation or pseudo-corporation has been little used in the real estate field because Subchapter S, which governs the use of such corporations, until 1983 prohibited the use of a pseudo-corporation if investment income, such as interest, dividends, rents, royalties, or other passive items, comprise more than 20 percent of the gross receipts of the corporation for any particular year.

The 1982 Congress, by the Subchapter S Revision Act, removed some of the technical barriers to utilization of the S corporation for real estate deals. However, some of the major objections to use of the S corporation for syndications still remain, and, except for a few restricted transactions, you will probably not see a large upsurge of S corporations in the real estate syndication field.

The 1982 act removed the prohibition against qualifying as an S corporation if you have rental income. However, while Congress expanded the number of shareholders from the original limit of 10 to a new limit of 35, that number will probably be too small for most real estate syndications.

The largest inhibition still limiting use of the S corporation for real estate syndications is the basis limitation. In the limited partnership or the general partnership, real estate investors are permitted to take losses not only on the capital they invest but also on any mortgage liability on the property itself. If you invest $1 of cash in a real estate deal, and the real estate is subject to $4 of mortgage, you can deduct up to $5 of losses. That leverage is very attractive to the real estate syndicate investor, because it can be the source of two for one, three for one, or other multiple deductions without limiting the investor to the "at risk" rules.

However, as soon as you take the piece of real estate and put it into an S corporation, your losses become limited to the basis you have for your stock. If the S corporation buys a real estate deal subject to $4 of mortgage and you add $1 to the transaction for the purchase of your stock, you would be limited to a $1 loss if you were an investor in an S corporation, while as illustrated above, you would get $5 of write-off if you were a limited partner.

It is true that if you borrow the money directly for the $4 of debt financing, and if you are personally responsible on that indebtedness, you can also get $5 of write-off in an S corporation. But that means that, as an S corporation investor, you are at a substantial business disadvantage.

If you go into the partnership, you really have only $1 at risk, but you can get $5 of write-off ($5 represents the total of your investment plus the mortgage indebtedness of the partnership). If you invest in an S corporation, you can only get $1 of write-off, unless you become liable for the borrowing on the mortgage.

You do not want to be at risk for the whole $5 in a typical transaction. You want $5 of write-off, but you don't want $5 of risk capital of your own.

The partnership will still be the favorite vehicle for most real estate syndications, because it offers leveraged write-offs without personal "at risk" investment.

S Corporation traps. In any case, as we mentioned above, if the entity is to use the S corporation technique of passing through profits and losses directly to the investors, thereby avoiding a double tax, it had better be spelled out in the agreement, and the general partner or corporate manager should be charged with making sure that the S elections are filed each year and that everything possible is done to keep the corporation qualified for S, lest there be a tax disaster if the technical requirements of the statute are not met.

Use of Dummies, or Corporate Nominees

The usury laws (which prohibit excessive rates of interest) and the desire to avoid any risk of personal liability in construction contracts have given rise to a particularly nasty problem for partnership syndications. What do you do if you need a corporation because a lender refuses to make a loan to a partnership since the interest rate is too high, or if you have to use a corporation because someone decides not to get involved in partnership form in a construction contract?

Suppose the partnership owns a piece of real estate and the lender insists that, before it will make a loan to the partnership, the partnership must convey title to a corporation and keep it there as long as the lender is making advances. This helps the lender to avoid the usury laws, but what happens to the investor partners?

The IRS could take two lines of attack. It could allow all the interest deductions on the ground that those deductions belong to the corporation that owns title and not to the partnership. The IRS also could argue that, when the property comes out of the corporation and is conveyed back to the partnership, the corporation is a collapsible corporation, and that the stockholders (the partners) have realized ordinary income in the form of a dividend by taking the property out. See Section 341 of the Internal Revenue Code for a discussion of collapsible corporations and the traps inherent therein.

Joint Ventures, Trusts, and Other Types of Syndicate Vehicles 49

How do you avoid the trap of the collapsible corporation, which can artifically impose a huge tax on the fair market value of the property when it is put back in the partnership name, or how do you avoid disallowance of the interest, which the partners desperately want as their own deductions?

A common method has been to form a special dummy corporation, to which title to the property is transferred for as short a period of time as necessary to have the corporation execute the mortgage and then to take title out of the corporation immediately afterward. In some cases, title has been thrown back and forth as each construction loan advance has come down, but this can be very expensive in terms of legal paperwork, and especially in those areas where the state or municipality has transfer taxes on conveying in and out.

Using the individual dummy. Of course, one of the ways out is to use an individual dummy rather than a corporate dummy. While this may avoid liability on a construction contract, it is a worthless technique if the usury laws are concerned, because it makes no difference whether the real owner is holding title or an individual dummy is holding title; only a corporation can get around the usury laws.

A whole batch of tax cases involve the subject of the use of corporate dummies, and occasionally the IRS will issue a ruling that a particular transaction is clean and that it will not attempt to disallow the deductions by taxing them to the corporate dummy.

On the other hand, one of the common techniques that appears to have passed both IRS scrutiny and the courts is the use of a corporate dummy owned by a lawyer or a title company in which the real owners of the property have no stock. The use of such a corporate dummy for a nominal fee of, say, $50 or $100, and in which the real owners have no interest, with the real owners and the corporate dummy entering into a written agreement in which it is stated that the dummy is being used solely to avoid usury laws and that the dummy will convey the property back to the real owners whenever they ask for it, is probably the safest way to handle the transaction and avoid loss of the deduction for interest or imposition of a collapsible corporation tax.

THE REAL ESTATE INVESTMENT TRUST

The real estate investment trust is a creature of the tax law. It goes back to the Revenue Act of 1961, which added Code Sections 856 (and those following) to the Internal Revenue Code. The purpose is to set up a vehicle or conduit that would pass through tax-free to the investors the benefit of a diversified real estate portfolio in much the same way that mutual funds pass through to their investors dividend income and capital gains, without double taxation.

Since Congress intended the real estate investment trust to be somewhat like the regulated investment company, many of the regulations and tax rulings are carryovers from the IRS's approach to the regulated investment company. Like the regulated investment company, the real estate investment trust is a conduit and does not pay any tax itself if all the technical requirements of the statute are met. But the real estate investment trust (REIT) is not a true conduit; it must be an association taxable as a corporation in format, which means that if the REIT's foot slips and if it does not comply with the statute rigidly, there will be taxable income.

Since the REIT is compelled to distribute 90 percent of its taxable income each year, it does not build up a treasury, and the imposition of a 50 percent corporate tax would be a disaster to the typical REIT. If it believed it were tax-free and paid out 90 percent of its earnings to the investors, and if a 50 percent tax then fell on it, where would the money come from to pay the tax?

Let us look at the technical tests that permit the REIT to escape corporate taxation. To begin with, the REIT must be taxable as a corporation, even though it has no taxable income, which means that it must satisfy three of the four corporate characteristics discussed earlier in Chapter 2 (see Regulation §301.7701–2). The four corporate tests, of which the REIT must pass three, are centralization of management, continuity of life, free transferability of interest, and limited liability. Typically, most REITs have no problem satisfying these requirements.

During 335 days of the entire taxable year there must be 100 or more beneficial shareholders (Section 856[a][5]). This means you need relatively broad distribution, so the typical real estate syndicate does not use the real estate investment trust as its vehicle. There are other disadvantages. The REIT must own passive real estate, not real estate requiring active and aggressive management (more about that later).

Furthermore, the REIT must be managed by one or more trustees during the entire taxable year. The trust agreement may grant the shareholders the right to elect or remove one or more of the trustees, and the trustees must have powers that will satisfy the centralization of management test.

One of the early problems involving the REIT, which prohibited the trustee from being an officer, employee, or owner of an independent contractor that furnishes or renders services pertaining to the REIT, has been removed. Many trustees also have a relationship with the management company.

Joint Ventures, Trusts, and Other Types of Syndicate Vehicles

The REIT must avoid holding property primarily for resale (dealer property), and no more than 50 percent in value of the beneficial interest (shares) may be owned by five or fewer individuals (Section 856[a][6]).

The Tax Election

When the REIT is established, it must file an election to be taxed as such.

As mentioned above, the income must be passive; the REIT cannot engage directly in aggressive management of property and cannot build or construct property that requires active management. The statute imposes two separate tests: a 75 percent test and a 90 percent test (Sections 856[c][3] and 856[c][2]).

The 75 percent test requires that at least 75 percent of the gross income come from rents from real property, interest on mortgages, gains from sale or other disposition of real estate, dividends or other distributions from the sale of interests in other REITs, and/or refunds of real estate taxes.

The 90 percent test requires that at least 90 percent of the gross income be derived from the same source as the 75 percent test, except that dividends, interest, and gains from the sale of stocks and securities may be included in passing the 90 percent test.

There is also a 30 percent test that prohibits 30 percent or more of the gross income from being derived from the gain on the sale of stocks or securities held for less than six months or from the sale of real property or interest therein held for less than four years. The REIT cannot be a speculative vehicle.

As far as interest income is concerned (in passing the 75 and 90 percent tests), there are some technical problems. To pass the 75 percent test, the income must be from interests in real property and cannot be a charge for personal services (which give rise to questions on standby commitment fees, discounts, financing charges, and so on).

Furthermore, in passing the passive income rental test (the 75 and 90 percent rules), rental income will be excluded if the REIT furnishes or renders services to the tenants or manages the property itself instead of through an independent contractor (see Section 856[d][3]).

Percentage rents are no good (Section 856[d][1]) if they are based on net income or profit of the tenant; they may, however, be based on percentages of gross sales. Rents will not pass the test if they come from a person in whom the REIT has an interest of 10 percent or more.

There is a whole batch of asset diversification tests entirely aside from the income tests discussed above. Thus, at the end of each taxable quarter, at least 75 percent of the REIT assets must be in real estate (the definition of real estate also includes real estate mortgages). Not more than 25 percent of the assets may be in other securities. The REIT cannot own securities of a single issuer in an amount greater than 5 percent of the REIT's total assets.

The REIT must declare, before the time for filing its tax return, and must distribute within 12 months of the close of the taxable year, 90 percent of the taxable income (Section 857[a][1]). Any nondistributed taxable income will be subject to corporate taxation.

Kinds of Real Estate Investment Trusts

There seem to be two major kinds of REITs and some hybrids. There are real estate equity trusts (which invest most of their assets in real estate equities of one sort or another), and there are real estate mortgage trusts (which invest their money mainly in mortgages of various types). In both cases, the trusts are convenient vehicles for taking the funds of small investors and putting them to work in real estate.

The equity trust would seem to be at a disadvantage with its competing vehicle, the real estate limited partnership. The limited partnership does not have the passive income tests and seems able to invest in a wider range of asset than the real estate investment trust can.

Furthermore, if the real estate partnership can qualify as a partnership under the safe harbor rules or under the four tests discussed in Chapter 2, the partnership would seem to have greater management flexibility as well as greater investment flexibility. What is more, the partnership can accumulate funds and does not have to distribute 90 percent of the funds each year, and the risks of having made an investment stake are smaller in the partnership than in the real estate investment trust, where erroneous investment policies can result in the imposition of a corporate tax (something not possible in the limited partnership).

Thus, the equity trusts seem never to have done very well in the stock market or as a public vehicle. On the other hand, the mortgage trusts have had quite a boom (since they were able to pass along to their investors earnings of 12 percent or better by offering a tax-free pass-through on diversified mortgage portfolios). The use of borrowed, leveraged funds at a time when interest rates were rising made the mortgage REITs a very popular Wall Street vehicle for a while. But in 1973 through 1975, the REITs overextended themselves in construction loans without permanent take-outs, and many went into bankruptcy or reorganization.

Joint Ventures, Trusts, and Other Types of Syndicate Vehicles

SUMMARY

The preferred vehicle for real estate equity syndication seems to be the limited partnership. The corporate vehicle has not been useful because of the double tax and the inability to pass losses through to stockholders. The other vehicles discussed in this chapter all lack the flexibility of the limited or general partnership discussed in Chapter 2, and, except for unusual circumstances, the general or limited partnership will be the preferred syndication vehicle.

The real estate investment trust is a specialized vehicle that has found greatest success (and greatest failure) in highly leveraged mortgage investments where the trust has raised money from the public in the form of equity investments and then used that equity to leverage bank borrowings and put them out in construction or development loans of various sorts, making the differential between the prime rate of its borrowings and the rate collected from its customers.

In general, the REIT is too cumbersome for equity real estate investments and suffers from the additional detriment of having to invest mainly in passive real estate, which does not offer great capital appreciation possibilities.

CHAPTER 4

Calculating Returns on Investment

During the last 30 years, most of us have been taught that the calculator and the computer are new, revolutionary tools that help us analyze with scientific accuracy the strengths and weaknesses of various alternatives. The computer has helped us put a man on the moon and has taken over the details of many routine jobs.

In the field of real estate syndication, the computer has enabled us, in a matter of minutes, to tell what the depreciation picture will be in the twentieth year, what difference an additional 5 percent added to rent roll can make in the bottom line of a deal, what difference one-quarter of a point more of mortgage interest can make, and how stretching a 20-year mortgage out to a 25-year mortgage affects cash flow. It tells the investor when the optimum time arrives to sell the real estate, at least from an income tax law viewpoint. In truth, the computer is an indispensable tool for real estate investment analysis.

In this chapter, you will familiarize yourself with the typical technique for comparing one real estate deal with another and how apparently equal deals are shown to be unequal through an analysis of the cash going in, the cash coming out, and the timing thereof. Without the computer or the pocket calculator, this great wealth of mathematical detail would not be readily available to us, and anyone who attempts to get involved in a piece of real estate today without at least taking a look at the computer run is clearly short-changing himself or herself.

THE COMPUTER IS NO MORE RELIABLE THAN THE ASSUMER

On the other hand, we must not get too hung up on computer returns. They are mathematical tests; they do not deal with the intangibles of real estate. Two deals with equal cash flow and equal timing will come out as equal on a computer run. One may be clearly superior in terms of location and will have a great future, and the other will be sick almost from its inception. All of the mathematical assumptions will crumble and all of the projections will be meaningless if the real estate is no good.

Real estate is still real estate, and the requirements of location, location, and location still prevail. Unfortunately, the computer has to ignore location, because it has no way of measuring it. Computer analysis is not a substitute for looking at the bricks, evaluating the tenancies, and determining whether the syndicate manager knows how to run a property. Beware of making decisions purely on the basis of computer analysis. This is almost as dangerous as agreeing to get married solely because the computer matched you up with a partner.

The most important technique in thinking through the strengths and weaknesses of a particular computer run is to examine the input sheet, which lists the assumptions the computer was asked to make in doing the mathematical computations.

COMPUTER DISASTERS

It can be disastrous to read a computer run without reading the input sheet first. The figures dance before your eyes; they are so overwhelming that the conclusion looks inescapable. The input sheet will tell you what useful life the computer assumed in making the depreciation calculations and whether this useful life will be allowed by the IRS. It tells you what tax bracket it put the investor in in making tax-saving computations and whether the investor will be in that tax bracket over the life of the investment.

What assumptions is the computer making about the kind of return an investor should expect on his or her money? Obviously, a return that assumes that an investor can make 6 percent on his or her money in competing investments is going to come out with an entirely different set of conclusions from those of one that assumes that the investor can make 10 percent on his or her money elsewhere. Which one of these two assumptions fits the investor? What is the effect on the com-

Calculating Returns on Investment

puter if you start changing assumptions by one-quarter point up or down? The computer may assume that you will refinance the property in the thirteenth year, that you will sell it in the fifteenth year, that rents will increase 2 percent per year, or that real estate will remain constant over the life of the investment. Are these all realistic assumptions?

Get the input sheet, read it carefully, and question the validity of each assumption before you read the computer run. Remember that mathematics is only part of the real estate investment decision. If you question the assumptions, the computer run will be extremely helpful to you.

MEASURING THE TIME VALUE OF MONEY

The problem facing the investor is difficult unless you get all investments on a comparable basis. Let us demonstrate the specifics of the problem by comparing a couple of different real estate deals (see Table 4.1).

As we look at the three alternative deals without the computer, each is a $3 million investment. The third deal brings you back $6 million at the end of four years, the first deal brings back $4.5 million, and the second deal brings back $5.1 million. Which is the best deal?

Even without the computer, you begin to see some variables. While the third deal produces the most dollars, it also asks for the most money up front, and it produces profits at the slowest rate. If you put up $3 million in shopping center 3, you don't get a dime until the end of the fourth year, when you then double your money.

THE EFFECT OF LESS UP-FRONT CASH ON RETURNS

Shopping center 2 requires the lowest amount of up-front cash and splits the total cash into two installments. What is more, shopping center 2 starts to produce cash in the second year, but it goes up slowly on an erratic basis.

Shopping center 1 also produces cash in the second year, but the cash starts coming in faster. Shopping center 2 produces more cash over the four years than 1 does, but which deal is the best?

I'll tell you the answer in advance: Shopping center 2 has the highest internal rate of return, 3 has the lowest, and 1 ranks in the middle. As for the whys and wherefores, you will have to go through the rest of the chapter, but first see if you can figure it out for yourself.

TABLE 4.1 WHICH DEAL IS BEST?

	Shopping Center 1		Shopping Center 2		Shopping Center 3	
	Cash in	Cash out	Cash in	Cash out	Cash in	Cash out
Initial investment	$3.0 million	–0–	$1.0 million	–0–	$3.0 million	–0–
First year	–0–	$1.5 million	$2.0 million	$0.8 million	–0–	–0–
Second year	–0–	$1.5 million	–0–	$1.7 million	–0–	–0–
Third year	–0–	$1.0 million	–0–	$1.6 million	–0–	–0–
Fourth year	–0–	$0.5 million	–0–	$1.0 million	–0–	$6.0 million
Total:	$3.0 million	$4.5 million	$3.0 million	$5.1 million	$3.0 million	$6.0 million

Calculating Returns on Investment
SOME DEFINITIONS AND CONCEPTS

Keep everything in perspective. These are mathematical tests. Nothing in this chapter will tell you which is a better piece of real estate. All we can expect the computer to do is measure mathematically which deal produces money fastest while calling for the least amount of money going in.

As you can see, the mathematical emphasis is on timing. If you can produce $1 of income the moment you put up $1 of risk money, your money is never out and never at risk, and the return is infinite. Because you need to put up very little money, you can even borrow it. And you don't even have to have a dime of your own in the deal, since the moment you put the money up, it comes back to you. That is a desirable real estate deal, by mathematical tests.

On the other hand, if you have to put up $1 today and you do not get anything back in 10 years, mathematically you are facing a number of risks. In the first place, you have to keep your money exposed longer; in the second place, you are exposing yourself to the continued erosion of inflation.

Defining the Variables

Let us define some of the terms we will be working with.

Cash flow.   Cash flow is what is left after you use the rent income from the real estate to pay all of the operating expenses of the property and both the interest and amortization (debt service) on any mortgages. There are two different kinds of cash flow: pretax cash flow and posttax cash flow. The posttax cash flow measures the impact of the income tax savings.

Tax savings.   Most investors are interested in posttax cash flow. They willingly pay more, in comparing two equivalent real estate deals, for the one that gives the most income tax shelter, because the deal has a hidden income factor—a contribution by the income tax collector—which gives rise to more spendable cash as far as the investor is concerned.

Tax savings are indispensable to the intelligent measurement of real estate investment. In some cases, if enough tax savings can be generated, it is the income tax collector's monies that can be used to finance purchase of the property.

A doctor who is faced with a $50,000 income tax bill on April 15 is readily prepared to invest that $50,000 on December 31. If the doctor's investment will wipe out his or her income tax bill, he or she is not giving up anything of his or her own, but is only paying the syndicate manager instead of the tax collector.

In many cases, the tax savings generated by a real estate deal may be more important than the pretax cash flow. Many real estate deals are put together today in which the return of cash (pretax cash flow on cash invested) is less than 6 percent, while the return generated from income tax savings may well exceed 100 percent in any particular year.

Obviously, a computer run that compares only pretax cash flow without taking into consideration the income tax impact is only telling part of the mathematical story. Bear in mind that most long-term computer runs that predict tax savings over a period of 20 years suffer from the inherent limitation of making the assumption that tax rates will remain constant over 20 years and that the taxpayer will stay in the same tax bracket over 20 years—two highly arguable assumptions.

One bright investment advisor I know concedes that you can measure two deals against each other on an after-tax basis to see which one is better. However, you should bear in mind that the tax saving dollars are less valuable than pure cash dollars. He argues that a real cash dollar can be spent for anything, but a tax saving dollar can be spent only to reduce your income tax bill, and, if you don't have an income tax bill, either because Congress changes the statute or your own income falls, a deal that depends on tax dollars does not shape up as well as a deal that depends on cash dollars.

Mortgage amortization. Typically, a portion of each annual mortgage payment on a real estate deal pays off part of the mortgage and builds up the investors' equity in the property, assuming that the property can be sold later for all cash above the mortgage or that the mortgage can be refinanced and reinstated to its original amount at a later date. These are also controversial assumptions.

We all know of investors who became rich by building up mortgage amortization on deals that show little cash flow. Over the last 20 or 30 years, it has been no trick to keep real estate running at an even level and to refinance it to its original mortgage many years down the line. Long-term inflation, rising construction costs, and rising rent rolls have permitted this.

But will it always be true? Isn't a mortgage amortization dollar less valuable than a pure cash dollar? Is it as good as a tax saving dollar? Here, too, all of the dollars will be rated the same mathematically, but wise investors recognize the limitations of mathematical projections.

Rent roll appreciation or valuation appreciation. Some computer runs assume that rents will climb faster than expenses by X percent a

Calculating Returns on Investment

year; others assume that construction costs will increase real estate values by Y percent a year. Some computer runs assume both; some assume neither. Again, all of these assumptions are controversial, and the amount of risk involved in swallowing these assumptions will depend on what percentage you allocate to X and Y and how long you have to stay in the deal before the X and Y percentages become meaningful.

To project that construction costs will rise 20 years from now is a rather wild thing to do, even though it may be safe to assume a 3 percent increase for the very next year.

The assumption that rents will increase faster than expenses was easier to make a couple of years ago, before rent control and recession.

COMPUTING INTERNAL RATE OF RETURN OR DISCOUNTED CASH FLOW

For many years, the Wall Street analysts have used a concept called internal rate of return or discounted cash flow. These computations take into account not only the total benefits achieved but also the time it takes to achieve those benefits and the speed required to put your money in.

These concepts come out of a study of compound interest. It is a familiar fact that if you put $1 in the bank, and if the bank pays you 5 percent a year compound interest (interest on the interest, as it builds up), at the end of year 1 you will have $1.05, and at the end of year 2 you will have $1.05 plus 5 percent of $1.05. A simple set of mathematical tables or relatively simple arithmetical computations will tell what the original $1 will mount up to at the end of year 5, year 10, year 50, and so on.

These computations might be called the mathematics of accumulated cash flow. The reverse might be the mathematics of discounted cash flow or the present value theory. That is what we are going to be working with now.

Obviously, the right to get $1 at some future date is not worth a full dollar now, because the investor has to give up use of the dollar until the time when it is returned. A present dollar can earn 5 percent interest. A future dollar, therefore, should be discounted at the rate of 5 percent per annum to see what it is worth today. The mathematics of that computation will depend on how many years, months, or days you have to wait to get your dollar. It also will depend on the assumed rate at which the discounting is being made; that is, a dollar discounted at 6 percent is worth less than a dollar discounted at 5 percent, since the 6 percent computation assumes you are giving up the right to make

6 percent on your money, while the 5 percent computation assumes you are going to give up the right to make 5 percent on your money.

NON-REAL-ESTATE YIELDS FOR COMPARISON PURPOSES

Again, it is easier to understand these computations if you go outside the real estate field. Suppose you could buy an annuity that gave you $1000 at the end of five years. Suppose you could put your money in the savings bank now to earn 5 percent a year for five years, or in a money market fund that would earn 10 or 12 percent. In order to determine how much you would pay for the annuity, you would compare it with your earnings if you put your $1000 in the savings bank. To make the comparison, all you do is compute the present value of $1000 discounted for five years on a compound basis at 5 percent.

In the real estate field, there is a problem. In the first place, real estate deals usually do not involve the present value of a single future payment but instead involve the right to receive a whole stream of payments occurring in different years and possibly in different amounts. The income stream in real estate is based on estimates of future rents and future expenses. Money may enter in a single piece, but it also may go in as a series of installments.

The investor has four variables to keep in mind, and it is these variables that we will play out on the computer. You have to tell the computer (1) what money is going in, and (2) when it will go in. You have to know (3) what money will be coming back, and (4) when it will be coming back.

USING THE COMPUTER TO COMPARE REAL ESTATE DEALS

If the investor compares two real estate deals, the one that requires the slower input of money and returns more money faster will be the superior deal—at least mathematically—assuming equivalent real estate values.

The computer tells you the amount of money going in and when it goes in, and it compares that with the amount of money coming out and when it comes out to compute the internal rate of return or the discounted present value of the income stream.

We will not discuss here the mathematics of how the computer does this, nor the programming. Even if you do not own a computer, internal rate of return computations can be made quickly, without programming, by using either the advanced Hewlett Packard or Texas Instruments pocket calculators.

CHAPTER 5

Tax Angles of Syndication and Joint Ventures

Real estate syndication has been a popular investment vehicle for many years now, because it offers higher than average current returns on investment plus the potential for future appreciation. The proportions of that product mix—current return and capital appreciation—have varied from time to time. In the early years of real estate syndication, back in the 1940s, current cash-on-cash returns (the amount of money you got each year on your investment) were attractive, because they offered investors better returns than they could get in their savings bank books. In those days, when savings banks were paying from 4½ to 5 percent interest and real estate syndications were paying from 10 to 15 percent current returns, investors were attracted by the high current cash yields.

In the 1980s, when money market funds offer investors the possibilities of making current cash-on-cash returns in the 12 to 14 percent area, and when cash-on-cash returns on real estate equities vary from as little as 1 or 2 percent to a maximum of 8 to 10 percent, investors are putting their money into real estate syndications because there are other attractions, not just current cash-on-cash returns.

It is important to know that the investors' current returns are composed of two parts: the cash distributions from the project (the money thrown off by the real estate after paying expenses and debt service) and the benefits on the investor's own personal income tax return (tax shelter or tax loss, which cuts the current income tax bill).

THE VALUE OF TAX SHELTER TO THE INVESTOR

If you are an investor in the 50 percent tax bracket, before considering the value of any tax shelters you may have, every dollar of tax loss is worth 50 cents to you on your personal income tax return. It really doesn't matter whether the dollar of tax loss is used to shelter the income from the real estate itself or to shelter other income you may have (from your salary or your business). If you are in the 50 percent tax bracket, a dollar of tax deduction is worth 50 cents to you.

Suppose you are in the 50 percent tax bracket and you are called on to invest $1 in a real estate syndication that produces $2 of tax loss for every $1 you invest. That means, if you invest $1 and it brings about $2 of tax loss on your income tax return, and if you are in the 50 percent tax bracket, a $2 tax loss saves you $1 on your tax return—so that you have had a full dollar of saving for every dollar you invested.

Put another way, if the deal you invest in can produce $2 of tax deduction for every $1 you put up, you are not really investing any of your own dollars; you are only investing the tax collector's dollars.

The deal is self-financing. Whenever you can find a real estate deal that will produce $2 of tax deduction for every $1 you put up, you are investing nothing in the transaction, because you are saving an equivalent amount on your personal income tax return (assuming you are in the 50 percent tax bracket).

Suppose, for every dollar you invest, the real estate syndicate is able to show you a $3 loss. That loss would be worth $1.50 on your personal income tax return (50 percent of $3) in tax savings. If you were able to find such a deal, you would have an instantaneous profit. Every dollar you invest in the deal would produce $1.50 of tax savings on your income tax return, so that your return would be 150 percent per annum on your investment. Not many kinds of investment will show you that kind of return. Stocks and bonds won't do it; money market funds and savings bank passbooks won't do it. Indeed, very few real estate deals will show you $3 of tax deduction for every dollar you invest.

However, this chapter will deal with the search for the maximum number of deductions for each investment dollar, with the techniques syndicate managers and investors use to maximize the tax deductions they buy for every dollar they invest.

In many ways, this is the most important chapter in this book. The pure cash benefits of real estate have shrunk steadily in past years to the point where equity investors are often content to buy real estate

Tax Angles of Syndication and Joint Ventures

for a cash return that is less than the return to the mortgage lender, even though the equity investor takes a greater risk. With mortgage rates going to 16 percent and equity investments in real estate rarely offering more than 8 percent on a current basis, the tax benefits are the key to successful real estate investing and successful real estate syndication.

TAX KNOW-HOW MAKES SICK DEALS SALEABLE

If a syndicate manager can increase the tax benefits of his or her particular syndication over those being offered by a competing syndication, he or she has a more saleable product, worth a premium price, which may enable him or her to make a better profit at the syndicator's level. Tax know-how is indispensable to real estate syndication.

Furthermore, since most real estate syndications offer highly leveraged (very fully mortgaged) investment positions, the imposition of an unexpected income tax on the property or the disallowance of substantial amounts of the tax losses can turn what looks like a very good real estate deal into a tax disaster. Leverage works both ways. If you are selling millions of dollars of real estate to investors, you can lose many millions of dollars for them if you do not understand the tax law.

Needless to say, this book cannot make you an instant tax expert. It is not possible to cover fully all of the tax aspects of real estate, or even of syndication, in a single chapter. The sole purpose here is to get you thinking about some of the tax problems and some of the benefits, so that you can assemble the information and ask questions of your tax advisors.

DEPRECIATION AND LEVERAGE

Perhaps the best deduction that can come out of a real estate deal is the depreciation deduction, because it does not involve the expenditure of cash. It is a book entry. Depreciation is computed on the total cost of the property, equity plus mortgage. Two factors increase the depreciation deduction: shortening the useful life and increasing mortgage leverage.

If you are going to depreciate a $1 investment on a five-year basis, you will have a deduction of 20 cents a year. If you are going to depreciate that same $1 on a 10-year basis, your deduction will be 10 cents a year. The shorter the useful life, the bigger the annual deduction.

Similarly, mortgage leverage increases the annual deduction per dollar invested. If you buy a piece of real estate that costs $100 with $1 of equity and $9 of mortgage, and if you are able to depreciate that $10 of investment over 10 years, or 10 percent per annum, you will get $1 of deduction each of the 10 years, based on the total $10 cost, even though you have only invested $1 of equity.

If you have the same 10-year life and buy something worth $20 for $1 of equity, you would have $2 of depreciation each year on your $1 investment.

These are hypothetical figures. Let's look at some more realistic figures to see the impact of mortgage-to-debt ratio in permitting you to buy more depreciation deductions per dollar of investment. Table 5.1 illustrates how leverage works. In each case, the 15-year useful life is assumed, as permitted under ACRS, pursuant to the Tax Relief Act of 1981.

It is obvious that the higher the equity-to-debt ratio, the less deduction you buy per dollar of investment. Thus, a one-to-nine equity-to-debt ratio gives you a 60-cent deduction in depreciation for every dollar you invest; while a one-to-five equity-to-debt ratio only gives you a 33-cent write-off.

Since the objective of most tax shelters is to buy $2 of write-off for every $1 of investment—or, better, if possible, if there were no other deductions in the deal but depreciation—you would have to buy $30 of mortgage for every $1 you invest in order to get a $2 deduction

TABLE 5.1 LEVERAGE

Equity Investment	Total Amount	Mortgage Amount	Depreciation Deduction at 0.0667 ($1/15$ per annum)
$1	$9	$8	60¢
1	8	7	53
1	7	6	46
1	6	5	40
1	5	4	33

Tax Angles of Syndication and Joint Ventures

for every $1 you invest. A $30 purchase price multiplied by the 0.0667 percentage (based on a 15-year useful life) would give you $2 of deduction. If you could buy that property with $1 of cash, you would be home free. Unfortunately, it is impossible under ordinary circumstances to buy real estate today with 3 percent cash and 97 percent mortgage.

SPREADING OUT YOUR PAYMENTS

One approach to the inadequate leverage found in higher equity-to-debt ratios is to pay in your capital contributions over a period of years instead of in a single year. Installment payments increase your write-off-to-equity-investment ratio.

See Table 5.2. This table will not permit you to utilize installment payments to get a 3 percent cash-to-debt ratio, nor will it permit you to come up with $2 of deductions for each $1 invested. However, it does demonstrate that installment payments permit you to time your investment dollars to coincide with the deductions that come out of the real estate. In other words, installment payments to the seller, instead of a single lump-sum cash payment up front, help you to buy more dollars of deduction per dollar of investment.

While this table does not come up with a two-to-one write-off, bear in mind, as you go through the chapter, that depreciation is not

TABLE 5.2 INSTALLMENT PAYMENTS

Assume a 15-year write-off, giving rise to 0.0667 depreciation deduction per dollar of investment.

Number of Years (Installments)	Amount Invested Per Year	Depreciation Deduction	Deduction/ Cash Ratio
1	$1.00	6.7¢	6.67%
3	0.33	6.7	20.00
5	0.20	6.7	33.50
6	0.17	6.7	39.40

Phasing in your money over six years increases the amount of write-off per dollar of investment, on an annual basis, by 600 percent.

the only deduction coming out of the real estate. The rest of this chapter will illustrate some other types of deduction. The installment payment, if acceptable to the seller, will always help you increase your leverage or permit you to use the tax collector's dollars to buy the real estate rather than the investor's dollars.

MORE BUILDING, LESS LAND

Ordinarily, when you buy real estate, you buy land and buildings. Land is not depreciable; buildings are. If you buy a piece of real estate for $1, and 10 percent of that value goes to land, then 90 cents is depreciable. Using a 0.0667 write-off on a 15-year basis gives rise to 6 cents of depreciation per annum per $1 of purchase price. If the land-to-building ratio becomes 50 to 50, so that you buy 50 cents of building for each $1 of investment, the depreciation deduction will go down to $3\frac{1}{3}$ cents per annum per $1 of investment.

Obviously, you want to buy as much building and as little land as possible for syndication purposes.

In some cases, the land-to-building ratio is tackled by the syndicator obtaining an outside appraisal. In other cases, the syndicator attempts to devalue the land by putting separate land-to-building ratios into the contract to purchase the property.

The IRS is not bound by either of these devices, but they are common in the syndication field. Ordinarily, the IRS looks to the land-to-building ratio found in the real estate tax assessor's books, the ratio found on the real estate tax bill, as evidencing a third-party, impartial opinion. You are faced with a fact question here; whether you or the IRS prevails depends on how good your evidentiary data is.

The problem is sometimes resolved by purchasing the building only and not the land. Perhaps the seller can be persuaded to keep the land and only sell you the building, subject to a land lease. In that case, every dollar of purchase price would give rise to a depreciation deduction, and none of your purchase price dollars would be wasted on buying land.

MORE INTEREST, LESS AMORTIZATION

Since almost all real estate purchased for syndication is purchased with mortgage debt on it, and since the syndicator's objective is always to buy as much deduction per dollar of investment as possible, it is common for the syndicator to try to renegotiate mortgage terms.

If $1 must go for debt service each year, it is better, from a tax write-off viewpoint, if that $1 goes to pay an interest deduction rather than to amortize the underlying debt. At the 50 percent tax bracket, that $1 is worth 50 cents in deductions if all of it goes to interest.

If the same $1 goes to pay off a 10-year loan, and 10 percent of it becomes mortgage amortization, then only 90 cents is deductible as interest, and that is only worth 45 cents of tax deduction.

If the same $1 amortizes a 20-year loan, then 95 cents of it is interest and 5 cents is amortization, and that $1 becomes worth 47½ cents in deductions to the syndicate.

THE WRAPAROUND MORTGAGE

The wraparound mortgage came into vogue because it gave real estate purchasers an opportunity to keep the benefits of older, below-market interest rate mortgages. If you were purchasing a piece of real estate that had an old mortgage on it with a 7½ percent interest coupon, and if the current mortgage market required a 15 percent interest coupon, every effort would be made to keep the old mortgage on the property, thereby saving the 7½ percent interest differential between the coupon rate and the current market rate.

If the old mortgage had no "due on sale" clause in it, the seller or a third-party lender would make a second mortgage loan and wrap it around the first mortgage. If the first (or underlying) mortgage required $7500 a year of debt service on $100,000 of principal, a new wraparound mortgage of $200,000 might be put on by the seller or a new lending institution at, say, 12 percent.

The $200,000 at 12 percent requires $24,000 of debt service. If a third-party lender were wrapping around the underlying first mortgage, which only required $7500 of debt service (7½ percent on $100,000), the 12 percent interest coupon on the $200,000 loan would require the new lender to pay out $7500 a year to the underlying mortgage lender, collecting $24,000 for itself but leaving $16,500 on a new investment of $100,000 a 16½ percent return on the $100,000 advanced.

The borrower's payments on the wraparound mortgage to the wraparound mortgage lender thus include enough money for the wraparound mortgage lender to pay the underlying mortgage and to pay interest on the second mortgage loan, both being wrapped together in a single wraparound mortgage.

The purchaser has achieved a benefit by getting a $200,000 loan at 12 percent instead of paying off the old loan and getting a $200,000 loan at 15 percent.

Note that the wraparound mortgage lender is required under the terms of its loan to make the necessary payments to the underlying first mortgage holder, thus protecting the purchaser–borrower from default of the underlying first mortgage loan, provided, of course, that the purchaser–borrower makes the wraparound mortgage loan payments.

THE WRAPAROUND MORTGAGE LOAN AND SYNDICATION

The syndicator found the wraparound mortgage loan a useful way of getting a free piece of the deal. The syndicator utilizes the purchase money wraparound mortgage loan to increase the purchase price, to get the free piece of the deal, and to increase the depreciable base to the syndicated partnership all at the same time.

Thus, if a piece of real estate is purchased by the syndicator at $100,000, and if the syndicator takes back a wraparound mortgage of $100,000 on top of the original purchase price, reselling the parcel to the newly formed limited partnership for $200,000, he or she has increased the depreciable base from $100,000 to $200,000, doubling the depreciation deduction by increasing the purchase price to the partnership.

Of course, before the IRS will permit the doubling of depreciation deductions and the doubling of tax base, it would have to agree that the fair market value of the real estate was equal to the $200,000 purchase price.

In other words, you cannot increase the depreciable base purely by a paper entry; the increase must relate to fair market value. Appraisals are often used to prove fair market value.

The wraparound mortgage permits the syndicator to create extra deductions, entirely aside from the increased depreciation deduction, by increasing interest deductions also.

Let's assume that the syndicator takes back a wraparound mortgage of $100,000 above the purchase price. The first thing the syndicator does, as mentioned above, is to increase the depreciation base by $100,000, and, assuming a 15-year useful life or a 0.0667 depreciation factor, adding the wraparound mortgage has increased the depreciation deductions by approximately $6670 a year.

If the syndicator puts a 12 percent interest coupon on that mortgage, that will increase deductions by another $12,000 a year (12 percent of $100,000); if the wraparound mortgage bears a 15 percent interest coupon, the total deductions of a 15 percent $100,000 wraparound mortgage

Tax Angles of Syndication and Joint Ventures

would be increased by a $6,667 additional depreciation deduction and a $15,000 interest deduction, adding total deductions of more than $21,000 to the syndicator.

If we assume that the syndicate investor wants to buy $2 of tax deduction for every $1 put in, the addition of a $100 wraparound mortgage at 15 percent should make the property worth $10,833.50 more to the investors, since $21,667 of increased deductions have been generated.

This is an oversimplification of a complicated problem, but it does illustrate the reason for the popularity of the wraparound mortgage.

HOW TO USE THE ACCRUAL METHOD TO GET MORE PARTNERSHIP DEDUCTIONS

The wraparound mortgage gives rise to another problem and to another tax-leveraged opportunity. It is typical for the cash flow of a real estate syndication to be rather low in the early years of the deal. If the syndicator is buying real estate at top dollar, the cash-on-cash return on the investment is bound to be rather small in the beginning. Similarly, if the syndicator is buying property with the intention of building up the rent roll or otherwise improving the bottom profit picture, it will take time to do that.

The property may be yielding relatively small cash returns in the early years. At the same time, the investors are interested in having maximum tax deductions and maximum tax losses in the early years. From the investors' viewpoint, the faster the tax losses come in, the faster they get back the money they are paying into the syndicate as an investment.

So, both the syndicator and the investors have every reason to want maximum losses in the early years, though the cash flow will be smallest in the early years.

Now, if the syndicator has taken back a wraparound mortgage, one way to maximize losses in the early years is to build up the interest coupon on the wraparound mortgage. In other words, if the syndicator compels the partnership to pay a high interest on the wraparound mortgage in the early years, the partnership will have relatively large tax losses in those years, which should make the investors very happy.

The problem goes something like this. There is not enough money coming into the partnership in the early years to pay excessively high interest rates. Of course, the partnership contributions that come from the limited partner investors can make up that deficit in the early years.

Therefore, if the limited partners' contributions are sufficient to make up the deficit in the higher interest rate, there would appear to be no problem from the partnership's viewpoint in the early years; the high interest rate will give rise to a high deduction, and everyone should be happy.

But what do you do after the limited partners' contributions stop? How do you make up the interest deficit in those years? Of course, if the property's earnings increase, there will be sufficient funds to pay the interest, and, again, everyone should be happy. The limited partners will not get those funds—they will go to the syndicator—but, presumably, the excess interest is something that has been contemplated and understood by both parties.

But what do you do if there isn't a sufficient increase in cash flow after the pay-in period to make up the excess interest deficit? Where will the money come from to pay the syndicator's wraparound mortgage at the higher interest rate?

That is where the accrual method of accounting comes in. Accruing an item on the books means entering it even though it is not paid in that particular period. If you are to keep proper bookkeeping records, and if you owe mortgage interest for the year ended 1985, you should enter the interest deduction on the books in 1985 even though you may not make the payment on the mortgage until, say, January 1, 1986. If you were to take a deduction for the interest in 1986 and leave it out of 1985, you would be distorting 1985's income by failing to take the deduction in the appropriate year.

To straighten out things like this, accountants have accruals and deferrals. An accrual is entering a matter on the books in the year in which it becomes due, and a deferral is taking a matter off the books and moving it to the year to which it is properly allocable even though it may have been paid in an earlier year. Here, we are concerned only with accruals.

Let us assume that there is a $1 million wraparound mortgage on the property taken back by the syndicator. The underlying mortgage was only 12 percent, but the syndicator took back a wraparound mortgage at 15 percent. Suppose the property only has a cash flow of $120,000. The partnership can only pay the syndicator $120,000, not the $150,000 called for by the wraparound mortgage.

You would accrue $150,000 on the books of the partnership but only pay $120,000, leaving a $30,000 balance due to be accounted for at a later date.

Of course, since the partnership has entered $150,000 on the books,

Tax Angles of Syndication and Joint Ventures

if all goes well the partnership will be permitted to take a $150,000 deduction on its tax return, and the limited partners will get the tax losses they bargained for.

When will the $30,000 missing payment be made? Typically, the partnership agreement and the wraparound mortgage state that if the whole $150,000 payment cannot be made in the year in which it accrues, payment will be deferred to a later date, but the bookkeeping entry will be made in the year in which it belongs.

That $30,000 can be paid on a resale or refinancing, or it will be paid when the cash flow catches up and the property begins to make more than $150,000 a year. Should that occur, there will be plenty of money to pay the current $150,000 a year, and, if there are any years in which the payments were not made, the excess cash flow (assuming that the property begins to earn more than $150,000 a year) can be utilized to pay off the old accrued but unpaid interest.

Accrual methods of accounting have been permitted for years, and, indeed, they are ordinarily preferred by both accountants and the IRS, because they more accurately state the income of a particular year and do not involve the distortions that occur merely because a check was put in the mail. Payment is typically more uneven and more distorting than accrual accounting.

Of course, like every other accounting technique, accrual accounting can be abused. The key questions are: Is the property worth the total amount of the wraparound mortgage plus the accrued but unpaid interest? Will the accrual be paid shortly into the future, or is the accrual a mere bookkeeping entry? Will there never be any source to pay off the accrued but unpaid funds? If that is so, there will be trouble. On the other hand, if the accrual method of accounting is realistic, the property is worth the value of the mortgage and unpaid interest, and if it is paid within a reasonably short time after the accrual, it is likely to pass not only accounting but also the IRS tests.

CASH OR ACCRUAL METHOD OF ACCOUNTING

A very important decision that should be spelled out in the partnership agreement is whether the partnership should report profits and losses on a cash or an accrual basis.

Some taxpayers prefer the cash basis, because it gives them relatively easy control over the timing of profits and losses. Pulling out the checkbook and writing a large number of checks at year-end may help the cash-basis taxpayer get additional deductions in a year in which they are needed.

Fashions change in syndications as they adapt to changing tax laws, and in recent years, as construction period losses, organizational expenses, and cash prepayment of interest expenses became less desirable, many syndications began to use accrual methods of accounting for their syndications.

You will have to plan where your syndicate will be during the early years and choose between the cash and accrual methods, depending on your particular circumstances. As mentioned above, the cash-basis taxpayer has a certain amount of control over tax timing. On the other hand, the accrual-basis taxpayer can get deductions for items for which he or she is not writing checks and has a smoother flow of income and expenses, thus avoiding an unexpected result when a piece of litigation recovers bunched-up income or when expenditures are made in a year in which deductions are not needed.

A good example of how the accrual basis produces deductions that are not available to a cash-basis taxpayer is a situation in which a property is in deep financial trouble. Interest on the mortgage continues to accrue, and deductions continue to be produced, so that tax benefits are achieved at a time when the deal can be in financial trouble. A partnership may not be paying interest on its mortgage, yet the investors may be accruing deductions.

While the partnership agreement need not decide in advance whether the cash or accrual basis will be used, the first tax return usually requires an election; once the election is made, it is almost impossible to change it without the permission of the IRS.

While it is not necessary for the partnership agreement to decide in advance which method will be used, it is desirable to include it in the partnership agreement, so that there is no misunderstanding by the partners. If there is going to be a disagreement between the limited partners and the general partners about which method shall be used, it is better to spell it out in the partnership agreement, so that nobody enters into the transaction with a misunderstanding.

If the limited partners are compelled to approve the general partners' decision, that should be stated in the agreement. If there is no coverage of the subject of whether cash or accrual shall be used, this is ordinarily left to the syndicate manager or general partner, who may have a different opinion from that of the investors on how the transaction should be treated.

TAX STRUCTURING YOUR DEAL

Cash outlays for expenses that are ordinary and necessary in carrying out a real estate business are deductible in the year in which they are paid out. Deductible items are called soft-dollar costs. Capital outlays, however, such as the cost of acquisition or construction of a building, can only be deducted or amortized over a period of years and are called hard-dollar costs. The investor, of course, wants deductions as soon as possible; therefore, as a syndicator, you should try to allocate as much of the investor's dollars as possible to soft-dollar costs.

The Tax Reform Act of 1976 limited the immediate deductibility of certain construction period costs by requiring them to be capitalized and thereby changed their status from soft- to hard-dollar costs.

Before the 1976 act, amounts paid during the construction period as interest and taxes were soft-dollar expenses and deductible in the year paid. Under Code Section 189 enacted by the 1976 act, construction period interest and taxes must be capitalized and amortized over a 10-year period. Since the enactment of Section 189, it is more favorable to syndicate an existing building than to construct a new building, because you don't have to wait for interest and tax deductions.

The 1976 act also enacted Code Section 709, which requires that partnership organization costs, such as the legal and accounting fees incurred in the organization of a partnership, be capitalized and amortized over at least a 60-month period. Section 709 also states that syndication expenses, which include costs incurred in marketing and promoting the sale of partnership interests such as brokerage fees, registration fees, and prospectus printing costs, must be capitalized.

In the good old days (until Revenue Ruling 68–643), it was popular for syndicators to put their deals together so that the money paid to acquire the property was labeled prepaid interest, which was deductible, rather than labeling the acquisition cost as principal, which was not deductible.

Up to five years of prepaid interest could be paid when acquiring the property under the old law, and this allowed the buyer soft-dollar deductions. In 1968, however, Revenue Ruling 68–643 limited the five-year prepaid interest deduction to only the current year's interest plus 12 additional months. Along came the 1976 act, which enacted Code Section 461(g) and completely took away soft-dollar prepaid interest. Section 461(g) now states that prepaid interest must be capitalized and deducted in the year in which it represents the cost of using the borrowed money.

In 1980, Code Section 195 was enacted, which permits previously nondeductible preopening or business investigatory expenses to be amortized over a period of at least 60 months. Preopening expenses would be expenses incurred by the syndicator in connection with the investigation of a real estate investment.

The tax laws have been changing frequently and will continue to change. Careful tax planning is essential to every real estate syndication. Since tax deductions are the key to successful real estate syndication, preplanning or tax structuring by the best tax advisor you can find can make the difference between a saleable and an unsaleable syndication.

If your deal can be structured so that your investors buy $2 of tax deductions for each $1 invested and if your investors are in the 50 percent tax bracket, they are buying real estate at no cost to themselves—the best of all investments. If each $1 invested produces $2 of tax deductions, a 50 percent tax deduction refunds the investors $1 at tax return time (50 percent of $2 deducted equals $1 of tax saving, refunding the investor's $1 investment, a 100 percent per annum return).

BEWARE OF THE MORTGAGE BASIS TRAP

Let's assume that you are going to use a partnership vehicle, that the syndicator is the general partner, and the investors are limited partners. That is the typical deal. Suppose the syndicator plans to construct an apartment house and to borrow several million dollars on a construction loan. When the syndicator goes to get the construction loan, the lender says, "We don't know if the project will actually be finished. We want you to be personally liable on the construction loan." This spells disaster for the syndicate!

To see why, you must understand the limitation on deductions that a partnership can take for its investor partners. When a partner (limited or general) buys into a partnership, the partner gets basis for the money he or she puts into it. If you put $1000 into a partnership in the form of cash, you get a cost basis of $1000 for your investment. If nothing else happens, the highest loss you can take off on your personal income tax return is $1000.

However, suppose you borrow some money on behalf of the partnership. Suppose you invest the $1000 and go to the bank and borrow another $1000. Under those circumstances, if you are not only an investor but also go to the bank and take out the loan personally, not only do you get a $1000 basis for the cash you invested but you also get a

Tax Angles of Syndication and Joint Ventures

$1000 basis for the $1000 borrowed from the bank that enables you to deduct up to $2000 of losses—$1000 on your equity and $1000 on your borrowing.

THE TAX BASIS PROBLEM FOR INVESTORS

Both kinds of money—borrowed money and invested money—are the same, as far as giving you basis is concerned. If the partnership loses $2000 that year, you are able to write off a $2000 deduction on your own personal income tax return.

However, suppose the partnership loses $5000 and the only basis you have is the $1000 you borrowed and the $1000 in cash you contributed. No matter how much the partnership loses, you can only write off on your personal income tax return your cost basis, which in this case consists of the money you borrowed plus the money you invested. These limitations are in Sections 704 and 753 of the Internal Revenue Code.

The regulations (1.752–1[e]) provide that the liabilities to which the partnership has taken subject are prorated among the various partners in accordance with the profit-and-loss ratio, provided that no partner has personal liability on the debt. If one partner has personal liability on the debt and the others do not, the partner who has the personal liability gets all the basis for the liability, and the other partners get none.

PRACTICAL TIPS ON TAX BASIS

Let's go back to the hypothetical situation in which there is one general partner and a number of limited partners. The general partner is the syndicator or developer, and the limited partners are investors. The investors put their money into the deal hoping to maximize their tax deductions, and they need every dollar of basis they can get in order to get tax deductions in excess of the cash they put in.

If they invest $100,000 in a deal that is going to have a $1 million mortgage, the investor–limited partners want to be sure that they get the $1 million mortgage tagged onto their $100,000 capital contributions so that they can get depreciation on $1,100,000 (the total of the cash invested plus the mortgage).

Suppose the general partner is the only one personally liable on the mortgage, because he or she personally guaranteed it to the construction lender. The investors will then get $100,000 basis for their cash contribution, but the general partner will get the $1 million worth of basis for signing the construction loan.

To the investor–limited partners, that is a disaster. It means that the general partner–syndicator will get 10 times as much depreciation as they do, 10 times as much construction loss as they do, and the investors who put up all of the money wind up with only 10 percent of the deductions.

PARTNERSHIP LIABILITIES AND TRAPS

The solution is that no partner should be personally liable on the mortgage if the limited partners are to get leverage and be able to increase their deductibles by the amount of the mortgage.

The partnership must take subject to the mortgage, or the mortgage must have an exculpatory clause that says that no one is personally responsible on the mortgage so the lender will look only to the property to collect. Sometimes a dummy is put on the mortgage so that none of the partners (neither general nor limited) is personally liable thereon.

This is a very important tax trap. If it is intended that the limited partners will get a basis for the partnership debts, it is imperative that the general partner not be personally liable on the mortgage, lest the limited partners lose tax base for the mortgage and discover that their losses are limited to their cash input.

SECTION 754 ELECTION

What happens when one partner gets out and is replaced with another partner? Suppose the new partner pays a higher price for his or her pro rata share of the partnership than the old partner did. Does the new partner get a different depreciation basis from what the old partner had? When the property is sold at a later date, does the new partner pay a tax on the appreciation of the property above its initial cost or above the price paid for it, which may be higher than initial cost?

It is possible for each individual partner in the partnership to have his or her portion of the partnership valued separately under Sections 754 and 743 of the Internal Revenue Code. The effect is that an investor who comes in after the initial organization and who buys the partnership interest from an original investor can get a basis benefit from his or her premium price.

Tax Angles of Syndication and Joint Ventures

In order to accomplish this, the partnership must file a 754 election, which means it has to file a form with the IRS agreeing to keep track of the various partnership interests and to make adjustments on its income tax return to reflect that information.

Use of the Section 754 election is desirable where there is a small group of investors with substantial investments; however, if you have a public partnership with hundreds or thousands of investors, Section 754 imposes a tremendous bookkeeping burden on the partnership itself, a burden with which most public partnerships are unwilling to comply.

SALE OF MORE THAN A 50 PERCENT INTEREST IN A PARTNERSHIP

Section 708(b)(1)(B) provides that where there is a sale of 50 percent or more of the total interest in capital and profits of the partnership within any 12-month period, such a sale will terminate the partnership for tax purposes.

The most important result is that the new partnership formed by the addition of a more-than-50-percent new partner may not qualify as an original user, whereas the old partnership may have qualified.

So, if an office building is completed, tenanted, and put into use in January of a particular year, and several months later one of the original partners gets out and sells a 60 percent interest to a new partner, the new partner's admission may terminate the old partnership at a time when it is impossible for a new party to enter and still be an original user. Only the earlier partnership, which was in possession before the tenants moved in and original occupancy started, can be the first user.

Everyone after that is taking second-hand property, and the termination of the old partnership by the admission of a new 60 percent partner can be a tax disaster.

TRAPS IN ADDING NEW PARTNERS

The admission of a new partner, who makes a second user out of the partnership, can cut double declining depreciation back to straight-line or 150 percent depreciation, as the case may be—a wipe-out of half of the tax shelter in an extreme case.

The rules for termination of a partnership as a result of admission of a new partner are quite complex, and your tax advisor must study Section 708 carefully to make certain that no tax trap exists if one partner sells out to a third party. The surviving partners, the partnership, and the new incoming partner can all be adversely affected by a cut in their depreciation benefits by as much as 50 percent through a mistake in this area. Check it out in advance, no matter which party you are or which you represent, and, if necessary, get a ruling from the IRS to avoid tax trouble.

DEPRECIATION RULES SINCE THE ECONOMIC RECOVERY TAX ACT OF 1981

The 1981 depreciation rules, called the accelerated cost recovery system (ACRS), is the most important aspect of the 1981 Economic Recovery Tax Act (ERTA) to syndicators. All buildings placed in service during 1981 or later must use the 15-year ACRS depreciation method, unless the syndicator elects straight-line depreciation over 15, 35, or 45 years. In commercial properties, an election of 15-year straight-line (6.67 percent per annum) will be desirable, because it will give you a quick return on your investment without the cost of ordinary income recapture.

Under ACRS, depreciation allowances are recovered over a period of 15 years in accordance with a schedule prepared by the Treasury Department. The schedule is based on the 175 percent declining balance method with a changeover to straight-line.

Under straight-line depreciation, which, if desired, must be elected, all annual deductions are equal. In the case of 15-year straight-line, the annual deduction can be figured by taking the full cost of the building and dividing by 15 (which is equal to 6.67 percent per annum).

ACRS or Straight-Line

As a syndicator, you must decide whether to use the 15-year accelerated method or to elect the 15-year straight-line method.

Although ACRS will allow your investors greater write-offs in the early years, the straight-line method is usually more desirable because it does not trigger the depreciation recapture rules and therefore results in capital gain taxation when the property is sold. For residential property, only the excess above straight-line is taxed at ordinary income rates under ERTA.

Depreciation Recapture under The 1981 Tax Act

When real estate is depreciated, each year the investors are allowed to deduct from their individual income taxes their proportionate share

Tax Angles of Syndication and Joint Ventures

of the total depreciation. These deductions reduce the property's basis and are taken by the investors at their ordinary income tax rates. When the property is sold, some or all of these deductions may be recaptured, depending upon which depreciation method was used.

If you use straight-line depreciation and hold the property for more than one year, when the property is sold there will be no recapture. Investors take their depreciation deductions, which reduce the property's basis, at ordinary income tax rates, and when the property is sold all gain is taxed at the more favorable capital gains rates.

If, however, you use the 15-year ACRS method and the property is sold before 15 years, some or all of the depreciation deductions will be recaptured and taxed to the investors at ordinary income tax rates. If the property depreciated is nonresidential, then all amounts previously deducted will be recaptured. If, however, the property is residential, recapture only affects the part of depreciation that is in excess of what would have been deducted if straight-line had been used.

Therefore, although ACRS allows greater deductions during the early years, it is usually more desirable for the syndicator to elect the 15-year straight-line method, because, by not triggering the recapture rules, it provides for full capital gain upon sale of the property.

Other ERTA Depreciation Changes

The Economic Recovery Tax Act of 1981 made substantial changes in the depreciation rules. Under ERTA, buildings may be depreciated without bothering to hassle over their useful lives or their salvage values. The new rules apply to buildings that were purchased or placed in service in 1981 or thereafter. The ACRS (the new name for depreciation) starts out by assuming that normal investment real estate will be written off on a 15-year basis, but you can take either a 35- or a 45-year write-off instead of a 15-year write-off.

However, you will have to elect to do that; otherwise, you will get the 15-year cost recovery rate. That rate—the 15-year life—will apply whether the buildings are newly constructed or you have repurchased an old one.

If you are not satisfied with the 15-year rate, as mentioned above, you could take a longer rate of either 35 or 45 years. However, what most people ask is, "Can I take an accelerated rate, even at the 15-year life?" You can take 175 percent declining balance method of depreciation based on a 15-year life, if you wish. You will swing over to a straight-line rate after the early years.

Indeed, low-income housing can get 200 percent declining balance method of depreciation, which will switch to straight-line in later years.

Should You Take Accelerated Depreciation under ACRS?

As mentioned elsewhere, most syndicators seek the fastest method of depreciation possible, because it produces the most tax shelter dollars in the early years. At first blush, it would seem that electing to take 175 percent or 200 percent depreciation would be better than straight 15-year life. However, there is a penalty for taking the accelerated depreciation, and that penalty applies particularly to commercial, nonresidential real estate.

Here is the penalty trap. You have commercial real estate and decide not to take the 15-year straight-line life, but instead elect to take the 175 percent accelerated rate. When you come to sell the property, all of the depreciation you took will be taxed at ordinary income rates (the so-called recapture).

On the other hand, if you decide not to take accelerated depreciation at the 175 percent rate on commercial structures you can take the slower, straight-line, 15-year rate. So, if you expect to hold the property for a decent period of time, you probably will take straight-line 15-year life instead of electing the accelerated method, because, after the first couple of years, the penalty of ordinary income rate recapture offsets the early years' tax savings.

You will have to make your computations on your own assumptions (whether you will hold the property for a long or a short period of time) and analyze what kind of a return you will make on the money you save in the early years and whether it offsets the penalty to be paid on resale.

Note that the full penalty of ordinary income recapture applies only to commercial real estate. Residential real estate will have ordinary income recapture under ACRS only if the property is not held for specific amounts of time, depending on whether it is low-income housing or ordinary residential housing.

The rules are complex, and you will want to check them with your tax advisor. It is not the purpose of this book to make you an expert in tax law but to point out some of the factors you must consider if you are to syndicate real estate and some of the questions to ask your advisor.

No More Component Depreciation

Under ACRS, only composite depreciation can be utilized on a single structure. In the past, you could break a building up into its components, and occasionally a building that had much short-lived

Tax Angles of Syndication and Joint Ventures

equipment in it was able to get more depreciation by being broken up into its component parts than by taking a single composite rate on the whole building.

Under ACRS, you have to take the flat 25-year rate unless you elect to take one of the longer ones; you can no longer break the building up into air-conditioning, plumbing, wiring, and so on.

The ERTA Antichurning Rules

During these times of tight money, real estate owners, builders, and developers in need of cash will syndicate their property and retain a small interest. If the syndicator retains an interest in the property, he or she may subject the new owners to depreciation under prior tax laws and bar the use of ACRS.

To prevent owners of pre-1981 property from engaging in sale activities for the sole purpose of bringing into play the post-1981 favorable ACRS depreciation rules, ERTA contains several provisions known as the antichurning rules. You may not use ACRS for any property acquired after 1980 that you or a related person owned at any time during 1980. Also, if you lease property back to its 1980 owner or a person related to the 1980 owner, you are barred from using ACRS.

So, if you are going to syndicate a piece of real estate, make sure that it won't be affected by the antichurning rules, so that your investors will be entitled to use ACRS depreciation.

These complex rules have been oversimplified here. You will want to check with your tax advisor about whether they apply to your situation. A typical problem arises when a person who owned a property before 1980 attempts to syndicate it in 1983 and wants to know whether the antichurning rules apply to the transaction. Similar questions arise concerning whether ACRS is available in transactions in which there is a sale leaseback and the seller occupied the premises as the owner before 1980.

Such questions can be answered only by carefully analyzing the tax law as it applies to your situation.

THE INVESTMENT INTEREST TRAP

The Revenue Act of 1969 made extensive changes in the deductibility of interest expenses incurred in connection with investments. In an effort to close the loophole that permitted taxpayers to deduct at ordinary income rates interest expenses on money borrowed with the intention of creating capital gains, Congress made some extensive changes in the deductibility of interest. As is usual in such statutory changes, they caused greater hardship for the innocent than for the tax avoider. The tax avoider studies the statutory material carefully, uses top legal and accounting advice, manages to work around the trap, and even discovers new loopholes.

But the innocent investor, not a student of such affairs, whose mind is concerned primarily with the business transaction itself rather than its tax avoidance potential, often falls into the pit set for the more wary competitor.

Congress was trying to prohibit, or make very expensive, the utilization of borrowed funds that give rise to ordinary income deductions for the purpose of creating capital gains, which are taxed at substantially lower rates. Congress's objection is important in understanding the rest of this section, since the rules themselves are arbitrary and make little sense except when seen in the light of that congressional purpose.

Some Investment Interest Rules

As mentioned above, the rule is attempting to disallow interest payments that exceed your investment income, so that you cannot go out and borrow funds to offset the income you earn in your business or from salaries.

However, the law recognizes that interest should be deductible to the extent that it enables you to earn investment income. Typical investment income is the money you make from interest you earn or dividends from stocks that you bought, or rents, royalties, and short-term capital gains from property sales that were purchased for investment.

Suppose you do have interest expense on borrowed funds that exceeds your investment income. This gets disallowed. You may, however, deduct investment interest equal to a flat $10,000 allowance plus any investment income you may have.

Someone with $100,000 of dividends and interest income can get deductions on interest on borrowed funds up to the amount of the interest and dividend income plus the $10,000 flat allowance.

Again, as with the other rules discussed here, the operation is more complicated than it is presented here. It requires a book on taxation and an expert advisor to lead you through the labyrinth of these rules.

CONSTRUCTION PERIOD TAXES AND INTEREST

In the past, it was common to write off all construction period interest and taxes as deductions, and utilization of those deductions,

Tax Angles of Syndication and Joint Ventures

particularly based on borrowed mortgage funds, gave rise to an enormous tax shelter which encouraged such construction. Congress, however, in order to inhibit those write-offs, has required that the construction period interest and taxes be capitalized and written off over a period of years instead of taking them in the year of the expenditure. There is a table that shows you how to do that, and, again, the rules are too complicated to lay out here; however, it is important to note that the construction period today gives rise, in most cases, to very small write-offs, and the syndication of such properties is thereby inhibited.

The property cannot take depreciation until construction is completed, so the only leveraged deduction you can get from borrowed funds starts when the building is completed rather than during the construction period.

THE NET LEASE TRAP

Section 57(c) of the Internal Revenue Code specifically provides that property subject to a net lease will be considered investment property (and therefore subject to the inhibitions of the interest disallowance rules discussed above) if the owner is guaranteed a specific return or is guaranteed in whole or in part against loss of income, or if the allowable deductions—which do not include interest, taxes or depreciation—are less than 15 percent of the actual rental income produced by the property.

The effect of these provisions is to limit the deductibility of interest paid in connection with net leased properties. However, you have to check each individual property mathematically to make sure that you don't fall into the trap inadvertently. Remember, if your property is leased, you must check the total of the interest, taxes, and depreciation; remove them from your expense roster; and see of the remaining expenses of your leased property exceed 15 percent of the rental income produced by the property.

An oversimplified summary of the effect of the partial disallowance of interest might be that interest involved in net leased properties, or interest involved in properties where the expenses (exclusive of interest, taxes, and depreciation) are less than 15 percent of the rent roll, is subject to these troublesome rules.

On the other hand, interest in properties that pass the 15 percent limitation and are not net leased will ordinarily be considered interest in connection with a trade or business and not subject to these rules.

Most apartment houses, office buildings, and hotels and motels that are owner-operated pass these tests. In any case, taxpayers who have substantial amounts of interest income are less concerned with these rules than taxpayers who have only earned income.

The investment interest rules are complex; their application must be studied by the best legal and tax accounting help you can find, because to fall into the trap unwittingly is disastrous. In some cases, if you study the transaction in advance, what starts out looking like a net leased property can pass the test and, through careful legal draftsmanship, you can avoid the penalty. If you plan for these transactions in advance, you may be able to avoid the trap; if you are not careful, you will almost certainly fall into it.

Syndicate investors have to be particularly careful, and syndicate promoters must be certain that they don't promise their investors deductions, only to discover afterward that they have given their investors tax preference income and disallowance.

IMPACT OF TEFRA ON SYNDICATIONS

The Tax Equity and Fiscal Responsibility Act of 1982 (TEFRA) imposes a number of penalties on real estate tax shelters, and they would be of interest not only to syndicators but also to their professional advisors and the investing public.

To begin with, a 10 percent civil penalty is imposed on all taxpayers under Section 6661(a) if they underpaid their taxes in a "substantial amount." The statute says that underpayment of taxes is substantial if it exceeds 10 percent of the tax shown on the face of the return. The IRS may waive the penalty if it is demonstrated that the taxpayer acted in good faith. The penalty will be waived if the taxpayer can show that there was "substantial authority" to back the taxpayer's position, or if the taxpayer's return "adequately disclosed" the facts dealing with the taxpayer's position.

Special Tax Shelter Rules

In the case of tax shelters, special rules were applied. A tax shelter is defined as a partnership, plan, arrangement, or entity whose principal purpose is avoiding or evading federal income tax. In tax shelters, the taxpayer must demonstrate that he or she had reason to believe that the way the item of deduction was treated on the return was "more likely than not" proper.

What all these words mean is still to be determined by litigation,

Revenue Rulings, and regulation, but many practitioners feel that the words "more likely than not" impose a stiff standard on tax shelters, their investors, and the sponsors.

New Penalties on Third Parties

In the past, most penalties were aimed at taxpayers. But the IRS felt that the promoters of tax shelters should be inhibited from peddling their wares, particularly if their merchandise consisted of "abusive" tax shelters. The IRS got Congress to go along by adding new civil penalties, which would be assessed not only against taxpayers but also on any person who aids, assists, procures, or advises with respect to any matters under the Internal Revenue laws, knowing that the material the advisor furnishes will be used for tax deduction purposes and knowing that an understatement of tax liability will result therefrom.

The penalty is $1000 in the case of individual returns and $10,000 in the case of corporate returns.

Congress went even further in imposing penalties on third persons who organized or sold tax shelters or who made statements concerning the tax deductions in the offering that the persons knew, or had reason to know, are false or fraudulent, or which statements involved a "gross valuation overstatement" regarding any particular set of facts. A gross valuation overstatement consists of a statement about the value of services or property that exceeds the correct value by 200 percent.

The penalty for promoting such abusive tax shelters is either $1000 or 10 percent of the gross income derived by the promoter, whichever is higher.

Finally, in connection with false or fraudulent statements, the commissioner may seek injunctive relief (Section 7408) to stop the promoter from continuing to sell abusive tax shelters.

Increased Fines

TEFRA increases the fines for criminal acts from $10,000 to $100,000 for tax evasion (and to $500,000 on corporate returns) with similar increases for willful failure to pay the tax, willful failure to keep records or report information, and/or perjury or the willful filing of false documents.

The impact of the above penalties on taxpayers, their advisors, and/or third-party promoters is to make them more conservative. Both the seller and the buyer must now fear the long arm of the tax collector.

Both should make certain that they have a reasonable basis in law for the claimed deductions if they are to convince the courts that they should not be assessed with the new penalty provisions.

Accountants, attorneys, appraisers, and other advisors should be more cautious in the future before going out on a limb.

CHAPTER 6

What Goes into the Joint Venture

The problems of drafting a syndication agreement and those of drafting a joint venture agreement are similar. There is no formal definition of the difference between a joint venture and a syndication. A joint venture is an agreement between a small group of one, two, or three partners, with each having almost equal bargaining power, while a syndication involves an agreement between an active syndicator and a larger group of investors, in which the syndicator clearly has the bargaining edge and draws the agreement more or less on a take-it-or-leave-it basis as far as the investors are concerned.

VENTURE PROSPECTS

A joint venture might be between a developer and an insurance company, between a developer and an owner of a substantial piece of land, between two developers with one supplying the money and the other supplying land and building skill, between a large and powerful tenant (such as a department store chain) and a developer, and so on.

In any event, whether the agreement is technically a joint venture or a syndication or a limited partnership, the problems to be covered by the agreement are almost identical. This chapter will deal with problems that are mainly business problems without regard to whether the agreement is a syndication agreement or a joint venture agreement.

WHY THE VENTURE?

The kind of transaction contemplated will have a large impact on the agreement. A syndication or venture that requires long-term development of a large site of vacant land is going to require an entirely different kind of agreement from one involving the development of a shopping center, and those two agreements will be different from one involving the purchase of an existing apartment house complex.

Whole sections of an agreement involving land speculation will deal with the problem of additional assessments in future years to pay carrying charges and real estate taxes, and additional large sections will be concerned with what happens to the proceeds of land sales and under what circumstances such sales can take place.

SHORT-FORM VENTURES

In a typical land speculation, the agreement is planned to be short-term; the agreement contemplates that in a certain period of years the venture will be finished and the cash proceeds distributed.

Perhaps the format of the land sales will be important enough so that the limited partners must be consulted on particular transactions (a sale of more than a certain amount or financing of certain types). But if we are dealing with a shopping center, the most important decisions will ordinarily be left to the developer, because timing and know-how are largely assumed to be within the developer's control, and he or she cannot consult his or her limited partners about leasing, timing, and operating decisions.

Furthermore, the question of why the team was put together will be of importance. In other words, if a developer is most anxious to move along a particular project in which he or she has already become deeply financially involved, that developer may make large concessions to the investors and may give them more control or a better share of the profits than would be available to them if the developer were merely trying to sell out a completed transaction to investors to yield them a limited return.

The "who" of the investment group is also important. A developer who needs financing will make a different kind of deal with an insurance company from the one he or she will make with a syndicator who is going to put together a deal to resell to a group of limited partner investors, and a different kind of a deal from what the developer will make if he or she deals with those limited partner investors himself or herself.

What Goes into the Joint Venture

SOME TAX PROBLEMS

Most real estate deals throw off tax losses, at least during the rent-up period. Who is to get the losses, and how are they to be allocated? If the syndicator is to allocate all of the losses to the investors (which is not uncommon), where will he or she get the money to pay his or her own income taxes, assuming there is taxable income allocated to the syndicator out of such items as management fees, sales at gains, and so on.

The agreement should deal with the tax problems of both the developer and the investors. Is the money going to the developer to be ordinary income? If so, will the partnership get a write-off for it? There is a conflict between the desires of the investors and those of the syndicator. The investors want to maximize the losses; the syndicator does not mind doing this but is reluctant to do so by picking up ordinary taxable income to himself or herself, unless there is some tax shelter in the transaction or unless there is a substantial amount of tax shelter available from another source.

AVOIDING TAX ON ORGANIZING THE VENTURE

Some tax problems come up as the developer turns over property to the partnership. Suppose the property cost the developer $5 and the partnership is going to pay $10 for it. Is the extra $5 ordinary income to the developer? If so, perhaps the developer could take it as a management fee that would be deductible to the partnership. Is it to be a capital gain to the developer? If so, is the investment group going to get basis for it? Or does the developer want to contribute the appreciated property in the form of a tax-free exchange and take the money later, in which case the partnership will get neither a step-up in basis nor a loss for the payment to the developer.

If the developer is a public corporation, it is earnings-conscious. Will the sale or contribution to the new partnership be reportable earnings from an SEC or accounting principles viewpoint? This becomes most important to an earnings-conscious developer.

The terms of the partnership agreement between the developer and the investors must be spelled out very carefully in accordance with SEC Accounting Release 95, which is now getting more rigorous enforcement by both the accounting profession and the SEC. The AICPA also has prepared accounting treatment rules governing the standards for reporting income by public corporations in real estate transactions.

ACCOUNTING REPORTING PROBLEMS FOR SELLERS

SEC Release 95 states that if there is uncertainty about the ultimate realization of profit by the developer, the profit should not be recognized for accounting purposes. The SEC points out that in order for there to be accounting recognition of a sale for earnings reporting purposes, the developer has to have substantial certainty at the time of reporting about his or her costs and expenses, and, if there is no certainty of profit, reporting the profit should await its actual determination.

The problem is particularly pertinent when the developer is earnings-conscious but the limited partners expect some guarantee of a return on their investment, failing which, they expect the buy-back of their position by the developer. Under those circumstances, many accountants and the SEC have taken the position that, since the sale is contingent upon future events, reporting the earnings may have to await the certainty of those events.

The accounting profession is constantly struggling with the problems of reporting earnings, particularly when the sale is contingent on profitable completion of the project or where substantial purchase money mortgages are taken back by the developer.

PURPOSE AND TERM OF AGREEMENT

The agreement should state whether the limited partnership is being formed to transact a single deal on a specific piece of real estate or whether it will own many pieces of real estate, and, if so, whether they are specific and presently in existence or the syndicator is going to go and look for them, in which case the investors should be told something about the kind of properties the syndicator will buy (the so-called blank check or blind pool of properties).

Similarly, the duration of the agreement becomes important. Will the partnership survive the sale of its first piece of property and continue as an investment group, reinvesting the proceeds in other parcels, or will the partnership wind up when the specific parcel contemplated in the initial transaction is disposed of?

Then there is the question of conflicts of interest and preemptions of opportunity. Will the syndicator give out contract work to subs he or she owns? Will the syndicator perform services for the syndicate for which he or she expects to be compensated? Or will all this work

What Goes into the Joint Venture

be given to outsiders? It certainly seems to make little sense to a syndicator with his or her own architectural staff and carpentry contracting shop to give the work to outsiders, but the investors must be informed.

DISCLOSING THE FACTS

On the other hand, the investors may be annoyed if they discover after putting their money into the deal that the syndicator is making more than one profit on them, especially if it was not revealed to them in advance.

With reference to conflicts of interest and preemptions of opportunity, what effect will future transactions have on the specific syndicate? Investors want to know if the syndicator is going to transact a competing deal across the street as soon as their deal is finished. Will the syndicator steal tenants from their syndicate to put in another parcel?

Suppose nothing is mentioned. What are the developer's rights to compete with his or her own syndicate? And what is competition? Is it competition if the syndicator builds another shopping center several miles from the first one and puts the same tenants in both, so that the tenants in shopping center 2 draw trade from shopping center 1, thus cutting down on the overages or percentage rentals available to the investors in shopping center 1? All this must be thought out carefully in advance and spelled out in the agreement to avoid trouble later.

CONTRIBUTIONS BY GENERAL PARTNER AND WITHDRAWALS BY LIMITED PARTNERS

What are the respective rights of the investors and the syndicator and their obligations, when putting money in and when taking it out?

Suppose the project needs working capital. Obviously, the typical plan contemplates that the investors put in a limited amount and therefore are limited partners. It is also generally assumed, if not specifically spelled out, that the general partner will make additional contributions at least to complete the project, particularly when the general partner is also the builder. In other words, typically, the risk of cost overruns falls on the builder–syndicator–developer, who is supposed to be the expert.

When does the general partner's liability stop? How far does it have to go? Is the general partner guaranteeing the deal forever? Must he or she continue to invest millions to keep the deal above water, when the investors have only put in a couple of hundred thousand? Can the general partner get off the hook by offering to refund their investment to the limited partners, or must he or she continue to subsidize a project that is under water until his or her own money runs out?

When excess capital funds become available from sales, refinancing, or operations, who gets them, in what percentages, and how do these distributions relate to the income tax consequences?

Ideally, the draftsperson, the developer, the investors, and their attorney should try to run the deal through their own minds from inception through sale, to visualize capital requirements, distribution of proceeds, sales and refinancing problems, and the tax consequences of each step.

Failure to think the deal through from its initial inception to the very last step, together with the tax and accounting consequences of each step, courts disaster for one or more of the parties.

CASH DISTRIBUTION PROBLEMS

A problem that often arises is an agreement that all cash distributions will go to investors until they receive a certain amount of money, since the syndicator subordinates his or her rights to theirs. Cash distributions, however, may not follow tax consequences unless the agreement makes this clear.

Thus, a general partner who is allocated a taxable profit and gets no share of the proceeds, because he or she is subordinate to the investors, may be in a tax bind on April 15.

If the limited partners are not to have any rights to withdraw their capital, this should be clearly spelled out. Otherwise, the general partner may find that the limiteds are asking for chunks of their money at a time when the general partner needs them.

RIGHTS AND POWERS OF
THE GENERAL PARTNER

It is very important to spell out in great detail the general partner's rights, not only to avoid conflicts between the general and limited partners but also to give the general partner a document to show third parties, in which his or her power to do something is specifically set forth.

What Goes into the Joint Venture

Mortgage lenders may not want to make loans, nor may title companies want to insure, nor may tenants want to sign leases with general partners unless the general partners can show specific authority, in writing, in the agreement signed by the limited partners. To leave any of these powers obscure is to tie the general partner's hands and make it very difficult for him or her to do business.

Typically, a limited partnership agreement involving real estate will give the general partner the broadest possible powers under the local statute and will spell out specifically rights permitting the sale, leasing, development, purchase, and marketing of real estate; the borrowing, mortgaging, pledging, modifying, consolidating, and extending, either with mortgage or without, regarding any of the partnership properties; the right to use dummies of nominees for the recording of title; the right to settle lawsuits, insurance claims, tax matters, and so on, and to hire such outside experts as architects, lawyers, insurance brokers, and real estate brokers; the right to file income tax returns and to make income tax elections; the right to litigate, compromise, arbitrate, waive, and contribute partnership rights and assets to third parties.

OTHER MANAGEMENT PROBLEMS

The largest part of limited partnership documents is often dedicated to the specifics of the transaction in which the general partner is authorized to act on behalf of the partnership. It is particularly important to spell this out in great detail to the investors so that their consent thereto can be obtained in writing in advance.

It is almost impossible to get all of the limited partners to agree on anything when a specific problem arises, unless you have gotten consent in advance. Many limited partners will not be able to understand complicated real estate transactions, and you will not be able to obtain their signatures at a later date if you didn't get them on the original agreement. Other limited partners, when they realize that their signatures are indispensable, may decide to hold up the partnership for additional financial considerations or emoluments. Get consent in advance, and save yourself trouble.

CHANGE IN PARTNERSHIP PERSONNEL

It is extremely important, from an income tax viewpoint and a business viewpoint, for the rights of limited partners to transfer their interests to third parties to be spelled out specifically. If partnership interests are to be freely transferable, the partnership agreement should so state; if the consent of the general partner is required before the limited partners can sell their shares to third parties, that also should be stated in the partnership agreement. Any other conditions also should be stated.

For example, in states where it is required that amendments to the limited partnership certificate be published, it is expensive to amend the limited partnership certificate to list a new limited partner. At the very least, a selling limited partner or his or her buyer should be required to pick up the tab for that advertisement. If you do not so provide in the agreement, you may find yourself with constant demands to transfer interests at a large cost to the partnership. In some cases, the cost of advertising bills and legal draftsmanship can exceed the amount collected by the selling limited partner.

Also, what happens in cases of death, bankruptcy, dissolution, or mental incompetency of a general partner should be discussed in the agreement; this is particularly important if there is only a single general partner. Who can replace the general partner if necessary, and is the partnership to terminate because of bankruptcy, insanity, death, or corporate dissolution?

RATIFICATION BY LIMITED PARTNERS

It is typical to provide that certain acts have to be ratified by the limited partners. In the simplest case, most partnerships require that a majority in interest of the limited partners must ratify a sale of the partnership assets. Particularly where the joint venture partner is the developer, provision should be made in great detail for all important management decisions that need be ratified by the limited partners.

Thus, in joint venture agreements in which the limited partner may be an insurance company, it often reserves for itself the right to approve tenants, leases of more than a certain amount, rents that involve less than a certain amount per foot, competing deals entered into by the developer, legal fees, architectural fees, leasing commissions, and so on, of more than a certain amount.

In some cases, all refinancing has to be approved by the limited partners; in other cases, only refinancing that does not fall within certain parameters requires consent (a refinancing may not require approval of a limited partner if it does not increase the total debt service above the existing debt service, or a debt service of a certain amount per month or per year may not require consent).

What Goes into the Joint Venture

DELINEATING SALES PROGRAM

In some cases, even sales parameters may be outlined in the agreement—parameters that do not call for the consent of the limiteds, provided that the developer acts within their confines. Thus, a sale of portions of the land subdivision, if they do not exceed a certain percentage of the total land and if they are at a price of not less than a certain amount, may take place without requiring investor consent.

If investor consent is required, it is important for the agreement to spell out how it is obtained. Do you write a registered letter? If you don't get an answer within a certain amount of time, is consent deemed to have been given, or must you get consent in writing? Generally, it is wise to provide that unless you get a negative response within a specific time, you should assume that consent is granted by the mere passage of time. Otherwise, particularly if there are large numbers of limited partners, the syndicator may be taking on an impossible burden, since people go away, get sick, and cannot be found when you need them most.

On page 167 is a limited partnership agreement that sets forth clauses that attempt to delineate the rights of the respective parties. Do not slavishly copy these documents; bear in mind that they are only one person's solution to a particular deal. Each partnership agreement has to be tailored to the particular transaction in mind. The first thing that must be done in putting together a syndication or venture is to visualize the transaction from initial offering right through to ultimate sale or dissolution. The transaction should be visualized not only from a management viewpoint but also from a liability viewpoint and, finally, from an income tax reporting viewpoint.

Similarly, pages 233 and 254 show two different forms of joint venture agreements, one favoring an owner or developer and the other favoring an institutional investor. You will also find checklists useful in putting together a real estate syndication and in putting together a joint venture.

CHAPTER 7

The Securities Laws and Syndication

Long before the SEC laws were passed as part of the New Deal, there was a history in the English and American courts of case law to protect investors from being defrauded in securities purchases. The law recognized for a long time that the typical investor was no match for the fast-talking securities salesperson. The SEC laws were passed to give investors more information and to require the information to be in formal prospectus form, uniform in nature of presentation (registration).

In other words, both the courts and the SEC have been attempting to protect the public from its own gullibility, greed, and ignorance—not by eliminating the investors' greed (a rather hopeless task)—but by making sure that the investors get enough information to make a sensible decision. That philosophy is called disclosure.

IMPORTANCE OF DISCLOSURE

This chapter discusses who must get such disclosure and how to give it. Bear in mind that there are three separate sets of regulatory bodies in the field. First, there is the SEC, which is a federal body that gets its jurisdiction from interstate commerce. Then there are the local state securities laws or blue-sky laws, which get their authority from the local state police powers. Finally, there is the old reliable court system, relying on such common law concepts as fraud and equity.

You must protect yourself at all three levels if you are a syndicator, and this can be done only by full disclosure of all material facts to your investors.

Who decides on what is adequate disclosure? In some cases, such as in interstate commerce, you may have both SEC rules and local state rules; in other cases, where there is no interstate commerce and everything is within a single state, you may only be dealing with the local securities laws or state courts. Your lawyer will have to check all three for you in each offering, to make sure you are not entrapped by one or the other. Sometimes there will be conflicts between state and federal rules and your lawyer will have to bridge the gap between them.

The local blue-sky laws are not treated in this book, nor is court-made law, because these would require a separate book. There are 50 different state laws and 50 sets of local courts. We will deal largely with the SEC statutes, however. Their first limitations come from the interstate commerce limitations.

NO SEC JURISDICTION IN INTRASTATE MATTERS

Section 3 of the 1933 Securities and Exchange Law provides an exemption from SEC registration requirements of "any security which is part of an issue *offered and sold* only to persons *resident within a single state or territory,* where the issuer of such security is a person *resident and doing business within such state or territory.*"

The intrastate exemption is designed only to apply to local financing of local businesses. If New York investors invest in a New Jersey real estate deal, the intrastate exemption is lost, because the securities are being offered in New York, while the group is doing business where the assets are located—in New Jersey.

ALL TESTS MUST BE PASSED

All of the following tests must be passed if the offering is to escape jurisdiction under the intrastate exemption:

1. The issuer (limited partnership or corporation) must be formed under the laws of a single state.
2. All of the limited partnership interests or corporate shares must be sold and offered to residents of the same state. Note that if a single nonresident is offered or buys a single security, the

The Securities Laws and Syndication

exemption is lost. The use of nominees to disguise the fact that a real buyer is a nonresident will not help you. Also, sales to residents who then resell to nonresidents make trouble for you. Indeed, any resale to a nonresident within nine months of the date of the last sale of the offering will disqualify the exemption.

3. The issuer must be a resident of the same state in which the securities are being offered.
4. At least 80 percent of the issuer's assets must be located within the same state as the investors and offerees. Also, the issuer must derive at least 80 percent of its gross revenues from within the state, and at least 80 percent of the proceeds derived from the offering must be used within the state.

In other words, the property, the investors, and the syndicator all must be located within a single state to escape SEC jurisdiction under the intrastate exemption.

THE NUMBER OF OFFEREES

If compliance with all of the above exists, the SEC does not have jurisdiction, and an intrastate exemption is available no matter how many offerees or purchasers there are. The offering might be made to literally hundreds of thousands of investors, but SEC registration will not be required if the offering, the offeror, the investors, and the property are all located within the confines of a single state.

Note, however, that we are only talking here about exemption from SEC jurisdiction. Even though all of the exempt features discussed above exist, some states still require compliance with the local blue sky laws. Some of the more important states requiring local registration, even though there is an exemption from the SEC, are New York, California, Texas, Illinois, and Ohio. You must check the laws of your state to find out if you have to register, even though you may escape the SEC's requirements.

EXEMPTIONS FOR PRIVATE PLACEMENT

Section 4(2) of the Securities and Exchange Law of 1933 exempts from registration transactions involving a *nonpublic offering*. What is a nonpublic or private offering? It is hard to define.

Here are some tests and observations to help you decide whether your offering is public or private. The legislative history of Section 4 of the Securities and Exchange Act of 1933 (House of Representative Report 85, 73rd Congress, First Session, page 5) states:

> The Act carefully exempts from its application certain types of securities transactions where there is no practical need for its application, or where the public benefits are too remote.

It was generally planned, according to the House of Representatives, that this kind of exemption would be available where sales of securities were being made to such sophisticated buyers as insurance companies, mutual funds, and banks. These organizations, according to Congress, were thoroughly competent to do their own analysis, and they did not need the protection of a prospectus or registration statement, since they would probably examine the underlying documents and the deal itself and not rely on any kind of summary information supplied in an offering statement or prospectus.

FINANCIAL SOPHISTICATION

Generally, offers should not be made to anyone unless the offeree has full disclosure of the facts and unless the offeree is sophisticated or knowledgeable enough to incur and understand the risks involved in the kind of security being offered.

There are two tests set forth above. The investor must have access to information, and he or she must know enough to be able to evaluate the information.

You cannot avoid registration merely by giving a novice investor access to all of your books and records and by saying, "There is nothing I can tell you. Look through the books and make up your own mind."

In passing the financial sophistication test where the investor uses an agent or business advisor to analyze the deal, the sophistication of the advisor is imputed to the investor, since it is the advisor who is making the investment decision.

An unsophisticated investor who is represented by a professional advisor (a business agent or the trust department of a bank) may find that the abilities of the advisor are imputed to him or her, so that a private offering arises out of the expertise of the advisor.

TESTS OF THE PRIVATE OFFERING

The principal factors to be found in the private offering test are set forth in *Edwards* v. *U.S.*, 374 F.2d 24. The tests were stated to be:

The Securities Laws and Syndication

1. The number of prospects and their relationship to one another and to the seller
2. The number of units offered
3. The size of the total offering
4. The manner of the offering
5. Whether the particular persons affected stand in need of the protection of a full registration (that is, their sophistication and financial expertise in the particular field of the offering)

SEC'S CURRENT GUIDELINES ON PRIVATE OFFERINGS

The SEC has for years recognized the difficulty in applying such subjective tests as financial sophistication and has made efforts to guide offerors into safe harbors, to enable them to avoid trying to guess whether they have prepared sufficient documentation to reasonably advise their investors of the facts.

From approximately 1972 to 1982, the SEC's advisory was called Rule 146, and it made an effort to simplify for offerors the determination of what is a private offering and what is not.

In 1982, in an effort to avoid some of the subjective language of Rule 146, a new regulation was propounded, called Regulation D, which attempts to codify the SEC's latest attitude toward private offerings.

Most of the books that offer real estate securities to investors (syndications) are attempts to follow Regulation D or its predecessor, Rule 146. Of course, your attorney will want to read Regulation D carefully and decide what should go into your prospectus. However, with some understanding of the changes effected by Regulation D, you will get a rough idea of the requirements and their practical impact on your ability to syndicate real estate investments.

One of the most interesting facets of Regulation D is that it provides an objective test for determining who is an accredited investor. Presumably, an accredited investor will not need all of the protection provided for the nonaccredited investor. An accredited investor is deemed to be anyone who has a net worth of $1 million or more, who has a $200,000-a-year income, and who is purchasing a syndication unit of $150,000 or more.

You may wonder what is the significance of the accredited investor. In the private offering field, the SEC wants you to have fewer than 35 investors. However, because of their deemed sophistication, accredited investors do not count. In other words, if you have 50 accredited investors, you can still have 35 nonaccredited investors in your deal. That makes 85, which is a good number of investors.

On the other hand, if you assemble a group of investors with $250,000 net worth, whose annual income is only $75,000 or $100,000, and who buy units in your syndication of only $75,000 apiece, these people will not be deemed to be accredited investors, and you had better not have more than 35 of them in your deal, or you will lose the private offering exemption.

SOME OTHER LIMITATIONS OF REGULATION D

Aside from providing a net worth and net income test as defined above, Regulation D gives some other tests that must be passed if you are to get a private offering exemption. As mentioned above, you may not have more than 35 purchasers (except for the accredited investors). If you do have accredited investors, they do not have to have offeree representatives to give them sophistication. Because they passed the net worth tests, they are deemed to have sophistication.

However, if you are going to use the private offering exemption, bear in mind that you cannot use general solicitations or general advertising, such as advertising in newspapers for investors, television or radio broadcasts, or the so-called general meeting or seminar that the public has been invited to attend. Such promotional devices are prohibited by the private offering rule.

It is important to note that just having accredited investors does not mean that you can eliminate the necessity of full disclosure, even to the accredited investors. The use of Regulation D does not provide an exemption from the antifraud, civil liability, or other provisions of the federal or state securities laws. It just eliminates the need for a full registration under Section 5 of the Securities Act of 1933. You still have to comply with state law; you still have to make certain that the investors have enough information, even though they are sophisticated, to make intelligent decisions; and you must not omit from your material any material facts; nor may you misinform them through the use of your private offering prospectus.

YOUR PROSPECTUS

If you have to register under the SEC or under a particular state statute, you will have to follow the current rules, regulations, and forms given out by the agency at that particular time. The prospectuses on page 222 may not be current at the time you register. But, even though

The Securities Laws and Syndication

the format is constantly changing, most issuers would like to make sure—even if they have a private offering or an intrastate exemption—that their investors do not sue them at a later date for failure to disclose some pertinent information in connection with the offering under court-made law.

It is important for you to decide in advance what kind of information is significant to an investor in making an investment decision on a syndication.

Guide 5, prepared by the SEC and amended by Release 33–6405 on June 3, 1982, which became effective on September 1, 1982, suggests that any prospectus dealing with a real estate offering should follow a more or less standard format with a standardized order and method of presentation, to give appropriate disclosure to investors in real estate securities.

You and your attorneys will want to read that document carefully. See pages 190 through 222. You must be sure to have the latest regulations before you. They are constantly changing.

In the interests of standardization, the guide suggests that the standardized format it lays out be followed and the materials covered in the order it recommends. The guide starts out by telling you what should be on the cover page of your book, how the tax aspects of the transaction are to be discussed, what use the proceeds being raised will be put to, what will happen if the proceeds of the offering are insufficient to meet the required need for funds, what kind of conflicts of interest arise between the general partner and the limited partner investors, and so on.

To give you a better idea of what goes into a prospectus, the table of contents of a recent Regulation D offering has been set forth on pages 223 through 228.

The instructions in Guide 5 are fairly specific. Just to give you an example, one of the items to be discussed in the prospectus, pursuant to Guide 5, is "Compensation and Fees to the General Partner and Its Affiliates."

The guide suggests that the section include a summary in tabular form, itemizing by category and specifying dollar amounts where possible all compensation, fees, profits, and other benefits (including reimbursement of out-of-pocket expenses) that the general partner and its affiliates may earn or receive in connection with the offering or operation of the partnership over its life.

The summary, according to Guide 5, should be organized to indicate clearly whether the compensation relates to the offering and organizational stage, the development of acquisition stage, the operational stage, or the termination and liquidation stage of the partnership.

PART TWO

Encyclopedia of Syndication and Joint Venture Forms and Checklists

Checklist for Syndicators	109
Subscription Agreement	112
Purchaser Representative Questionnaire	132
Investor Suitability Standards	137
Broker-Dealer Sell Sheet	140
Limited Partnership Agreement	167
General Partnership Agreement	186
Regulation D Private Offering Sample Table of Contents	223
Joint Venture Checklist	229

CHECKLIST FOR SYNDICATORS

The first form is a checklist for syndicators. It is based on a logical, step-by-step order for syndicating, from the beginning to the end, and it includes all of the traps I have discovered in four decades of syndication experience.

Each item in the checklist is based on the experience of myself or one of my clients, for which all of us have paid dearly. I have not attempted to make recommendations in the checklist, because you will want to tailor the transaction to meet your own needs, but you should find each point in the checklist worth thinking about.

As you move along in the syndication business, you may want to expand this checklist based upon your own experience. Needless to say, some of the points in the checklist are technical and must be reviewed with your professional advisors; some involve pure business judgment.

CHECKLIST FOR SYNDICATORS

1. Find an appropriate parcel.
2. Make certain it has an adequate return to:
    a. Attract investors.
    b. Absorb your syndication costs.
    c. Ensure a safety factor.
    d. Structure, as the key to syndication.
3. Contract to buy the property.
4. Prepare a sales prospectus or brochure from:
    a. The sales viewpoint.
    b. The legal viewpoint.
5. Select your format:
    a. General partnership with or without leaseback.
    b. Limited partnership with or without leaseback.

    c. Use of wrap mortgage, use of soft costs.
    d. Corporation, thin or tax-sheltered.
    f. Other (joint venture, trust, tenancy in common, or real estate investment trust).
6. How will you recoup your syndication costs?
    a. Sell extra units.
    b. Take back subordinated units.
    c. Postpone first payment to investors.
7. What will you use for working capital?
    a. Sell additional units.
    b. Hold off on distribution to the investors to build up a fund.
8. Who will sell your units?
    a. You.
    b. An outside sales organization.
    c. A combination of both.
    d. Part-time commission people (accountants, real estate or stock brokers, lawyers, insurance people).
9. Is your advertising campaign acceptable:
    a. Under state law?
    b. SEC law?
    c. The tax laws?
10. If you use a leaseback:
    a. How will refinancing proceeds be split?
    b. What percentage return (rent) to the investors?
    c. When do payments start?
    d. Will there be any inflation or overage clause?
    e. Any action to buy out the investors?
    f. Shall you use a dummy or a release clause?
    g. Will the lease be guaranteed for any particular period?
11. The syndicator's equity share:
    a. Is it subordinated?
    b. What is its dollar valuation?
    c. What is its tax status?
12. How will you raise the deposit money for the contract?
13. Specialized consultation:
    a. Who will help you write the brochure?
    b. Is tax counsel available for a depreciation ruling, review of all syndicate documents?
    c. SEC and blue-sky problems.
    d. Local real estate counsel.
    e. Accounting personnel.

Checklist for Syndicators

14. Your syndicate agreements:
    a. Management clauses.
    b. Compensation of syndicate manager.
    c. Transferability of shares.
    d. Continuity past death.
    e. Limited liability.
15. The syndicator's tax advantage over the publicly held real estate investing corporation:
    a. Avoidance of double tax that would fall first on the corporation, then on the stockholders.
    b. Direct use of the tax-free depreciation deduction by the investors.
    c. What the new investment trust will mean to you.
16. Getting the cash flow to the investor at minimum tax cost: the corporation thinly capitalized repaying its bonds as it makes money.
17. What is an unincorporated association (which will be taxed as a corporation)? It will have one or more of the following:
    a. Continuity despite death or resignation of members.
    b. Transferability of interests.
    c. Centralized management (in which investors turn over control to a board or manager).
    d. Limited liability to investors.

SUBSCRIPTION AGREEMENT

The next document is a subscription agreement, filled out, signed, and initialed on each page by the subscriber or potential investor.

In substance, this is a short document in which the potential investor acknowledges receipt of a copy of the full placement memorandum, that he or she understands the purchase price and the installments involved, that he or she understands that if payments are not made he or she may lose the investment, and that, until he or she gets a countersigned subscription agreement and acceptance from the partnership, all he or she may be entitled to is a refund if the deal falls apart for any reason.

Furthermore, if the purchaser has used a purchaser representative (a professional advisor, such as a financial analyst, an accountant, or a lawyer), the purchaser is asked for the name, address, and telephone number of that representative (as you proceed through the forms, you will see a special form for the representative to fill out).

Purchaser representatives are often compensated by the partnership for their services. You might say they receive a fee from the partnership for the work they do in analyzing the transaction and for their help in selling it to the investor.

The subscriber is asked to represent his or her net worth and income, to determine whether he or she is an accredited investor within the meaning of Regulation D of the securities law, and is also asked to represent that he or she is purchasing for his or her own account and not with a view toward resale.

There are a number of other technical clauses in the subscription agreement, but most are self-explanatory. Since the subscriber may never meet the general partner, he or she is asked to have documentation notarized so there is no dispute later about whether or not he or she signed it.

SUBSCRIPTION AGREEMENT—LIMITED PARTNERSHIP INTERESTS

You have advised me that _____ (the "Partnership") a _____ limited partnership, has been formed for the purpose of acquiring and operating _____ an office building located in _____, all as more fully set forth in the Private Placement Memorandum, dated _____ (the "Memorandum"), which has been furnished to me, and in the documents contained in the exhibits thereto. I understand that certain words used herein, whose initial letters are capitalized, may be defined in the Memorandum in terms of a meaning different from common usage, that said meanings are incorporated herein, and I acknowledge that I have consulted the Memorandum for such meanings.

I am writing to advise you of the following terms and conditions under which I offer and agree to subscribe to the amount of Class A Limited Partnership Interests of the partnership set forth herein (each being hereinafter referred to as a "Unit").

1. *Subscription*

A. Interest Being Subscribed For and Manner of Payment. Subject to the terms and conditions hereinafter set forth in this agreement (the "Subscription Agreement"), the undersigned hereby offers to purchase $_____ (the "Purchase Price") (Investor to fill in amount subscribed for) of Class A Limited Partnership Interest(s) (the "Unit"). You are urged to read with care the memorandum before signing this subscription agreement. Payment of the Purchase Price will be made in five (5) unequal installments pursuant to the following schedule for a full Unit:

_____
(Initial here)

Dates	Amounts*	
At execution hereof, to be applied at my Admission	$_____	(_____% of Purchase Price)
June 1, 1985	$_____	(_____% of Purchase Price)
June 1, 1986	$_____	(_____% of Purchase Price)
June 1, 1987	$_____	(_____% of Purchase Price)
June 1, 1988	$_____	(_____% of Purchase Price)
Total	$_____	(_____% of Purchase Price)

    I, the undersigned, hereby agree that the installments of the Purchase Price and interest due after my Admission under the Investor Note shall be made by checks of the undersigned payable to _____, as agent for collection for the Partnership, and paid, subject to collection, on or before the due dates.

    It is further understood that upon any failure to pay any of the Investor Installments of principal or interest, pursuant to the terms of the Investor Note, the General Partners may (1) accelerate, without prior notice, all Investor Installments, making them immediately due and payable, (2) borrow from any person sums in the amount of the Investor Installments of principal and interest unpaid from time to time, to the extent unpaid and charge the Class A Limited Partners' interest for such loan, (3) commence an action for the entire amount owed, together with interest as permitted by law, and/or (4) foreclose on the undersigned's Class A Limited Partnership Interest, to recoup the amounts due to the Partnership, the amount of any loans plus interest and in each instance legal or other fees in connection therewith, and such other costs or fees actually incurred by the Partnership in connection with the collection of such sums, all as more particularly set forth in the Partnership Agreement.

    The undersigned understands that foreclosure of his or her Class A Limited Partnership Interest upon a default on any Investor Installment may result in the loss of the undersigned's entire investment and may have adverse tax consequences. (See Memorandum, "Tax Aspects—Gain or Loss on Sale of Partnership Interest.")

_____
(Initial here)

_____
* For half Units, the aforesaid figures will be one-half of the listed figures.

Subscription Agreement

2. Conditions of offer

You or the Partnership shall have the right to accept or reject this Subscription or to rescind the sale of the Unit, for any reason whatsoever.

3. Instructions

If the undersigned has authorized a Purchaser Representative to act with or for him or her, please complete the following:

Name of purchaser representative: _____
Address: _____
Telephone: _____

4. Representations and warranties of the undersigned

The undersigned, in order to induce you to accept this Offer, hereby warrants and represents as follows:

A. He or she is over the age of twenty-one (21) years and resides at the address set forth below and has no present intention of becoming a resident of any other state or jurisdiction.

B. He or she has sufficient liquid assets to pay, promptly when due, the amounts owed under this Subscription Agreement, and the Investor Note.

C. He or she meets the requirements for an accredited investor (see paragraph D below), or he or she and/or his or her Purchaser Representative, as the case may be, is experienced in investment and business matters and familiar with the concept of tax shelter investments in real estate and has such knowledge and experience in financial and business matters that he or she is capable of evaluating the merits and risks of the prospective investment in the Interests being offered on the terms and conditions set forth in the Memorandum. The undersigned, either alone or with his or her Purchaser Representative, has read and fully understands the Memorandum. In connection with his or her review of the Memorandum, he or she has consulted with such independent legal counsel or other advisors considered appropriate to assist in evaluating the proposed investment in the Partnership. In particular, and not in limitation of the foregoing, he or she has taken full cognizance of and understands that:

_____
(Initial here)

i. Substantial compensation and other benefits are being paid to the General Partners, the Special Limited Partner, and the Manager and their affiliates (as set forth in the Memorandum, in the section entitled "Compensation of the General Partner, Special Limited Partner, and the Manager," and elsewhere in the Memorandum).

ii. A service fee is being paid by the Partnership to appropriate Purchaser Representatives (as set forth in the Memorandum, in the section entitled "The Offering—Compensation of Purchaser Representatives, Broker-Dealers, and Other Professionals").

iii. None of the consideration to be paid by the Partnership, whether for services or for its partnership property, necessarily represents fair market value, and none of the compensation or other benefits were determined as a result of arm's-length negotiation.

iv. There are substantial Risk Factors and Conflicts of Interest described in the Memorandum under those topical headings, and, in addition, there are numerous tax consequences of a complicated and potentially adverse nature that are described in the section of the Memorandum entitled "Income Tax Aspects."

v. The Units are speculative investments that involve a *high degree of risk of loss* of an Investor's entire investment in the Partnership.

vi. There are substantial restrictions on the transferability of the Units, and the Units will not be and the Investors in the Partnership have no right to require that the Units be registered under the act; there will be no public market, and, accordingly, the undersigned may have to hold the Unit indefinitely, and it may not be possible for an Investor to liquidate an investment in the Partnership.

vii. He or she has consulted with and been advised by his or her own tax advisor in connection with the income tax aspects of this transaction, including but not limited to the reasonableness or availability of the various income tax deductions or other benefits hypothetically projected or suggested in the "Projections" and elsewhere in the Memorandum.

viii. Any income tax benefits that may be available to the undersigned may be lost through, among other matters, adoption of new laws, amendments to existing laws, or changes or differences in the interpretation of existing laws and regulations.

D. He or she (i) has adequate means of providing for current needs

_____

(Initial here)

Subscription Agreement

and reasonably anticipated future needs and contingencies and has no need for liquidity of his or her investment in the Partnership; (ii) can afford (a) to hold his or her Unit for an indefinite period of time and, in any event, to satisfy various state blue-sky requirements, for a period of not less than 12 months, and (b) to sustain a complete loss of the entire amount of his or her investment and, at the same time, bear the tax liability that may result if his or her investment is lost as a result of the foreclosure of the Property or a forfeiture or foreclosure of his or her Unit; (iii) has no reason to anticipate any changes in personal circumstances, financial or otherwise, that may cause or require any sale or distribution of his or her unit; (iv) anticipates recognition of income from other sources during the period when contributions are required under the Partnership Agreement at a level that will enable him or her to utilize losses allocated to him or her during each year of such period, in production of income of which some portion would be subject to combined federal, state, and local income taxes at a rate of not less than 50 percent (46 percent for corporations); and (v) confirms that there has been no material adverse change in the information, financial and other, previously given to the Partnership in order to induce the Partnership to send the undersigned the Memorandum and this form of Subscription Agreement except as set forth below.

He or she meets one of the following suitability requirements (Check either i or ii, or both, as applicable):

____i. (For Accredited Investors as defined under Regulation D of the Act.) He or she represents that (a) he or she has an individual net worth or, together with his or her spouse, a joint net worth (total assets in excess of total liabilities) in excess of $1 million, or (b) he or she has had in each of the two most recent years, and reasonably expects to have during the current year, an individual income in excess of $200,000.*

____ii. He or she (a) has a personal net worth equal to not less than 2.5 times his or her investment in the Partnership (excluding from

_____
(Initial here)

---

* For this purpose, a person's income is the amount of individual adjusted gross income (as reported on a federal income tax return) increased by the following amounts: (1) any deduction for long-term capital gains (Section 1202 of the Internal Revenue Code—the "Code"), (2) any deduction for depletion (Section 611 *et seq.* of the Code), (3) any exclusion for interest on tax-exempt municipal obligations (Section 103 of the Code), and (4) any losses of a partnership allocated to the individual limited partner (as reported on Schedule E of Form 1040).

consideration his or her investment in the Partnership and any personal residence, home, and personal automobiles), and (b) he or she anticipates, in 1984, a gross income in excess of $100,000 (reduced pro rata for fractional Units) and taxable income (exclusive of losses from "Tax Shelter Investments") some portion of which will be subject to combined federal, state, and local taxes at a rate of 50 percent (46 percent for corporations) or more.

E. Either directly or through his or her Purchaser Representative, he or she has been:

i. Furnished with a copy of the Memorandum, a copy of the Exhibits thereto, and such other information in connection with this transaction as has been requested.

ii. Afforded the opportunity to ask questions of and receive answers from the General Partners or persons acting on their behalf concerning the terms and conditions of this transaction and to obtain any additional information, to the extent that the Partnership possesses such information or can acquire it without unreasonable effort or expense, necessary to verify the accuracy of the information furnished; and has availed himself or herself of such opportunity to the extent that he or she considers appropriate in order to evaluate the merits and risks of the proposed transaction.

F. The Unit being subscribed for in the Partnership is being acquired by the undersigned solely for the account of the undersigned for investment and not with a view to, or for resale in connection with, any distribution as that term is contemplated under the Act. By such representation, the undersigned means that no other person has a beneficial interest in the Unit subscribed for hereunder, and that no other person has furnished or will furnish, directly or indirectly, any part of, or guarantee the payment of any part of, the consideration to be paid to the Partnership in connection therewith. The undersigned does not intend to dispose of all or any part of such Unit and understands that any Unit that may be issued is being offered pursuant to a specific exemption under the provisions of the Act, which exemption depends, among other things, upon the investment intent of each subscriber, including the undersigned. The undersigned realizes that, in view of the requirements of the Act and the Rules and Regulations promulgated by the Securities and Exchange Commission, a purchase now with an intent to resell by reason of any foreseeable specific contingency or an anticipated change in market value of the Units or in connection

(Initial here)

Subscription Agreement

with a contemplated liquidation or settlement of any loan obtained by him or her for the acquisition of such Unit and for which such Unit is pledged as security, would represent a purchase with an intent inconsistent with the foregoing representation to you, and that such a sale or disposition might be regarded as a deferred sale as to which the exemption is not available.

G. He or she is purchasing the Unit in the state of the undersigned's residence; all of the undersigned's contacts with this offering have been in such state.

H. He or she is aware that if he or she has a Purchaser Representative, such representative may receive a fee for his or her services of up to 10 percent of his or her aggregate Unit Purchase Price as and when Investor Installment cash payments are received by the Partnership.

The undersigned certifies that each of the foregoing representations and warranties set forth in subsections (A) through (H), inclusive, of this Section 4 are now and will be true as of the date of making of the payments due to the Partnership before his Admission and shall survive such dates. If in any respect such representations and warranties shall not be true and accurate prior to his Admission, the undersigned shall give written notice of such fact to the General Partners specifying which representations and warranties are not true and accurate and the reasons therefor, whereupon the General Partners may elect to terminate the Subscription Agreement pursuant to Section 12.

5. *Nonpublic offering*

The undersigned acknowledges his or her understanding of the following:

A. The Unit being subscribed for has not been registered under the Act in reliance on an exemption under Section 4(2) of the Act and pursuant to Rule 506 promulgated under the Act and, therefore, cannot be resold in any event unless the Unit is registered under the Act or unless an exemption from registration is available; and the undersigned further understands that he or she is purchasing a Unit in the Partnership without being furnished any offering literature or prospectus other than the Memorandum and Exhibits thereto.

B. This Offer of Units in the Partnership has not been reviewed by the Attorney General of the State of _____ (the "Attor-

_____
(Initial here)

ney General'') because of the Partnership's representations that this is intended to be a nonpublic offering pursuant to Rule 506 under the Act, and that if all of the conditions and limitations of said Rule is not complied with, the offering will be resubmitted to the Attorney General for amended exemption or for registration.

C. The Partnership has no obligation or present intention to register under the Act the Unit proposed to be acquired by the undersigned or to make available to the public information (in the form of reports pursuant to Sections 1, 13, or 15 of the Securities Exchange Act of 1934 or otherwise) without which resale without registration pursuant to Rule 144 of the General Rules and Regulations under the Act will not be available, and no representations to the contrary have been made by any person on behalf of the General Partners or the Partnership in connection with this proposed investment.

6. *Availability of documents*

The undersigned acknowledges that all documents, records, and books pertaining to this transaction have been made available for inspection by his or her attorney and/or his or her accountant and/or his or her Purchaser Representative and himself or herself. The undersigned further understands that the books and records of the Partnership will be available upon reasonable notice for inspection by Investors during reasonable business hours at its principal place of business.

7. *Indemnification*

The undersigned understands that the Partnership Interest is being offered without registration under the Act in reliance upon the exemption pursuant to Section 4(2) of the Act, and, in _____ State, pursuant to an exemption from registration obtained by the Partnership from the office of the Attorney General of the State of _____; that the availability of such exemptions is in part dependent upon the truthfulness and accuracy of the representations made by the undersigned herein; that the General Partners and the Partnership will rely on such representations in accepting any subscription for a Unit or Units; that the General Partners and the Partnership may take such steps as they consider reasonable to verify the accuracy and truthfulness of such representations in advance of accepting or rejecting the undersigned's subscription. The undersigned agrees to indemnify and hold harm-

_____
(Initial here)

Subscription Agreement

less the General Partners and the Partnership against any damage, loss, expense, or cost, including reasonable attorney's fees, sustained as a result of any misstatement or omission on the undersigned's part.

8. *Appointment of attorney-in-fact*

The undersigned does hereby nominate, appoint, and constitute the General Partners and any successor or additional General Partners of the Partnership designated as such in accordance with the terms and conditions of the Partnership Agreement (in the form annexed as an Exhibit to the Memorandum), and each of them, in the undersigned's name, place, and stead, to take all such action, from time to time, including but not limited to the execution of the Partnership Agreement in such form, the Certificate of Limited Partnership, or any amendment to the Agreement or Certificate of Limited Partnership as may be required in order to effectuate any of the provisions of the Partnership Agreement concerning admission of an additional or successor General Partner(s), or Limited Partners, or substituted Limited Partners, or otherwise, and to amend the Certificate or Agreement of Limited Partnership to set forth any changes resultant from the making of capital contributions of any type, and to make, execute, sign, acknowledge, and swear to all instruments and file all documents to accomplish the foregoing, including but not limited to the following:

A. All business certificates, necessary certificates of Limited Partnership, and amendments thereto from time to time as required by the Partnership Law of _____.

B. All documents that may be required to effect the dissolution of the Partnership and the cancellation of its Certificate of Limited Partnership, as amended from time to time.

C. All such other instruments, documents, and certificates that may be required from time to time by the laws of _____ or the United States of America.

The foregoing power of attorney is irrevocable and coupled with an interest in recognition of the fact that each of the Partners under the Partnership Agreement will be relying upon the power of the General Partners to act as contemplated by the Partnership Agreement in such filing and other action by them on behalf of the Partnership. All such powers of attorney shall, to the extent permitted by law, survive the death,

_____
(Initial here)

incapacity, and bankruptcy of the undersigned and any assignment by the undersigned of the whole or any part of the Unit.

9. *No waiver*

Notwithstanding any of the representations, warranties, acknowledgments, or agreements made herein by the undersigned, the undersigned does not thereby or in any manner waive any rights granted to the undersigned under federal or state securities laws.

10. *Transferability*

The undersigned agrees not to transfer or assign this Agreement, or any interest herein, and further agrees that the assignment and transferability of the Unit acquired pursuant hereto shall be made only in accordance with the Partnership Agreement, which severely restricts such transferability.

11. *Revocation*

The undersigned agrees that he or she shall not cancel, terminate, or revoke this Agreement or any agreement of the undersigned made hereunder, and that this Agreement shall survive the death or disability of the undersigned.

12. *Termination of subscription agreement*

The undersigned acknowledges having been advised by the General Partners that the General Partners may elect to terminate this offering or the undersigned's subscription for any reason. If the General Partners elect to cancel this Subscription Agreement, provided that they return to the undersigned, without interest, all sums paid by the undersigned, then this Agreement shall be null and void and of no further force and effect, and neither party shall have any rights against any other party hereunder or under the Partnership Agreement.

13. *Miscellaneous*

A. All notices or other communications given or made hereunder shall be in writing and shall be mailed by registered or certified mail, return receipt requested, postage prepaid, to the undersigned at the address set forth below.

_____

(Initial here)

Subscription Agreement

B. This Agreement shall be construed in accordance with and governed by the laws of the State of _____.

C. This Agreement constitutes the entire agreement among the parties hereto with respect to the subject matter hereof and may be amended only by a writing executed by all parties.

14. *Assignability*

I understand that you may assign payments due by me hereunder. In such event, upon notice from you, I shall make all payments due after such notice to the assignee designated by you.

15. *Certification*

The undersigned certifies that he or she has read this entire Subscription Agreement and initialed all pages in his or her own handwriting and that every statement set forth herein is true and complete.

16. *Set forth is my:*

Business name and Address: _____

_____

Home address: _____

_____

Social Security number: _____

Home telephone number: _____

Business telephone number: _____

In witness whereof, the undersigned has executed this Subscription Agreement on the date his or her signature has been subscribed to below.

_____
Investor (Print name)

_____
Investor (Signature)
Dated: _____

_____
(Initial here)

State of _____

County of _____ ss:

City of _____

On _____, before me personally came _____, to me known and known to me to be the individual(s) described in and who executed the foregoing instrument, and duly acknowledged to me that he or she (they) executed the same.

_____
Notary Public

_____
(Initial here)

Accepted this ____ day of _____, ____.

By _____
General Partner

_____
(Initial here)

PROSPECTIVE OFFEREE QUESTIONNAIRE

The purpose of the offeree questionnaire is to give enough factual information to the general partner so that the general partner can decide whether the offeree (subscriber) qualifies as an accredited investor. The subscriber's net worth and taxable income are the major criteria for determining the accreditation, and accreditation is most important if the partnership is to comply with the exemption available under Regulation D.

The offeree questionnaire further elicits information about where the offeree (subscriber) resides—a fact that is significant in determining whether a blue-sky registration is necessary in a particular state—and gives banking references and a background description to help the general partner determine the sophistication of the investor, to determine his or her accreditation.

If the subscriber uses a purchaser representative—that is, a professional advisor—some of the information relating to the purchaser's sophistication will not be necessary, but the background of the purchaser representative will be elicited by another form, which follows this questionnaire.

PROSPECTIVE OFFEREE QUESTIONNAIRE

The information contained herein is being furnished to _____ _____, as General Partners of _____ (the "Issuer") in order to assure the Issuer that the undersigned meets the standards required by the General Partners for purchasers of Class A Limited Partnership Interests which the Issuer proposes to offer (the "Interests"). The undersigned understands that (1) the Issuer will rely upon the information contained herein for purposes of its determination, (2) the Interests will not be registered under the Securities Act of 1933 (the "Act") in reliance upon the exemption from registration provided by Section 4(2) of the Act and Rule 506 promulgated thereunder, and (3) this questionnaire is not an offer to sell the Interests to the undersigned.

The undersigned further represents to the Issuer that (1) the information contained herein is complete and accurate and may be relied upon by the Issuer, and (2) the undersigned will notify the Issuer immediately of any material change in any of such information occurring before the purchase of the Interests, if any purchase is made, by the undersigned.

The undersigned understands and agrees that, although the issuer will use its best efforts to keep this questionnaire strictly confidential, the issuer may present this questionnaire to such parties as it deems advisable if called upon to establish the availability under any federal or state securities laws of an exemption from registration of the private placement.

The undersigned realizes that this letter is not an offer to sell interests but merely a request for information.

The undersigned will send one completed copy of this questionnaire, and will send or cause to be sent a copy of the Purchaser Representative Questionnaire, along with his or her Subscription Agreement and payment, to _____ in the enclosed return envelope as soon as possible. The other copy will be retained for the undersigned's files.

(Please type or print.)

1. Name: _____ Date of birth: _____
   Social Security no.: _____ Marital status: _____
   Citizenship: _____ Number of dependents: _____
   County and state where registered to vote: _____
   State of issuance of driver's license: _____
2. Home address: _____
   Home telephone number: (___) _____

   (Strike out the alternative that is not relevant.)
3a. (First alternative.) The undersigned has such knowledge and experience in financial and business matters that he or she is capable of evaluating the merits and risks of an investment in the Interests and is not utilizing any other person to be his or her Purchaser Representative in connection with evaluating such merits and risks. The undersigned offers the information contained herein as evidence of his or her knowledge and experience in these matters.
3b. (Second alternative.) The undersigned acknowledges the following professional or business advisors or other named person(s) to be his or

Prospective Offeree Questionnaire

her Purchaser Representative(s) in connection with evaluating the merits and risks of an investment in the Interests.

List the name(s) and address(es) of Purchaser Representative(s):

_____   _____

_____   _____

The named Purchaser Representative(s) has (have) furnished to the undersigned a complete and executed Purchaser Representative Questionnaire, a copy of which is delivered to you herewith.

The undersigned and the named Purchaser Representative(s) together have such knowledge and experience in financial and business matters that they are capable of evaluating the merits and risks of an investment in the Interests.

4. The undersigned is a person who is able to bear the economic risk of an investment in the Interests in the amount of at least his or her investment, the purchase price of which is $_____ per Unit. In making this statement, consideration has been given to whether the undersigned could afford to hold the Interests for an indefinite period and whether at this time he or she could afford a complete loss. The undersigned has adequate means of providing for current needs and possible personal future contingencies and has no need for liquidity with respect to this investment. The undersigned offers the information contained herein as evidence of ability to bear the economic risk of loss of his or her investment.

5. Name and address of principal bank: _____

    _____

    _____

    Bank officer serving your account: _____

6. Firm name: _____

    Nature of business: _____

    Position: _____

    Nature of duties: _____

    Business address: _____

    Business telephone number: (____)_____

7. a. Undersigned's employment, positions, or occupations during the past five years (and the inclusive dates of each) are as follows. (What

is sought is a sufficient description to enable the Issuer to determine the extent of vocationally related experience in financial and business matters.)

Employment, Position, or Occupation	Nature of Duties	From	To

b. Undersigned's general, business, or professional education, and the degree received, are as follows:

School	Degree	Year Received

8. In your federal income tax returns for 1983 and 1984, check which of the following tax tables you used:
Married Individuals Filing Joint Returns _____
Heads of Household _____
Unmarried Individuals _____
Married Individuals Filing Separate Returns _____

9. Undersigned's income from all sources for the latest complete calendar year was more than (check highest one applicable):

_____ $40,000 _____ $100,000
_____ $60,000 _____ $200,000
_____ $80,000 _____ $500,000

a. Approximate percentage of my income as shown above remained, for my discretionary use, after payment of federal, state, and local taxes and after payment of all ordinary and necessary living expenses: _____ percent.

10. I reasonably anticipate that my average annual income from all sources for the four-year period ending December 31, 1985, will be in excess of (check highest applicable average):

Prospective Offeree Questionnaire

    ____ $40,000   ____ $100,000
    ____ $60,000   ____ $200,000
    ____ $80,000   ____ $500,000

11. Undersigned's present net worth (together with his or her spouse), exclusive of home, home furnishings, and personal automobiles, is in excess of (check highest applicable one):

    Less than   ____ $ 200,000
    ____ $ 75,000   ____ $ 500,000
    ____ $ 75,000   ____ $ 750,000
    ____ $100,000   ____ $1,000,000
    ____ $150,000   or greater

    a. The following percentages of my net worth as shown above are presently invested in (i) investments in marketable securities (stocks, bonds, debentures, or notes), (ii) investments in unmarketable or restricted securities, and (iii) cash or equivalent:

    i. _____%   ii. _____%   iii. _____%

12. Undersigned's present net worth (together with his or her spouse), inclusive of home, home furnishings, and personal automobiles, is in excess of (check highest applicable one):

    Less than   ____ $ 200,000
    ____ $ 75,000   ____ $ 500,000
    ____ $ 75,000   ____ $ 750,000
    ____ $100,000   ____ $1,000,000
    ____ $150,000   or greater

13. Set forth below are any other investments or contingent liabilities which the undersigned reasonably anticipates could cause me to require cash in excess of the amount of cash readily available to me (please specify use and estimated amount).

    _____
    _____
    _____

14. Investment experience:

    a. The frequency of my investment in marketable securities is: ( ) often ( ) occasionally ( ) seldom ( ) never.

    b. The frequency of my investment in tax-sheltered partnership ventures is: ( ) often ( ) occasionally ( ) seldom ( ) never.

c. The frequency of my investment in real estate is: ( ) often ( ) occasionally ( ) seldom ( ) never.

d. The frequency of my investment in securities purchased on margin is: ( ) often ( ) occasionally ( ) seldom ( ) never.

e. The frequency of my investment in unmarketable securities is: ( ) often ( ) occasionally ( ) seldom ( ) never.

f. In addition, as indicated below, the undersigned has previously purchased the following securities which were sold in reliance on the private offering exemption from registration under the Securities Act of 1933, pursuant to Section 4(2) under the Act and/or Rule 146 or Regulation D, promulgated under the Act.

Year	Type of Securities	Seller	Business of Seller	Total Amount Invested

15. Further, especially if the undersigned is acting without a Purchaser Representative, in the space provided below, specifically set forth any prior real estate syndication investment experience he or she has had and any other additional information (to the extent there is any) that may be helpful in enabling the Issuer to determine that the knowledge and experience of the undersigned in financial and business matters is sufficient to enable the undersigned to evaluate the merits and risks of this prospective investment. Your ability to participate in this investment may depend on the nature and quality of your response to this question.

16. The undersigned (is) or (is not) acting for his or her own account. (Strike out inapplicable phrase.)

 a. To the extent that the undersigned is not acting for his or her own account (complete the following):

  i. The undersigned is acting as (Agent, Trustee, otherwise). (Circle one.)

Prospective Offeree Questionnaire

    ii. The name, address, and telephone number of persons that the undersigned represents are: _____

_____

_____

    iii. Attached is evidence of the authority of undersigned.

Note: Any individuals represented must also meet suitability standards.

To the best of my information and belief, the above information supplied by the undersigned is true and correct in all respects.

_____
(Signature of Prospective Offeree)

_____
Print name)

PURCHASER REPRESENTATIVE QUESTIONNAIRE

Typically, the purchaser representative is an accountant, an attorney, a financial analyst, a stock broker, a lawyer, or a real estate person.

Assuming no ethical or registration problem in the case of the advisor, the advisor will receive a fee based on the amount of the investor's capital contributions. These fees or commissions may range from as little as 3 or 5 percent of the investment to 8, 10, or 12 percent. Typically, they are paid by the limited partnership out of the gross proceeds of the offering.

The questionnaire is self-explanatory and is an effort to adduce the purchaser representative's professional qualifications, so that it does not appear that the partnership is selling units to unsophisticated investors who have no professional advisor.

PURCHASER REPRESENTATIVE QUESTIONNAIRE

The information contained herein is being furnished to _____, the General Partners of _____ (the "Issuer"), in order to assure the Issuer that the undersigned meets the standards required by the General Partners of a Purchaser Representative for _____. The undersigned understands that (1) the Issuer will (name of Purchaser)
rely upon the information contained herein for purposes of its determination, (2) the Class A Limited Partnership Interests the Issuer proposes to offer (the "Interests") will not be registered under the Act in reliance upon the exemption from registration provided by Section 4(2) of the Securities Act of 1933 (the "Act") and Rule 506 promulgated thereunder, and (3) this questionnaire is not an offer to sell the Interests to the undersigned or to the above-named Prospective Purchaser.

Purchaser Representative Questionnaire

The undersigned further represents to the Issuer that (1) the information contained herein is complete and accurate and may be relied upon by the Issuer, and (2) the undersigned will notify the Issuer immediately of any material change in any of such information occurring before the purchase of the Interests, if any purchase is made, by the undersigned.

The undersigned understands and agrees that, although the Issuer will use its best efforts to keep this questionnaire strictly confidential, the Issuer may present this questionnaire to such parties as it deems advisable if called upon to establish the availability under any federal or state securities laws of an exemption from registration of the private placement.

The undersigned will complete, sign, date, and return one copy of the questionnaire to _____ (the General Partners of Issuer) at the above address in the enclosed return envelope as soon as possible. The other copy will be retained for the undersigned's files.

(Please type or print.)
1. Name: _____
   Age: _____
   Business address: _____
   _____

2. The undersigned has such knowledge and experience in financial and business matters that the undersigned is capable of evaluating the merits and risks of an investment in the Interests. The undersigned offers the information contained herein as evidence of his or her knowledge and experience:
   _____
   _____
   _____

3. Present occupation or position, indicating period of such practice or employment and field of professional specialization, if any (what is sought is a sufficient description to enable the Issuer to determine the extent of vocationally related experience in financial and business matters):
   _____
   _____
   _____

4. List any business or professional education, indicating degrees received, if any:

_____

_____

_____

5. List any professional licenses or registrations, including bar admissions, accounting certificates, real estate brokerage licenses, investment adviser registrations and SEC or state broker–dealer, salesperson, or agent registrations, held by you:

_____

_____

_____

6. Describe generally any business, financial, or investment experience that would help you to evaluate the merits and risks of this investment:

_____

_____

_____

7. State how long you have known the Prospective Purchaser(s), and in what capacity:

_____

_____

_____

8. In advising the Prospective Purchaser in connection with his or her prospective investment in the Issuer, will you be relying in part on the expertise of an additional Purchaser Representative or Representatives?

_____ Yes   _____ No

If yes, give the name and address of each such additional Purchaser Representative:

_____

_____

_____

The undersigned understands that the Issuer will be relying on the accuracy and completeness of his or her response to the foregoing questions, and the undersigned represents and warrants to the Issuer as follows:

Purchaser Representative Questionnaire

A. The undersigned is acting as Purchaser Representative for the Prospective Purchaser in connection with his or her prospective investment in the Issuer.

B. The answers to the above questions are complete and correct and may be relied upon by the Issuer in determining whether the offering in connection with which the undersigned has executed this questionnaire is exempt from registration under the Act and state securities laws.

C. The undersigned is not an affiliate, director, officer, or employee of the Issuer, or the beneficial owner of 10 percent or more of any class of the equity securities of the Issuer or 10 percent or more of the equity interest in the Issuer.

D. Except as disclosed to the Prospective Offeree in writing, there is no material relationship (meaning any relationship that a reasonable investor might consider important in the making of a decision whether to acknowledge the undersigned as his or her Purchaser Representative) between the undersigned or affiliates of the undersigned and the Issuer and its affiliates, which now exists or which is mutually understood to be contemplated or which has existed at any time during the previous two years, nor, except as previously disclosed in writing to the Prospective Purchaser, has any compensation been received, or is any compensation to be received, by the undersigned as a result of any such relationship. A copy of the written disclosures referred to herein, if any, is attached as Exhibit A hereto and incorporated by reference herein.

E. The undersigned has agreed to read and become familiar with the Private Placement Memorandum pertaining to the above investment and understands that he or she is invited to ask questions of and receive answers from the General Partners of the Issuer as set forth in the Private Offering Memorandum, concerning the terms and conditions of the investment and the Offering and to obtain any additional information, to the extent that the Issuer possesses such information or can acquire it without unreasonable expense, necessary to verify the accuracy of the information contained in the Private Placement Memorandum.

F. In acting as Purchaser Representative, the undersigned is and will be acting solely in the interest of the Prospective Purchaser.

G. The undersigned will notify the Issuer immediately of any material change in any statement made herein occurring before the closing of any purchase by the Prospective Purchaser of any interest in the proposed investment.

In witness whereof, I have executed this Questionnaire this _____ day of _____, _____.

_____
(Signature of Purchaser Representative)

This letter is not an offer to sell securities but merely a request for information.

INVESTOR SUITABILITY STANDARDS

The syndicator wants to know he or she is complying with Regulation D. The earlier Prospective Offeree Questionnaire gives the information needed to determine if the investor fits the private exemption pattern. The following Investor Suitability Standards discuss the factors that qualify the investor. Such a discussion is usually found in the front of the prospectus.

INVESTOR SUITABILITY STANDARDS

This Offering is intended to be made as a private placement, pursuant to Section 3(b) or 4(2) of the Act and Regulation D promulgated thereunder and pursuant to exemptions provided for under applicable state securities laws. As for persons who are not accredited under Regulation D, the Limited Partnership Interests are being offered by the Partnership to such persons who, before making any sales hereunder, the General Partner has reasonable grounds to believe, either alone or together with their Purchaser Representatives, have such knowledge and experience in financial and business matters that they are capable of evaluating the merits and risks of this investment unless the General Partner waives the requirement.

The determination of whether a person is accredited will be made by the General Partner based upon the information to be furnished in and along with the Subscription Agreement.

An investment in the Partnership is expected to provide a limited Cash Flow to the Investor, which is not guaranteed (see "Summary of Partnership Agreement"), will involve a high degree of risk, and will be nonliquid. Accordingly, the financial benefits, if any, derived from an investment herein will depend to a large degree on the income tax bracket of the Investor; and because the sale or transfer by an Investor of a Limited Partnership Interest may result in substantial adverse tax consequences, the Partnership will not sell a Limited Partnership Interest to any Investor who is not an accredited investor, unless he or she represents, among other things, that he or she has, apart from the amount of investment hereunder (1) adequate means of providing for current needs and reasonably anticipated future needs and contingencies, (2) no need for liquidity with respect to this investment, (3) a personal net worth equal to not less than two and one-half times his or her investment in the Partnership (exclusive of the investment in the Partnership, homes, home furnishings, and personal automobiles), or such higher amount as may be required by the applicable state law, and (4) anticipated gross income in 1984 in excess of $100,000 (reduced pro rata for fractional units) and should anticipate, although it is not required, 1984 taxable income (exclusive of losses for tax purposes from tax-shelter investments), some portion of which will be subject to combined federal, state, and local income taxes at a rate of 50 percent (46 percent for corporations) or more.

Investment in the Partnership is not recommended for Investors who are unable to hold their Limited Partnership Interest for an indefinite period of time and who cannot afford a complete loss of their investment, or for Investors who do not anticipate taxable income, some portion of which, notwithstanding tax-shelter investments, will be taxed at the rate of 50 percent (46 percent for corporations) or more for at least the next five years. (See "Risk Factors—Disposition of Property or Interests," and "Income Tax Aspects—Sale or Foreclosure of the Property.")

The Suitability Standards set forth above represent minimum suitability requirements for Investors, and the satisfaction of such standards by a prospective Investor does not necessarily mean that the Units are a suitable investment.

Additionally, before the purchase of a Unit, each prospective Investor will also be required to represent, among other things, that (1) he or she has the requisite knowledge or relied upon the advice of his or her own counsel, accountants, business advisors, or Purchaser Representatives with regard to the tax and other considerations involved in making such an investment, (2) he or she is acquiring the Limited Partnership Interest for his or her own account and not with a view to resale or public distribution thereof, (3) he or she meets the Suitability Standards set forth above, (4) he or she has no reason to anticipate any change in personal circumstances, financial or otherwise, which may cause or require any sale of the Unit, (5) he or she is familiar with the nature of and risks attending investments in real estate and securities, and has determined independently, or on the basis of consultation with business and tax advisors or an appropriate Purchaser Representative, that the purchase of the Units is consistent with his or her investment objectives and income prospects, (6) he or she is aware that no trading market for the Units will exist at any time, and

Investor Suitability Standards

the Units will at no time be freely transferable or transferable without potential adverse tax consequences, and (7) he or she realizes that, since the Units cannot be readily transferred, he or she may not readily liquidate the investment for an indefinite period of time, and, in any event, to satisfy various state blue-sky requirements, he or she must hold the Unit for a period of not less than 12 months. A prospective Investor, therefore, must not purchase a Unit unless he or she has sufficient liquid assets to assure himself or herself that such purchase will cause no undue financial difficulties.

For purposes of this paragraph and this Memorandum, the term "Purchaser Representatives" means any person or persons not affiliated with the Partnership, the General Partner, or any of his or her affiliates who, the General Partner reasonably believes:

1. Has such knowledge and experience in financial or business matters that he or she, either alone or together with other legal or business advisors, or the prospective Investor, is capable of evaluating the merits and risks of the prospective investments.

2. Is acknowledged by the prospective Investor, is writing, to be his or her Purchaser Representative in connection with evaluating the merits and risks of the proposed investment.

3. Has before disclosed to the prospective Investor, in writing, the acknowledgment specified above any material relationship between such person or his or her affiliates and the Partnership or the General Partner or any of his or her affiliates, which then exists, is mutually understood to be contemplated, or which has existed at any time during the previous two years, and any compensation received or to be received as a result of such relationship (including but not limited to any Purchaser Representative's fees paid, or to be paid, hereunder).

In addition to the above standards, prospective Investors will also be required to meet the suitability standards imposed by the particular jurisdiction in which the Units are offered and sold. In order to ensure compliance with all applicable suitability standards, Investors will be required to submit statements and questionnaires confirming certain information. (See the Subscription Agreement and Prospective Offeree Questionnaire.)

It is anticipated that comparable suitability standards will be imposed by the Partnership in connection with any resale of the Units. Any such resale is subject to various restrictions and may result in substantial adverse tax consequences.

BROKER–DEALER SELL SHEET

The annexed Broker–Dealer Sell Sheet is a brief summary intended to be addressed to professionals who act as advisors to syndicate investors. The sell sheet is intended to summarize, in capsule form, the highlights of the material included in the formal prospectus.

By examining this particular Broker–Dealer Sell Sheet, you will get a chance to see what the underwriter deemed significant in alerting offeree representatives to why the particular syndication is a desirable investment.

However, only by reading the full prospectus can the offeree representative or the investor make certain that the facts they deem significant are appropriately covered.

Note that the Rule of 78s mentioned in this Sell Sheet has been outlawed by a Revenue Service opinion since June 1983.

BROKER–DEALER SELL SHEET

Dear _____.

Thank you for your interest in reviewing one of _____ most recent real estate limited partnerships. At the request of _____, enclosed is a copy of the Confidential Offering Memorandum for _____.

Certain highlights of this offering include:

1. The property is located in _____ and is leased to seven tenants. Of the seven tenants three are major national companies.
2. The wrap mortgage is self-liquidating. (There is no balloon payment.)
3. The write-off for 1985 is 2.91 to 1.
4. The write-off over the pay-in period is 2.70 to 1.
5. The total write-off over 15 years is 3.78 to 1.
6. No letter of credit needed.

Broker–Dealer Sell Sheet

7. The payment notes are interest-free.
8. Half-units are available.
9. An MAI appraisal has been prepared by _____ for a value in excess of the purchase price to the Partnership.
10. As has been the practice in the past, we anticipate that _____ will continue to prepare the tax returns and audited Financial Statements for the Partnership.

_____ has already successfully syndicated 10 other real estate offerings this year. By early indications, this offering should close quickly. Therefore, if you have any interested investors, please contact me soon.

Sincerely,

SUMMARY OF THE OFFERING

22 UNITS OF $135,000
$2,970,000 OF LIMITED PARTNERSHIP INTERESTS

August 1, 1985

This summary is for use by broker–dealers, attorneys, accountants, and investment counsel only. The investment described herein involves a high degree of risk. This summary should not be reproduced nor used, given, shown, or read to any potential purchaser or any other party. This material does not constitute an offer to sell, nor is it a solicitation of an offer to buy any of the securities referred to. The securities may be offered and sold through the use of an accurate, complete, and current private placement memorandum, which contains information relevant to the risks and/or merits attendant on such an investment, which information is not contained in this document.

(For reference purposes only—not to be used for solicitation.)

	Price to Limited Partners	Selling Commissions	Proceeds to Partnership
Per Unit	$ 135,000	$ 13,500	$ 121,500
Total Offering	$2,970,000	$297,000	$2,673,000

SUITABILITY

The Units specified herein will only be sold to investors who can satisfy the suitability requirements imposed by the applicable state blue-sky laws and who have a net worth, in respect of each Unit purchased, of at least $250,000, and have and anticipate continuing to have future income, some portion of which, after taking into consideration losses anticipated to result from an investment in the Units, will be subject to a federal income tax rate of at least 45 percent.

For marketing information, contact: _____

Partnership Objectives

The partnership expects to realize:

1. Cash flow from operations.
2. Appreciation in the value of the property.
3. Cash from the refinancing or disposition of the property.
4. Tax benefits exclusive of cash flow as follows.

Tax benefits per unit

Broker–Dealer Sell Sheet

	Invest-ment	Income (Loss)	Loss Ratio	Tax Savings 45% Bracket	Tax Savings 50% Bracket
1982	$ 16,250	$ (47,268)	2.91:1	$ 21,271	$ 23,634
1983	35,450	(96,627)	2.73:1	43,482	48,314
1984	30,650	(82,614)	2.70:1	37,176	41,307
1985	27,750	(72,839)	2.62:1	32,778	36,420
1986	24,900	(65,154)	2.62:1	29,319	32,577
1987	0	(33,962)		15,283	16,981
1988	0	(27,961)		12,582	13,981
1989	0	(22,822)		10,270	11,411
1990	0	(18,371)		8,267	9,186
1991	0	(14,483)		6,517	7,242
1992	0	(11,062)		4,978	5,531
1993	0	(8,036)		3,616	4,018
1994	0	(5,348)		2,407	2,674
1995	0	(2,952)		1,328	1,476
1996	0	(809)		364	405
	$135,000	$(510,308)	3.78:1	$229,638	$255,157

Note: Please review the Projections at the end of the Summary.

Product Profile

A. The Offering

$2,970,000 in 22 Limited Partnership Units at $135,000 per Unit. Fractional Units may be accepted at the discretion of the Managing General Partner.

B. The Property

The property to be acquired by _____ (the "Property") consists of (1) approximately 10.5 acres of land located in _____ (the "Land"), and (2) various one-story retail stores and other improvements constructed on the Land (the "Premises"), and (3) the landlord's interest under various leases of the Land and the Premises (the "Operating Leases") to _____ and five other tenants.

The Premises, completed in 1970, consist of various one-story, fully sprinklered buildings totaling 128,322 square feet. The department store occupies 82,857 square feet. The supermarket occupies 33,460 square feet. The drugstore occupies 7200 square feet. The buildings are fully heated and air conditioned and parking is provided for more than 600 automobiles.

The borough of _____ is located in _____ County in the southwest portion of _____. The population as of 1980 was 199,917, which reflects a 15.8 percent increase from 1970. This predominately residential community is bordered on the north by _____ on the west by _____ and, 9½ miles south of downtown _____.

The Property has an excellent location on the east side of _____, which is a heavily traveled roadway. The surrounding properties consist of commercial establishments and residential homes.

C. Summary of Key Sales Considerations

Investment in _____ throughout (the "Partnership") is an attractive opportunity for many high-income investors. The reasons are as follows:

1. Minimum risk from nonrecourse financing. Liability of the investors will be limited to their capital contributions. No investor will be personally liable for the wraparound mortgage or the underlying first or second mortgage. Since the investment will be in real estate, the "at risk" limitations of the Internal Revenue Code should not apply.

2. Extended pay-in. The $135,000 purchase price for each Unit will be payable over five calendar years: $16,250 per Unit upon subscription; $35,450 per Unit on January 10, 1985; $30,650 per Unit on January 10, 1986; $27,750 per Unit on January 10, 1987; and $24,900 per Unit on January 10, 1988.

3. Depreciation. The depreciation used will be straight-line over 15 years. Since accelerated depreciation will not be used, the risk of depreciation recapture is eliminated and preference income will not be generated.

Broker–Dealer Sell Sheet

4. Credit Tenants. _____ is a multinational retailer distributing a broad range of variety, footwear, apparel, and department store merchandise through more than 6900 stores and leased departments in the United States, Puerto Rico, Virgin Islands, Canada, and many foreign countries.

_____ had sales of more than $7.2 billion in the fiscal year ending January 31, 1984.

_____ Corporation, a New York Stock Exchange listed company, operates a chain of supermarkets under the _____ name. As of January 31, 1983, _____ operated 287 stores in the northeast United States. Its income for its fiscal year ending January 31, 1983, was $26.1 million on sales of $2.6 billion.

_____ Drug Company of _____, a division of _____, is one of the 12 largest drug store chains in the United States. It operates more than 350 stores in more than 20 states.

5. Managing general partner. _____ has extensive experience in the ownership and management of commercial real estate.

6. Substantial Write-offs.

1984:	2.91:1
Over the pay-in period:	2.70:1
Total write-off over 15 years:	3.78:1

7. Only tax dollars used. If an individual makes this investment, he or she will be using money he or she otherwise would have paid as income tax.

8. Tax benefits in excess of investment. As a result of substantial write-offs, each investor should receive tax benefits exceeding his or her investment.

9. Legal opinion. Counsel to the Partnership will render an opinion that, for federal income tax purposes:

a. The Partnership should be subject to the partnership provisions of the Internal Revenue Code of 1954, as amended, and will not be an association taxable as a corporation.
b. The Partnership should be deemed to be the owner of the Property.
c. Each Limited Partner's basis in his or her Partnership interest should be deemed to include his or her pro rata portion of the partnership wraparound notes.

d. The Partnership may elect to utilize the accrual method of accounting and should be allowed to deduct interest expense arising from the partnership wraparound notes using the Rule of 78s.

10. MAI appraisal. The Property has been appraised by _____, a member of the American Institute of Appraisers, for a value in excess of the purchase price to the Partnership.

11. Partnership accounting. _____ will prepare the initial tax return and audited financial statement for the Partnership. The Partnership will elect the accrual method of accounting for federal income tax purposes.

12. Financial projections. The comprehensive projections at the end of this summary detail the after-tax benefits for an investor in the 50 percent bracket as well as the Income and Expense and Cash Flow of the Partnership.

13. Commissions. The commissions paid to the Broker by the Partnership are capitalized, rather than attempting to pay and deduct them through an affiliated company.

14. Self-liquidating wraparound mortgage. The Partnership wraparound mortgage is fully self-amortizing. There is no balloon payment at any time. The interest rate is at a constant 16.75 percent.

15. Upside potential. The investor may realize appreciation in his or her investment from a percentage rent clause in the operating leases, increases in base rents of operating lessees, and the company lease. Percentage rent paid in 1984 under the operating leases was $16,326.

16. Communications. Each Limited Partner and Sales Representative will receive the following information and documents:

a. Confirmation of purchase.
b. Copy of the Partnership Agreement.
c. Photograph of the Property.
d. Income tax information.
e. Periodic reports.

D. The Parties to the Transaction

_____ (the "Partnership") is a _____ limited partnership that will acquire the Property.

Broker–Dealer Sell Sheet

The General Partners of the Partnership are _____ (the "General Partner") _____ and sole shareholder of _____, the sponsor of this offering.

_____ (the "Company") will convey the Property to the Partnership. The Company is a wholly owned subsidiary of _____.

E. Structure of the Transaction

The Partnership will purchase the Property from the Company.

The total purchase price for the Property will be $3,460,889, which amount is payable $246,712 at the closing and the balance by delivery of the 36 partnership wraparound notes in the aggregate principal amount of $3,214,177. The partnership wraparound notes are secured by the partnership wraparound mortgage. Under the partnership wraparound mortgage, the Company will be obligated to make all payments due under the senior mortgages, the company wraparound mortgage, and the contract of sale.

Immediately after the sale of the Property to the Partnership, the Partnership will lease the Property to the Company for a term of 35 years, five months. The Company, through its leaseback, will be entitled to the operating lease rents and will be responsible for all physical and financial operations of the Property.

1. The company lease.

Landlord:	Partnership
Tenant:	Company
Term:	35 years, five months
Rent:	1984: $ 10,000
	1985–1988: $ 24,000/year
	1989–2004: $557,500/year
	2005–2019: $677,500/year
Percentage rent:	70 percent of the aggregate rents (including tenant reimbursements) received by the Company for the Property in excess of $387,751 per annum, minus the amount by which the Company's costs (excluding company lease rent) in operating and maintaining the Property exceed $117,935.

2. The partnership wraparound mortgage notes.

    Payor: Partnership
    Payee: Company
    Aggregate principal: $3,214,177
    Interest: 16.75% per annum, compounded monthly
    Debt service: 1984: $676,000
                          1985: $583,528
                          1986: $619,047
                          1987–1988: $291,630/year
                          1989–2019: $532,500/year
    Balance due: Self-liquidating

    a. There will be 36 separate notes. One note will be payable on December 31 of each year from 1984 through 2019. The specified debt service includes principal plus interest on the note currently due.

    b. The Partnership will deduct in each year as interest expense, in accordance with the Rule of 78s, the amount of interest that accrues on all of the then outstanding notes.

    c. The partnership wraparound mortgage is subject to the senior liens, the operating leases, and the Company's obligations under the contract of sale and wraps around the Company's obligations under the contract of sale (except the obligation to pay the Agent under the leasing agreement), and the senior mortgage. The Company will be responsible for satisfaction of such obligations as they come due.

3. The contract of sale.

    Buyer: Company
    Sellee: _____
    Date: As of August 1, 1984
    Amount: $25,000 upon execution of the contract of sale; $325,000 on closing; $400,000 in two principal installments of $200,000 each, plus 12% per annum simple interest with payment due August 1, 1985, and August 1 1986; $2,174,884 plus interest 9% per annum with payment due $19,568 per month from August 1, 1984, through July 1, 2004; "additional interest" until the first mortgage is fully paid, equal

Broker–Dealer Sell Sheet

to 3% of monthly fixed rent in excess of $6,600 plus 2% of the fixed and percentage rent paid by all the other tenants in excess of $21,366. The Company is entitled to a cumulative priority of $35,000 per year regarding its cash flow from the Property and may reduce its regular interest payments by an amount sufficient to obtain that priority by up to $33,400 per year. Those unpaid amounts will be deferred and repaid upon full payment of the purchase price under the contract of sale and may be paid in monthly installments of $19,568 beginning August 1, 1984, through July 1, 2004. If the Company's cash flow in any year exceeds $35,000, the Company will pay, as additional interest, 20% of the excess to the seller.

4. The senior mortgage.

Mortgagee:	_____
Principal:	$1,890,363.79
Interest:	8⅛%
Date:	December 8, 1980
Term:	237 months
Debt service:	$16,055 per month commencing on December 1, 1984

5. The leasing agreement.

Agent:	_____
Dated:	August 12, 1970
Term:	2 years
Commissions:	Agent is entitled to commission of 5% of the fixed and percentage rent paid under the _____ leases and 2½% of the fixed and percentage rent paid under the _____ lease. These commissions are payable throughout the initial and any renewal terms of these leases.

6. The operating leases.

See exhibits for summary of operating leases.

EXHIBITS

August 1, 1984

A. Summary of Operating Leases

B. Projected Cash Flow

C. Projected Income and Expense

D. Projected Investment Summary—50 Percent Tax Bracket

E. Projected Results of Reinvesting Benefits—50 Percent Tax Bracket

F. Projected Cash Flow Including Anticipated Increases from Percentage Rents

G. Projected Income and Expense Including Anticipated Increases from Percentage Rents

H. Projected Investment Summary—50 Percent Tax Bracket—Including Anticipated Increases from Percentages Rents

I. Projected Results of Reinvesting Benefits—50 Percent Tax Bracket—Including Anticipated Increases from Percentage Rents

J. Performance of _____

All projections contained herein are based upon the following assumptions:

1. For federal income tax purposes, the Partnership will be recognized as a limited partnership, the Partnership will be deemed to be the owner of the Property, each limited Partner's basis for his or her Partnership interest will include a pro rata share of the Partnership's obligations under the partnership wraparound notes, and the Partnership may elect the accrual method of accounting and deduct interest expense using the Rule of 78s.

2. The fair market value of the Property is not less than the Partnership's purchase price of $3,460,889, of which $3,287,889 relates solely to the Premises.

3. Neither the company lease nor the operating leases will be canceled or terminated before the expiration of the term of the company lease, that all payments on the company lease, the senior mortgage, the con-

tract of sale, the leasing agreement, and the partnership wraparound mortgage will be paid as they become due and that they will not be prepaid, and that the Partnership will incur no expenses other than those expressly set forth therein.

PROJECTED CASH FLOW
(August 1, 1984–December 31, 2019)

	SOURCE OF FUNDS				APPLICATION OF FUNDS					
	Capital Contributions									
Year	Rental Income[1]	Limited Partners	General Partners	TOTAL SOURCE	Cash for Acquisition	Debt Service Wraparound Mortgage[1]	Managing General Partner's Fee	Marketing Fees	Other Expenses[2]	TOTAL APPLICATION	Cash Available for Distribution
1984	$ 0	$357,500	$3,612	$361,112	$246,712	$ 0	$ 5,400	$99,000	$10,000	$361,112	$ 0
1985	10,000	779,900	7,877	797,777	0	676,000	11,777	99,000	10,000	796,777	1,000
1986	24,000	674,300	6,812	705,112	0	583,528	10,184	99,000	10,000	702,712	2,400
1987	24,000	610,500	6,166	640,666	0	619,047	9,219	0	10,000	638,266	2,400
1988	48,000	547,800	5,533	601,333	0	583,260	8,272	0	5,000	596,532	4,801
1989	557,500	0	0	557,500	0	532,500	0	0	5,000	537,500	20,000
1990	557,500	0	0	557,500	0	532,500	0	0	5,000	537,500	20,000
1991	557,500	0	0	557,500	0	532,500	0	0	5,000	537,500	20,000
1992	557,500	0	0	557,500	0	532,500	0	0	5,000	537,500	20,000
1993	557,500	0	0	557,500	0	532,500	0	0	5,000	537,500	20,000
1994	557,500	0	0	557,500	0	532,500	0	0	5,000	537,500	20,000
1995	557,500	0	0	557,500	0	532,500	0	0	5,000	537,500	20,000
1996	557,500	0	0	557,500	0	532,500	0	0	5,000	537,500	20,000
1997	557,500	0	0	557,500	0	532,500	0	0	5,000	537,500	20,000
1998	557,500	0	0	557,500	0	532,500	0	0	5,000	537,500	20,000
1999	557,500	0	0	557,500	0	532,500	0	0	5,000	537,500	20,000
2000	557,500	0	0	557,500	0	532,500	0	0	5,000	537,500	20,000
2001	557,500	0	0	557,500	0	532,500	0	0	5,000	537,500	20,000
2002	557,500	0	0	557,500	0	532,500	0	0	5,000	537,500	20,000
2003	557,500	0	0	557,500	0	532,500	0	0	5,000	537,500	20,000
2004	557,500	0	0	557,500	0	532,500	0	0	5,000	537,500	20,000

Year						
2005	677,500	0	677,500	0	5,000	537,500	140,000
2006	677,500	0	677,500	0	5,000	537,500	140,000
2007	677,500	0	677,500	0	5,000	537,500	140,000
2008	677,500	0	677,500	0	5,000	537,500	140,000
2009	677,500	0	677,500	0	5,000	537,500	140,000
2010	677,500	0	677,500	0	5,000	537,500	140,000
2011	677,500	0	677,500	0	5,000	537,500	140,000
2012	677,500	0	677,500	0	5,000	537,500	140,000
2013	677,500	0	677,500	0	5,000	537,500	140,000
2014	677,500	0	677,500	0	5,000	537,500	140,000
2015	677,500	0	677,500	0	5,000	537,500	140,000
2016	677,500	0	677,500	0	5,000	537,500	140,000
2017	677,500	0	677,500	0	5,000	537,500	140,000
2018	677,500	0	677,500	0	5,000	537,500	140,000
2019	$677,500	$ 0	$677,500	$ 0	$ 5,000	$537,500	$140,000

[1] Receipts of rent and payments of debt service due December 31, 1984, 1985, 1986, and 1987 are anticipated to occur in January of the following year.

[2] Legal expense: $5,000 in 1984

PROJECTED INCOME AND EXPENSE
(August 1, 1984–December 31, 2019)

Year	Rental Income	Interest Expense Wraparound Mortgage	Depreciation	Managing General Partner's Fee	Other Expenses[1]	Total Expenses	Income (Loss)	Cumulative Income (Loss)
1984	$ 10,000	$ 958,670	$ 91,330	$ 5,400	$5,000	$1,060,400	$(1,050,400)	$ (1,050,400)
1985	24,000	1,935,291	219,193	11,777	5,000	2,171,261	(2,147,261)	(3,197,661)
1986	24,000	1,625,485	219,193	10,184	5,000	1,859,862	(1,835,862)	(5,033,523)
1987	24,000	1,409,225	219,193	9,219	5,000	1,642,637	(1,618,637)	(6,652,160)
1988	24,000	1,239,399	219,193	8,272	5,000	1,471,864	(1,447,864)	(8,100,024)
1989	557,500	1,088,026	219,193	0	5,000	1,312,219	(754,719)	(8,854,743)
1990	557,500	954,654	219,193	0	5,000	1,178,847	(621,347)	(9,476,090)
1991	557,500	840,459	219,193	0	5,000	1,064,652	(507,152)	(9,983,242)
1992	557,500	741,558	219,193	0	5,000	965,751	(408,251)	(10,391,493)
1993	557,500	655,149	219,193	0	5,000	879,342	(321,842)	(10,713,335)
1994	557,500	579,132	219,193	0	5,000	803,325	(245,825)	(10,959,160)
1995	557,500	511,891	219,193	0	5,000	736,084	(178,584)	(11,137,744)
1996	557,500	452,153	219,193	0	5,000	676,346	(118,846)	(11,256,590)
1997	557,500	398,897	219,193	0	5,000	623,090	(65,590)	(11,322,180)
1998	557,500	351,292	219,193	0	5,000	575,485	(17,985)	(11,340,165)
1999	557,500	308,654	127,862	0	5,000	441,516	115,984	(11,224,181)
2000	557,500	270,409	0	0	5,000	275,409	282,091	(10,942,090)
2001	557,500	236,078	0	0	5,000	241,078	316,422	(10,625,668)
2002	557,500	205,251	0	0	5,000	210,251	347,249	(10,278,419)
2003	557,500	177,577	0	0	5,000	182,577	374,923	(9,903,496)
2004	557,500	152,756	0	0	5,000	157,756	399,744	(9,503,752)
2005	677,500	130,526	0	0	5,000	135,526	541,974	(8,961,778)

Year					
2006	677,500	110,657	0	115,657	561,843	(8,399,935)
2007	677,500	92,951	0	97,951	579,549	(7,820,386)
2008	677,500	77,229	0	82,229	595,271	(7,225,115)
2009	677,500	63,337	0	68,337	609,163	(6,615,952)
2010	677,500	51,134	0	56,134	621,366	(5,994,586)
2011	677,500	40,497	0	45,497	632,003	(5,362,583)
2012	677,500	31,315	0	36,315	641,185	(4,721,398)
2013	677,500	23,487	0	28,487	649,013	(4,072,385)
2014	677,500	16,923	0	21,923	655,577	(3,416,808)
2015	677,500	11,543	0	16,543	660,957	(2,755,851)
2016	677,500	7,270	0	12,270	665,230	(2,090,621)
2017	677,500	4,039	0	9,039	668,461	(1,422,160)
2018	677,500	1,787	0	6,787	670,713	(751,447)
2019	$677,500	$ 458	$ 0	$5,458	$ 672,042	$ (79,405)

[1] Legal expense: $5,000 in 1984; accounting expense: $5,000 per year, 1985–2019.

PROJECTED INVESTMENT SUMMARY—50% BRACKET
Investment of $135,000

Year	Amount Invested	Taxable Income (Loss)	Tax Savings (Cost)[1]	Cash Flow	Annual Benefits[2]	Cumulative Annual Benefits	Investment Interest Subject to Limitation before $10,000 Exclusion	Cumulative Benefits Net of Investment[3]
1984	$16,250	$ (47,268)	$23,634	$ 0	$23,634	$ 23,634	$ 450	$ 7,384
1985	35,400	(96,627)	48,314	45	48,359	71,993	1,080	20,343
1986	30,650	(82,614)	41,307	108	41,415	113,408	1,080	31,108
1987	27,750	(72,839)	36,420	108	36,528	149,936	1,080	39,886
1988	24,900	(65,154)	32,577	216	32,793	182,729	1,080	47,779
1989	0	(33,962)	16,981	900	17,881	200,610	9,864	65,660
1990	0	(27,961)	13,981	900	14,881	215,491	9,864	80,541
1991	0	(22,822)	11,411	900	12,311	227,802	9,864	92,852
1992	0	(18,371)	9,186	900	10,086	237,888	9,864	102,938
1993	0	(14,483)	7,242	900	8,142	246,030	9,864	111,080
1994	0	(11,062)	5,531	900	6,431	252,461	9,864	117,511
1995	0	(8,036)	4,018	900	4,918	257,379	7,811	122,429
1996	0	(5,348)	2,674	900	3,574	260,953	5,123	126,003
1997	0	(2,952)	1,476	900	2,376	263,329	2,727	128,379
1998	0	(809)	405	900	1,305	264,634	584	129,684
1999	0	5,219	(2,610)	900	(1,710)	262,924	0	127,974
2000	0	12,694	(6,347)	900	(5,447)	257,477	0	122,527
2001	0	14,239	(7,120)	900	(6,220)	251,257	0	116,307
2002	0	15,626	(7,813)	900	(6,913)	244,344	0	109,394
2003	0	16,872	(8,436)	900	(7,536)	236,808	0	101,858
2004	0	17,988	(8,994)	900	(8,094)	228,714	0	93,764
2005	0	24,389	(12,195)	6,300	(5,895)	222,819	0	87,869

Year							
2006	25,283	(12,642)	6,300	(6,342)	216,477	0	81,527
2007	26,080	(13,040)	6,300	(6,740)	209,737	0	74,787
2008	26,787	(13,394)	6,300	(7,094)	202,643	0	67,693
2009	27,412	(13,706)	6,300	(7,406)	195,237	0	60,287
2010	27,961	(13,981)	6,300	(7,681)	187,556	0	52,606
2011	28,440	(14,220)	6,300	(7,920)	179,636	0	44,686
2012	28,853	(14,427)	6,300	(8,127)	171,509	0	36,559
2013	29,206	(14,603)	6,300	(8,303)	163,206	0	28,256
2014	29,501	(14,751)	6,300	(8,451)	154,755	0	19,805
2015	29,743	(14,872)	6,300	(8,572)	146,183	0	11,233
2016	29,935	(14,968)	6,300	(8,668)	137,515	0	2,565
2017	30,081	(15,041)	6,300	(8,741)	128,774	0	(6,176)
2018	30,182	(15,091)	6,300	(8,791)	119,983	0	(14,967)
2019	$ 30,242	$(15,121)	$6,300	(8,821)	$111,162	$ 0	$ (23,788)

[1] Taxable income (loss) time tax bracket.
[2] Tax savings (cost) plus cash flow.
[3] Cumulative of annual benefits minus amount invested.

PROJECTED RESULTS OF REINVESTING BENEFITS—50% BRACKET

Year	Net Annual Savings[1]	10% Interest After Taxes[2]	Cash Flow[3]	Total Benefits
1984	$ 7,384	$ 92	$ 0	$ 7,476
1985	12,863	1,267	45	21,651
1986	10,657	2,654	108	35,070
1987	8,669	3,971	108	47,819
1988	7,677	5,257	216	60,969
1989	16,981	6,977	900	85,827
1990	13,980	9,443	900	110,150
1991	11,411	11,870	900	134,331
1992	9,186	14,296	900	158,712
1993	7,241	16,752	900	183,606
1994	5,531	19,272	900	209,308
1995	4,018	21,882	900	236,109
1996	2,674	24,613	900	264,296
1997	1,476	27,494	900	294,165
1998	405	30,554	900	326,023
1999	(2,610)	33,746	900	358,060
2000	(6,347)	36,929	900	389,542
2001	(7,119)	40,166	900	423,490
2002	(7,813)	43,666	900	460,243
2003	(8,436)	47,458	900	500,165
2004	(8,994)	51,581	900	543,651
2005	(12,194)	55,973	6,300	593,730
2006	(12,641)	61,155	6,300	648,543
2007	(13,040)	66,830	6,300	708,633

Year			
2008	(13,394)	73,055	6,300	774,594
2009	(13,706)	79,890	6,300	847,078
2010	(13,981)	87,405	6,300	926,802
2011	(14,220)	95,672	6,300	1,014,554
2012	(14,427)	104,774	6,300	1,111,201
2013	(14,603)	114,800	6,300	1,217,698
2014	(14,750)	125,850	6,300	1,335,098
2015	(14,872)	138,033	6,300	1,464,560
2016	(14,968)	151,470	6,300	1,607,362
2017	(15,040)	166,291	6,300	1,764,913
2018	(15,091)	182,645	6,300	1,938,767
2019	$(15,121)	$200,692	$6,300	$2,130,639

[1] Net annual savings are tax savings (cost) less amount invested and are assumed to be available on a quarterly basis beginning September 30, 1984.
[2] Interest is assumed to be paid quarterly from net annual savings and total benefits of the previous years.
[3] Cash flow is assumed to be available at one time at the end of the year.

PROJECTED CASH FLOW
(August 1, 1984–December 31, 2019)
(including anticipated increases from percentage rents[1])

SOURCE OF FUNDS

Year	Rental Income[2]	Capital Contributions — Limited Partners	Capital Contributions — General Partners	TOTAL SOURCE
1984	$ 0	$357,500	$3,612	$ 361,112
1985	10,058	779,900	7,877	797,835
1986	34,750	674,300	6,812	715,862
1987	40,193	610,500	6,166	656,859
1988	86,042	547,800	5,533	639,375
1989	579,852	0	0	579,852
1990	734,835	0	0	734,835
1991	751,474	0	0	751,474
1992	769,703	0	0	769,703
1993	789,670	0	0	789,670
1994	811,538	0	0	811,538
1995	835,481	0	0	835,481
1996	861,692	0	0	861,692
1997	890,381	0	0	890,381
1998	921,777	0	0	921,777
1999	955,990	0	0	955,990
2000	992,993	0	0	992,993
2001	1,033,470	0	0	1,033,470
2002	1,077,742	0	0	1,077,742
2003	1,131,003	0	0	1,131,003

APPLICATION OF FUNDS

Year	Cash for Acquisition	Debt Service Wraparound Mortgage[2]	Managing General Partner's Fee	Marketing Fees	Other Expenses	TOTAL APPLICATION	Cash Available for Distribution
1984	$246,712	$ 0	$ 5,400	$99,000	$10,000	$361,112	$ 0
1985	0	676,000	11,777	99,000	10,000	796,777	1,058
1986	0	583,528	10,184	99,000	10,000	702,712	13,150
1987	0	619,047	9,219	0	10,000	638,266	18,593
1988	0	583,260	8,272	0	5,000	596,532	42,843
1989	0	532,500	0	0	5,000	537,500	42,352
1990	0	532,500	0	0	5,000	537,500	197,335
1991	0	532,500	0	0	5,000	537,500	213,974
1992	0	532,500	0	0	5,000	537,500	232,203
1993	0	532,500	0	0	5,000	537,500	252,170
1994	0	532,500	0	0	5,000	537,500	274,038
1995	0	532,500	0	0	5,000	537,500	297,981
1996	0	532,500	0	0	5,000	537,500	324,192
1997	0	532,500	0	0	5,000	537,500	352,881
1998	0	532,500	0	0	5,000	537,500	384,277
1999	0	532,500	0	0	5,000	537,500	418,490
2000	0	532,500	0	0	5,000	537,500	455,493
2001	0	532,500	0	0	5,000	537,500	495,970
2002	0	532,500	0	0	5,000	537,500	540,242
2003	0	532,500	0	0	5,000	537,500	593,503

Year	Col2	Col3	Col4	Col5	Col6	Col7
2004	1,184,380	0	0	532,500	0	5,000	537,500	646,880
2005	1,362,736	0	0	532,500	0	5,000	537,500	825,236
2006	1,426,529	0	0	532,500	0	5,000	537,500	889,029
2007	1,496,256	0	0	532,500	0	5,000	537,500	958,756
2008	1,572,463	0	0	532,500	0	5,000	537,500	1,034,963
2009	1,655,742	0	0	532,500	0	5,000	537,500	1,118,242
2010	1,746,740	0	0	532,500	0	5,000	537,500	1,209,240
2011	1,846,163	0	0	532,500	0	5,000	537,500	1,308,663
2012	1,954,781	0	0	532,500	0	5,000	537,500	1,417,281
2013	2,073,435	0	0	532,500	0	5,000	537,500	1,535,935
2014	2,203,040	0	0	532,500	0	5,000	537,500	1,665,540
2015	2,344,595	0	0	532,500	0	5,000	537,500	1,807,095
2016	2,499,191	0	0	532,500	0	5,000	537,500	1,961,691
2017	2,668,016	0	0	532,500	0	5,000	537,500	2,130,516
2018	2,852,367	0	0	532,500	0	5,000	537,500	2,314,867
2019	$3,053,657	$ 0	$ 0	$532,500	$ 0	$ 5,000	$537,500	$2,516,157

[1] Assume a 9% per annum increase in gross sales, a 5% per annum increase in the Consumer Price Index, and a 4% per annum increase in local taxes and expenses.

[2] Receipts of rent and payments of debt service due December 31, 1984, 1985, 1986, and 1987 are anticipated to occur in January of the following year.

PROJECTED INCOME AND EXPENSE
(August 1, 1984–December 31, 2019)
(including anticipated increase from percentage rents[1])

Year	Rental Income	Interest Expense Wraparound Mortgage	Depreciation	Managing General Partner's Fee	Other Expenses[2]	Total Expenses	Income (Loss)	Cumulative Income (Loss)
1984	$ 10,058	$ 958,670	$ 91,330	$ 5,400	$5,000	$1,060,400	$(1,050,342)	$ (1,050,342)
1985	34,750	1,935,291	219,193	11,777	5,000	2,171,261	(2,136,511)	(3,186,853)
1986	40,193	1,625,485	219,193	10,184	5,000	1,859,862	(1,819,669)	(5,006,522)
1987	41,999	1,409,225	219,193	9,219	5,000	1,642,637	(1,600,638)	(6,607,160)
1988	44,043	1,239,399	219,193	8,272	5,000	1,471,864	(1,427,821)	(8,034,981)
1989	579,852	1,088,026	219,193	0	5,000	1,312,219	(732,367)	(8,767,348)
1990	734,835	954,654	219,193	0	5,000	1,178,847	(444,012)	(9,211,360)
1991	751,474	840,459	219,193	0	5,000	1,064,652	(313,178)	(9,524,538)
1992	769,703	741,558	219,193	0	5,000	965,751	(196,048)	(9,720,586)
1993	789,670	655,149	219,193	0	5,000	879,342	(89,672)	(9,810,258)
1994	811,538	579,132	219,193	0	5,000	803,325	8,213	(9,802,045)
1995	835,481	511,891	219,193	0	5,000	736,084	99,397	(9,702,648)
1996	861,692	452,153	219,193	0	5,000	676,346	185,346	(9,517,302)
1997	890,381	398,897	219,193	0	5,000	623,090	267,291	(9,250,011)
1998	921,777	351,292	219,193	0	5,000	575,485	346,292	(8,903,719)
1999	955,990.	308,654	127,862	0	5,000	441,516	514,474	(8,389,245)
2000	992,993	270,409	0	0	5,000	275,409	717,584	(7,671,661)
2001	1,033,470	236,078	0	0	5,000	241,078	792,392	(6,879,269)
2002	1,077,742	205,251	0	0	5,000	210,251	867,491	(6,011,778)
2003	1,131,003	177,577	0	0	5,000	182,577	948,426	(5,063,352)
2004	1,184,380	152,756	0	0	5,000	157,756	1,026,624	(4,036,728)

Year						
2005	1,362,736	130,526	0	5,000	1,227,210	(2,809,518)
2006	1,426,529	110,657	0	5,000	1,310,872	(1,498,646)
2007	1,496,256	92,951	0	5,000	1,398,305	(100,341)
2008	1,572,463	77,229	0	5,000	1,490,234	1,389,893
2009	1,655,742	63,337	0	5,000	1,587,405	2,977,298
2010	1,746,749	51,134	0	5,000	1,690,615	4,667,913
2011	1,846,163	40,497	0	5,000	1,800,666	6,468,579
2012	1,954,781	31,315	0	5,000	1,918,466	8,387,045
2013	2,073,435	23,487	0	5,000	2,044,948	10,431,993
2014	2,203,040	16,923	0	5,000	2,181,117	12,613,110
2015	2,344,595	11,543	0	5,000	2,328,052	14,941,162
2016	2,499,191	7,270	0	5,000	2,486,921	17,428,083
2017	2,668,016	4,039	0	5,000	2,658,977	20,087,060
2018	2,852,367	1,787	0	5,000	2,845,580	22,932,640
2019	$3,053,657	$ 458	$ 0	$5,000	$ 3,048,199	$25,980,839

[1] Assumes a 9% per annum increase in gross sales, a 5% per annum increase in the Consumer Price Index, and a 4% per annum increase in local taxes and expenses.
[2] Legal expense: $5,000 in 1984; accounting expense: $5,000 per year, 1985–2019.

PROJECTED INVESTMENT SUMMARY—50% BRACKET
Investment of $135,000
(including anticipated increase from percentage rents[1])

Year	Amount Invested	Taxable Income (Loss)	Tax Savings (Cost)[1]	Cash Flow	Annual Benefits[2]	Cumulative Annual Benefits	Investment Interest Subject to Limitation before $10,000 Exclusion	Cumulative Benefits Net of Investment[3]
1984	16,250	$ (47,265)	$ 23,633	$ 0	$23,633	$ 23,633	$ 453	$ 7,383
1985	35,450	(96,143)	48,072	48	48,120	71,753	1,564	20,053
1986	30,650	(81,885)	40,943	592	41,535	113,288	1,809	30,938
1987	27,750	(72,029)	36,015	837	36,852	150,140	1,890	40,040
1988	24,900	(64,252)	32,126	1,928	34,054	184,194	1,982	49,194
1989	0	(32,956)	16,478	1,906	18,384	202,578	9,864	67,578
1990	0	(19,981)	9,991	8,880	18,871	221,449	9,864	86,449
1991	0	(14,093)	7,047	9,629	16,676	238,125	9,864	103,125
1992	0	(8,822)	4,411	10,449	14,860	252,985	8,597	117,985
1993	0	(4,035)	2,018	11,348	13,366	266,351	3,810	131,351
1994	0	370	(185)	12,332	12,147	278,498	0	143,498
1995	0	4,473	(2,237)	13,409	11,172	289,670	0	154,670
1996	0	8,341	(4,171)	14,589	10,418	300,088	0	165,088
1997	0	12,028	(6,014)	15,880	9,866	309,954	0	174,954
1998	0	15,583	(7,792)	17,292	9,500	319,454	0	184,454
1999	0	23,151	(11,576)	18,832	7,256	326,710	0	191,710
2000	0	32,291	(16,146)	20,497	4,351	331,061	0	196,061
2001	0	35,658	(17,829)	22,319	4,490	335,551	0	200,551
2002	0	39,037	(19,519)	24,311	4,792	340,343	0	205,343
2003	0	42,679	(21,340)	26,708	5,368	345,711	0	210,711
2004	0	46,198	(23,099)	29,110	6,011	351,722	0	216,722

Year						
2005	55,224	0	(27,612)	37,136	9,524	361,246	226,246
2006	58,989	0	(29,495)	40,006	10,511	371,757	236,757
2007	62,924	0	(31,462)	43,144	11,682	383,439	248,439
2008	67,061	0	(33,531)	46,573	13,042	396,481	261,481
2009	71,433	0	(35,717)	50,321	14,604	411,085	276,085
2010	76,077	0	(38,039)	54,416	16,377	427,462	292,462
2011	81,030	0	(40,515)	58,890	18,375	445,837	310,837
2012	86,331	0	(43,166)	63,778	20,612	466,449	331,449
2013	92,023	0	(46,012)	69,117	23,105	489,554	354,554
2014	98,150	0	(49,075)	74,949	25,874	515,428	380,428
2015	104,762	0	(52,381)	81,319	28,938	544,366	409,366
2016	111,911	0	(55,956)	88,276	32,320	576,686	441,686
2017	119,654	0	(59,827)	95,873	36,046	612,732	477,732
2018	128,051	0	(64,026)	104,169	40,143	652,875	517,875
2019	$137,169	$ 0	$(68,585)	$113,227	$44,642	$697,517	$562,517

[1] Taxable income (loss) times tax bracket.
[2] Tax savings (cost) plus cash flow.
[3] Cumulative of annual benefits minus amount invested.

PROJECTED RESULTS OF REINVESTING BENEFITS—50% BRACKET
(including anticipated increases from percentage rents[1])

Year	Net Annual Savings[2]	10% Interest After Taxes[3]	Cash Flow[4]	Total Benefits
1984	$ 7,383	$ 92	$ 0	$ 7,475
1985	12,621	1,257	48	21,401
1986	10,293	2,614	592	34,900
1987	8,264	3,938	837	47,939
1988	7,226	5,252	1,928	62,345
1989	16,478	7,101	1,906	87,830
1990	9,990	9,499	8,880	116,199
1991	7,046	12,332	9,629	145,206
1992	4,411	15,242	10,449	175,308
1993	2,018	18,276	11,348	206,950
1994	(185)	21,477	12,332	240,574
1995	(2,236)	24,889	13,409	276,636
1996	(4,170)	28,559	14,589	315,613
1997	(6,014)	32,535	15,880	358,014
1998	(7,792)	36,869	17,292	404,385
1999	(11,576)	41,539	18,832	453,180
2000	(16,146)	46,430	20,497	503,962
2001	(17,829)	51,638	22,319	560,090
2002	(19,519)	57,400	24,311	622,282
2003	(21,340)	63,787	26,708	691,438
2004	(23,099)	70,899	29,110	768,348
2005	(27,612)	78,712	37,136	856,583
2006	(29,495)	87,800	40,006	954,894
2007	(31,462)	97,931	43,144	1,064,507
2008	(33,530)	109,231	46,573	1,186,781
2009	(35,717)	121,841	50,321	1,323,227
2010	(38,039)	135,918	54,416	1,475,521
2011	(40,515)	151,633	58,890	1,645,530
2012	(43,165)	169,181	63,778	1,835,323
2013	(46,011)	188,776	69,117	2,047,205
2014	(49,075)	210,655	74,949	2,283,734
2015	(52,381)	235,084	81,319	2,547,756
2016	(55,956)	262,356	88,276	2,842,432
2017	(59,827)	292,800	95,873	3,171,279
2018	(64,026)	326,778	104,169	3,538,200
2019	$(68,584)	$364,696	$113,227	$3,947,539

[1] Taxable income (loss) times tax bracket.
[2] Net annual savings are tax savings (cost) less amount invested and are assumed to be available on a quarterly basis beginning September 30, 1984.
[3] Interest is assumed to accrue quarterly from net annual savings and total benefits of the previous years.
[4] Cash flow is assumed to be available at one time at the end of the year.

LIMITED PARTNERSHIP AGREEMENT

The following pages cover a full agreement of limited partnership utilized by a publicly offered limited partnership. It deals with such issues as continuity, transferability, limited liability, and delegation of management—all as discussed in greater detail in the preceding chapters.

This full limited partnership agreement will let you see some of the subjects it covers. Such an agreement must be drafted to meet the needs and laws of your state.

AGREEMENT OF LIMITED PARTNERSHIP

Agreement of Limited Partnership made as of _____, by and among _____, a _____ corporation, as General Partner (the "General Partner"), and _____, as Limited Partner. Such Limited Partner and any additional Limited Partners hereafter admitted to the partnership as herein provided are collectively referred to as "Limited Partners," and the Limited Partners, as constituted from time to time, and the General Partner are collectively referred to as the "Partners."

The Partners desire to form a Limited Partnership to engage in the business described in Paragraph 3 upon the terms and conditions hereinafter set forth.

It is therefore agreed:

1. *Formation*

The parties do hereby form a Limited Partnership (the "Partnership") pursuant to the provisions of Article VIII of the Partnership Law of the State of _____.

2. Name and office

The name of the Partnership shall be _____. The office of the Partnership shall be located at _____, or at such other place or places as the General Partner may from time to time determine.

3. Purposes

The purposes of the Partnership are (a) to purchase, lease, sell, own, develop, and construct improvements upon; to finance the acquisition, operation, and development of, and the construction of improvements upon; and to operate and maintain for any uses, real property, or interests therein, wherever located; (b) to purchase, lease, sell, own and operate, and finance the acquisition and operation of personal property; (c) to incur indebtedness, secured or unsecured, for any of the purposes of the Partnership; (d) to lend any of the monies or other assets of the Partnership with or without security; (e) to invest and reinvest the assets of the Partnership in and to purchase or otherwise acquire, hold, sell, transfer, exchange, or otherwise dispose of or realize upon securities of all types and descriptions and any other interests in business ventures; and (f) any other purposes as are necessary to protect or enhance the assets of the Partnership.

4. Term

The term of the Partnership shall commence on the date of filing of a Certificate of Limited Partnership in the office of the County Clerk of _____ County and shall terminate December 31, 2068, provided, however, that the Partnership shall be terminated before such date (a) upon the bankruptcy, withdrawal, or liquidation of the General Partner; (b) by decision of the General Partner, concurred in by Limited Partners holding more than 50 percent of the Units of the Partnership which are held by Limited Partners; or (c) by decision of Partners holding more than 66⅔ percent of the Units of the Partnership.

5. Capital

The capital of the Partnership shall be measured in terms of Units and may be increased from time to time by contributions in cash or in property as hereinafter provided.

6. Distributions to partners and allocation of profits and losses among partners

a. Distributions of cash to the Partners may be made from time to time, at the discretion of the General Partner, in amounts not to exceed

Limited Partnership Agreement

the Gains and Earnings Account described in subparagraph 7(c) as of the date designated by the General Partner for the determination of the persons entitled to receive such distribution as provided in subparagraph f of this paragraph. The Gains and Earnings Account shall be decreased by the amount of each distribution made, the decrease to be effected as of such designated date.

b. Distributions of cash made in any fiscal year of the Partnership (as distinct from the allocation of net profit or net loss, which shall be as provided in subparagraphs c and d of this paragraph) shall be divided among the Partners as follows:

i. First, to the extent necessary, to satisfy the Annual Distribution Preference for such fiscal year and then, to the extent that it has not been satisfied for all preceding fiscal years ending after January 1, 1971, to satisfy the annual distribution preference for all such fiscal years.

ii. The balance, if any, as follows: 25 percent to the General Partner and 75 percent to all Partners divided among the Partners in proportion to the number of Units held by them as of the end of such fiscal year.

The term "annual distribution preference" for any fiscal year of the Partnership shall mean an amount equal to the excess, if any, of 8 percent (or, for a fiscal year of less than 365 days, 8 percent multiplied by a fraction, the numerator of which is the number of days in such fiscal year and the denominator of which is 365) of the daily average capital for such year over one-half of the net loss, if any, for such year. For purposes of the computation of the annual distribution preference, the net loss shall be deemed to be the net loss stated on the federal income tax return originally filed by the Partnership for the applicable fiscal year and shall not thereafter be adjusted notwithstanding any subsequent adjustment in the net loss for such fiscal year from any cause. Any such subsequent adjustment will be reflected in the computation of the annual distribution preference for the fiscal year in which the adjustment is made.

The annual distribution preference, to the extent satisfied, shall be divided among the Partners in proportion to the number of Units held by them as of the end of the fiscal year.

c. The net profit of the Partnership for any fiscal year shall be allocated as follows:

i. To the extent available, an amount equal to 8 percent of the daily average capital for such fiscal year among the Partners in proportion to the number of Units held by them as of the end of such fiscal year.

ii. The balance, if any, as follows: 25 percent to the General Partner and 75 percent to all Partners allocated among the Partners in proportion to the number of Units held by them as of the end of such fiscal year.

d. The net loss of the Partnership for any fiscal year shall be allocated among the Partners in proportion to the number of Units held by them as of the end of such fiscal year.

e. The terms "net profit" and "net loss" of the Partnership shall mean the net profits or losses, as the case may be, from the operations of the Partnership, as determined for federal income tax purposes.

f. The General Partner shall designate a date for the determination of the owners of Units who shall be entitled to receive any distribution to be made according to the number of Units held, and such distribution shall be to the owners of the Units as of such date.

g. Any Unit that was not outstanding at the beginning of the fiscal year in which or for which any allocation or distribution is made shall be deemed for the purposes of such allocation or distribution (except in connection with the liquidation of the Partnership) to be a fraction of a Unit, the numerator of which shall be the number of days from the date of the issuance of such Unit to the end of such fiscal year and the denominator of which shall be the number of days in such fiscal year. The owner of each such Unit shall receive in respect thereof the same fractional portion of all allocations or distributions (except in connection with the liquidation of the Partnership) made in or for the fiscal year in which such Unit was issued in respect of each Unit that was outstanding at the beginning of the year.

h. If any distribution is made for any fiscal year before the annual distribution preference for such year is determined, the General Partner shall estimate the amount of the annual distribution preference for such year and such distribution shall be allocated by the General Partner on the basis of such estimate. Distributions made within three months after the end of a fiscal year, if so designated by the General Partner, shall be deemed to have been made for such fiscal year.

i. Any allocation or distribution not otherwise specifically provided for herein shall be among the Partners in proportion to the number of Units held.

7. *Memorandum accounts for determination of unit values*

For purposes of the computation of Unit Values as defined in paragraph 8, the following shall apply:

Limited Partnership Agreement

a. All contributions to the Partnership, whether in cash or in property and whether by way of initial investment, new investment, or reinvestment shall be credited to the capital of the Partnership. The capital of the Partnership will be divided into two accounts, the Aggregate Capital Investment Account and the Capital Cash Account. The Aggregate Capital Investment Account is the sum of the capital investments in each of the Partnership properties and other assets. The capital investment in each property or asset is the total net expenditures paid from the Capital Cash Account for the purchase of, capital improvements to, or capitalized carrying costs for, such property or asset, less all amounts by which such capital investment has been reduced pursuant to subparagraph c of this paragraph. If a property or other asset is contributed to the Partnership, the initial capital investment for such property or asset will be equal to the value at which the contribution was accepted. The Capital Cash Account shall be equal to the excess of the capital over the Aggregate Capital Investment Account.

b. The Amortization Account for each property or other asset shall be the cumulative sum of the amortization of indebtedness then encumbering such property or asset which has been paid from the Gains and Earnings Account, less all amounts by which such Amortization Account has been reduced pursuant to subparagraph c of this paragraph.

c. The Gains and Earnings Account shall consist of the excess of the gross cash receipts of the Partnership (other than contributions to the capital) over the gross cash payments and distributions of the Partnership (other than from the Capital Cash Account and other than payments for capitalized costs of organization of the Partnership and expenses of offering and sale of interests in the Partnership), subject to the following:

i. The net proceeds of borrowings not related to or secured by a particular property and of borrowings secured by purchase money indebtedness described in subdivision v of this subparagraph shall be added, in the discretion of the General Partner, either to the Gains and Earnings Account or to the Capital Cash Account. The account to which such borrowings are added shall be reduced when and to the extent they are repaid.

ii. The net proceeds of a borrowing related to or secured by a particular property, to the extent they exceed the amount to be used (x) to repay other indebtedness related to or secured by such property, (y) for improvements on such property or on an adjoining and related property or (z) for the purchase of such property or of an adjoining and related property, shall be applied to the extent available in the following manner:

A. First to increase the Gains and Earnings Account by up to the amount of the Amortization Account for such property, and the Amortization Account for such property shall be reduced by the amount of such increase.

B. Then to increase the Capital Cash Account by up to the amount of the capital investment in such property, and the Capital Investment Account for such property shall be reduced by the amount of such increase.

C. Then to increase the Gains and Earnings Account.

iii. In the event of a sale or other disposition, voluntary or involuntary, of the entire interest of the Partnership in a property, the proceeds thereof shall be applied in the following manner:

A. First the Gains and Earnings Account shall be increased by the amount of the Amortization Account for such property, and the Amortization Account for such property shall be reduced to zero.

B. Then the Capital Cash Account shall be increased by the amount of the capital investment in such property, and the Capital Investment Account for such property shall be reduced to zero.

C. Then the Gains and Earnings Account shall be increased by the excess, if any, of the net proceeds of such sale or disposition over the sum of the Amortization Account for and the capital investment in such property (before they were reduced as provided in clauses A and B above). If the sum of the Amortization Account for and the capital investment in such property exceeds such net proceeds, the Gains and Earnings Account (after it has been increased as provided in clause A above) shall be reduced by the amount of the excess.

iv. In the event of a sale or other disposition, voluntary or involuntary, of less than the entire interest of the Partnership in a property, to the extent that the net proceeds thereof exceed the amount thereof to be used to repay indebtedness related to or secured by such property, for improvements on such property or on an adjoining and related property, and for the purchase of an adjoining and related property, they shall be applied to the extent available in the following manner:

A. First to increase the Gains and Earnings Account by up to the amount of the Amortization Account for such property, and the Amortization Account for such property shall be reduced by the amount of such increase.

Limited Partnership Agreement 173

B. Then to increase the Capital Cash Account by up to the amount of the capital investment in such property, and the Capital Investment Account for such property shall be reduced by the amount of such increase.

C. Then to increase the Gains and Earnings Account.

v. If the proceeds of a sale or other disposition shall consist, in whole or in part, of evidences of indebtedness, the increases in the respective accounts to be effected in the event of such sale or other disposition as provided in subdivisions iii and iv of this subparagraph shall be deemed to have been effected by the addition to such accounts, in the order specified in such subdivisions, first of the cash, if any, received upon such sale or other disposition to the extent available and then of such evidences of indebtedness. Subsequent principal payments on, or the proceeds of a sale of, such indebtedness shall be substituted for the portions of the indebtedness in each such account in the order in which they were deemed to have been added thereto.

If on final disposition of any such evidence of indebtedness, as determined by the General Partner in its sole discretion, the Partnership shall realize in cash less than the principal amount thereof, if such indebtedness was received by the Partnership upon the sale or other disposition of the entire interest of the Partnership in a property, the Gains and Earnings Account shall be reduced by the deficit; and if such indebtedness was received by the Partnership upon the sale or other disposition of less than the entire interest of the Partnership in a property, the accounts to which such indebtedness was deemed to have been added shall be reduced by the deficit in reverse order of application.

If the Partnership shall acquire any property, by foreclosure or otherwise, that was security for indebtedness owed to the Partnership, then the capital investment in such property shall be equal to the unpaid amount of such indebtedness plus the expenses of foreclosure or other means of acquisition, less any monies actually collected from persons obligated to pay such indebtedness.

vi. The Gains and Earnings Account shall be decreased by all amounts paid in respect of obligations of the Partnership except for capital investments and except for capitalized costs of organization of the Partnership and expenses of offering and sale of interests in the Partnership. If the amount paid in respect of any such obligation exceeds the Gains and Earnings Account, the Capital Cash Account shall be reduced by the amount of such excess, and if the obligation so paid pertains to a particular property, the capital investment for such property shall be increased by the amount by which the Capital Cash Account was so reduced, or, if the obligation so paid does not pertain to a particular property, the amount by which the Capital Cash Account was so reduced shall be carried forward in a special account until it has been repaid as provided in the next sentence. As amounts become available in the Gains and Earnings Account for the purpose, the Gains and Earnings Account shall be reduced by the amount by which the Capital Cash Account was so reduced and the Capital Investment Account shall be decreased and the Capital Cash Account shall be increased accordingly.

vii. The provisions with respect to properties of the Partnership in subdivisions i through vi of this subparagraph shall also apply to any other assets of the Partnership.

8. *Capital contributions*

a. *Initial.* Each Partner shall make a contribution in cash to the capital of the Partnership in the aggregate amount specified in Schedule A to this Agreement at the time or times set forth in a schedule promulgated by the General Partner. Upon payment of the total contribution the Partner shall be credited with the number of Units specified in Schedule A or upon payment of a portion of the contribution in accordance with such schedule, he or she shall be credited with the pro rata share of such number of Units.

b. *Additional.* The General Partner may permit the Partners (including persons who are concurrently admitted as Limited Partners as provided in paragraph 9) to make additional contributions, at such times and in such amounts as the General Partner in its sole discretion shall determine, either as a reinvestment of distributions or as a new investment in cash or in property.

i. Reinvestment. If the General Partner shall have elected to permit the reinvestment, in whole or in part, of a distribution ("reinvestment"), each Partner, whether listed on Schedule A hereto or admitted pursuant to paragraph 9 hereof, may reinvest all or any part of the distribution received by him or her (limited to his or her proportionate part of the reinvestment) by contributing it to the capital and upon such contribution shall be credited with the additional number of Units determined by dividing the amount of the contribution by the reinvestment unit value. The reinvestment unit value is equal to the sum total of the capital, the Gains and Earnings Account, and the Amortization Account, all as constituted on the effective date of the reinvestment and immediately after giving effect to such distribution, divided by the number of Units then outstanding. At least 15 days before the distribution, the General

Partner shall deliver to each Limited Partner a statement showing the amount of the proposed distribution, the effective date of the reinvestment, and the reinvestment unit value as of the effective date of the reinvestment. If a Limited Partner desires to reinvest, he or she shall before the effective date of the reinvestment advise the General Partner of the portion of such distribution that he or she desires to reinvest, and the General Partner shall as of the effective date of the reinvestment transfer the applicable amount to the capital and credit the Partner with the number of Units computed as provided above.

ii. New investment. From time to time, at the option of the General Partner, each Partner (including persons who are concurrently admitted as additional Limited Partners as provided in paragraph 9) may be permitted to make a new investment ("new investment") by contributing cash or property to the capital and to acquire the number of additional Units determined by dividing the amount of the contribution by the new investment unit value. The new investment unit value is equal to the sum total of the capital, the Gains and Earnings Account, the Amortization Account, and the value of the intangible appreciation of the Partnership, all as constituted on the effective date of the new investment and immediately after giving effect to any concurrent distributions and reinvestment of distributions, divided by the number of Units then outstanding. The value of the intangible appreciation of the Partnership will be determined by the General Partner in its sole discretion, whose determination shall be final and binding on the Partners, and will include increased but unrealized market value of properties, the value of project planning and work in progress, the value of the Partnership as a going business, and all other factors of an intangible nature which nevertheless have value.

c. *Limitations on capital contributions.* No Limited Partner may make additional contributions to the capital if such Partner owns or, after giving effect to such additional contribution, would own more than 10 percent of the then outstanding Units, provided, however, that such limitation shall not apply to any reinvestments as provided in subparagraph b (i) of this paragraph.

The General Partner, in its sole discretion, may refuse any new investment by any Limited Partner without refusing it to all Limited Partners, may refuse anyone admission as an additional Limited Partner while accepting others, and may allow new investment by additional Limited Partners without first allowing such new investment by existing Partners. Reinvestment, however, is a right of the Partners and may not be refused or limited to any Partner unless it is refused or limited to all.

d. *Contributions of the general partner.* The General Partner may, in addition to its initial contribution specified in Schedule A, make additional contributions in cash to the capital of the Partnership in the manner specified in subparagraph b of this paragraph. The General Partner shall be permitted to reinvest in the manner provided in subparagraph b(i) of this paragraph both its distributions on its Units and the amounts distributed to it pursuant to subdivision ii of subparagraph 6(b).

e. *Contributions in property.* The General Partner, at its option, may accept contributions of property in exchange for Units. The Partners agree that, in such cases, gain, loss, and depreciation shall be allocated as provided on the date of this Agreement in Section 704(c) (1) of the Internal Revenue Code.

f. *Fractional units.* Fractional Units may be issued for reinvestment purposes and in other instances at the discretion of the General Partner.

9. *Admission of additional limited partners*

The General Partner is authorized to admit additional Limited Partners to the Partnership at any time. Upon their initial contribution to the capital, the additional Limited Partners shall receive Units computed as provided in subparagraph b(ii) of paragraph 8. Upon the admission of such additional Limited Partners, an amendment to the Certificate of Limited Partnership of the Partnership, reflecting such admissions and increases in contributions to the capital, shall be filed. To accomplish the purposes of this paragraph, the General Partner is authorized to do all things necessary to effect the admission of such Limited Partners. A new Partner shall become a party hereto by executing an appropriate supplement to this Agreement pursuant to which he or she agrees to be bound by the terms and provisions of this Agreement; provided, however, that no such supplement shall become binding and effective until it has been executed by the General Partner. The admission of any additional Limited Partner pursuant to this paragraph shall not be cause for dissolution of the Partnership.

10. *The general partner*

a. The General Partner shall have the exclusive right and power to manage and operate the Partnership and to do all things necessary to carry on the business of the Partnership for the purposes described in paragraph 3. The General Partner shall devote so much of its time to the business of the Partnership as in its judgment the conduct of its business shall reasonably require and shall not be obligated to do or perform any act or thing in connection with the business of the Partnership not expressly

Limited Partnership Agreement

set forth herein. The General Partner may engage in business ventures of any nature and description independently or with others, including but not limited to business of the character described in paragraph 3 hereof (or any part thereof), and neither the Partnership nor any of the other Partners shall have any rights in and to such independent ventures or the income or profits derived therefrom.

b. The General Partner is specifically authorized and empowered, on behalf of the Partnership, without any further consent of the Limited Partners, to do any act or execute any document or enter into any contract or any agreement of any nature necessary or desirable, in the opinion of the General Partner, in pursuance of the purposes of the Partnership, including, without limitation, to enter into and to perform the following agreements:

(1) A contract with _____ Real Estate Corporation Incorporated, or any subsidiary or to act as the managing agent of the Partnership, providing that:

(A) The managing agent will (i) find and negotiate the acquisition of suitable investments for the Partnership, (ii) perform the day-to-day investment and administrative operations of the Partnership, (iii) act as the investment advisor and consultant for the Partnership in connection with policy and investment decisions, and (iv) prepare reports to the Partners as provided in paragraph 20.

(B) The managing agent shall be paid for its services an annual fee for each fiscal year equal to 2 percent of the sum of the average daily Aggregate Capital Investment Account and the average daily Amortization Account and one-half of 1 percent of the average daily Capital Cash Account, which shall be calculated and payable not more often than in quarterly installments. Such fee shall not be deemed to be a Partnership distribution. The contract shall be nonassignable and shall contain an exculpatory clause with respect to the managing agent substantially similar to subparagraph e of this paragraph.

(C) All expenses of the Partnership, including without limitation expenses of operation and administration, shall be paid by the Partnership, except that the managing agent shall provide without expense to the Partnership office space and facilities. Any amounts advanced by the managing agent for payment of expenses or obligations of the Partnership shall be deemed to be debts and liabilities of the Partnership to the managing agent.

(2) Contracts with agents, attorneys, accountants, appraisers, or other independent consultants or contractors, whether or not any of

such persons may also be employed by the managing agent or any real estate investment trust or other entity for which the General Partner or the managing agent shall be acting as an advisor, manager, sponsor, or underwriter.

(3) Agreements with real estate investment trusts or other entities underwritten, advised, managed, or sponsored by the General Partner or by the managing agent, providing essentially for the sale of a property or properties to any such entity for the cost of such property or properties to the Partnership or, if a property has been improved while owned by the Partnership, at the then fair value of that property as determined by the General Partner, and for the simultaneous leasing of such property or properties by the Partnership for a net rental not greater than the stipulated value of the property or properties multiplied by a factor not greater than the product of two times the average of the prime lending rates charged at the date of execution of the lease by the _____ Bank, the _____ Bank, and the _____ Bank and providing, further, that such entity may have the option to require the Partnership to repurchase such property at the stipulated value in the event of an assignment of the lease of such property by the Partnership. The stipulated value will be the price at which the property was sold by the Partnership, adjusted annually on the basis of increases in the cost-of-living index for the United States published by the Department of Labor, or, if such index is unavailable, any other index that the General Partner considers appropriate. Such agreements may also provide that the Partnership may lease on similar terms other properties from any such entity.

(4) Agreements to borrow money on a secured or unsecured basis from real estate investment trusts or other entities underwritten, advised, managed, or sponsored by the General Partner or by the managing agent, on terms competitive in the judgment of the General Partner with borrowings from other sources.

c. The General Partner, on behalf of the Partnership, shall not be prohibited from employing, purchasing, or leasing real or personal property from or to or otherwise dealing with a Partner, the managing agent, an officer, director, or stockholder of the General Partner or of the managing agent, or a member of the family of a Limited Partner or of an officer, director, or stockholder of the General Partner or of the managing agent, or any firm, corporation, or fund which any of such persons is directly or indirectly interested in or connected with, or with any fund or trust managed or advised by the General Partner or by the managing agent, and neither the Partnership nor any of the Partners shall have any rights

Limited Partnership Agreement

in or to any income or profits received by any such person in a transaction with the Partnership.

d. In addition to the specific rights and powers herein granted to the General Partner, it shall possess and may enjoy and exercise all rights and powers of general partners as provided in the Partnership Law of the State of _____.

e. The General Partner shall not be liable to the Partnership or the Limited Partners for any act or omission performed or omitted by it in good faith pursuant to the authority granted to it by this Agreement, but only for fraud, bad faith, or gross negligence.

f. The Partnership shall indemnify and save harmless the General Partner from any loss or damage incurred by it by reason of any act performed by it on behalf of the Partnership or in furtherance of its interests; provided, however, that the foregoing shall not relieve the General Partner of liability for its fraud, bad faith or gross negligence; and further provided, however, that in the case of any loss or damage arising from an action brought pursuant to Section 115–a of the Partnership Law of the State of _____, the indemnification pursuant to this provision shall be limited to the reasonable expenses, including attorneys' fees, actually and necessarily incurred by the General Partner in connection with the defense of such action, or in connection with an appeal therein, except that there shall be no indemnification in relation to matters about which the General Partner is adjudged to have breached its duty to the Partnership, and the indemnification shall not include amounts paid in settling or otherwise disposing of a threatened action, or pending action, with or without court approval, or expenses incurred in defending a threatened action, or pending action, which is settled or otherwise disposed of without court approval.

11. *Assignment of the general partner's interest*

The General Partner shall not assign or sell its interest as General Partner in the Partnership or enter into any agreement as a result of which any person, firm, or corporation shall become interested with it in its interest in the Partnership, except that it may at any time sell or assign any Units held by it.

12. *Bankruptcy, withdrawal, or liquidation of the general partner*

In the event of the bankruptcy, withdrawal, or liquidation of the General Partner, the Partnership shall be dissolved and terminated.

13. *Limited partners*

No Limited Partner shall take any part in the conduct or control of the Partnership's business nor have any right or authority to act for or on behalf of the Partnership. No Limited Partner shall be liable for any debts, obligations, or losses of the Partnership in excess of his or her contribution to the capital of the Partnership.

14. *Substitution and assignability of limited partners' interests*

a. Except as provided in this paragraph, without the prior written consent of the General Partner, a Limited Partner may not assign or sell his or her interest (or any part thereof) in the Partnership, nor substitute an assignee, and no attempted substitution shall be binding upon the Partnership or General Partner in the absence of such written consent.

b. If a Limited Partner shall die or be adjudicated insane or incompetent, his or her legal representatives shall be deemed to be an assignee of, and may, with the prior written consent of the General Partner, be substituted for, such Limited Partner.

c. As a condition to admission as a substituted Limited Partner, an assignee or the legal representatives of a Limited Partner, as the case may be, shall execute and acknowledge such instruments, in form and substance satisfactory to the General Partner, as the General Partner shall deem necessary or desirable to effect such admission and to confirm the agreement of the person being admitted as such substituted Partner to be bound by all of the terms and provisions of this Agreement.

15. *Withdrawal by limited partners*

No Limited Partner shall at any time be entitled to withdraw all or any part of his or her contribution to the capital of the Partnership without the prior written consent of the General Partner.

16. *Death of a limited partner*

The death of a Limited Partner shall not dissolve or terminate the Partnership.

17. *Advances*

If any Partner shall advance any monies to the Partnership in excess of his or her contribution to the capital of the Partnership, the amount of any such advances shall not increase his or her contribution or entitle him or her to any increase in the distributions of the Partnership; but

Limited Partnership Agreement

the amount of any such advance shall be a debt of the Partnership to such Partner and, unless otherwise provided and agreed, shall be repaid without interest and shall be payable or collectible only out of the Partnership assets.

18. *Interest on capital contributions*

No Partner shall receive any interest on his or her contribution to the capital of the Partnership.

19. *Accounting*

a. The fiscal year of the Partnership shall be the calendar year.

b. The General Partner shall keep, or cause to be kept, full and accurate records of all transactions of the Partnership.

c. The records and books of accounts shall be audited by a firm of independent Certified Public accountants, selected by the General Partner, as of the end of each fiscal year of the Partnership and at any other time that the General Partner may deem it necessary or desirable.

d. The General Partner shall prepare, or cause to be prepared, a federal income tax return for the Partnership and, in connection therewith, make any available or necessary elections, including elections with respect to the useful life of the properties of the Partnership and the rates of depreciation of such properties.

20. *Reports and statements*

a. As soon as practicable after the end of each fiscal year of the Partnership, the General Partner shall deliver to each Partner:

i. Such information as shall be necessary for the preparation by such Partner of his or her federal and state income or other tax returns.

ii. A statement prepared by the General Partner, accompanied by a report of a firm of independent Certified Public Accountants selected by the General Partner, which statement shall set forth, as of the end of and for such fiscal year, the following:

A. A profit-and-loss statement and a balance sheet of the Partnership.

B. The computation of the annual distribution preference and the allocation to each Partner of the net profit or net loss, as the case may be, of the Partnership for such year.

C. The balances in the capital, the Capital Cash Account, the Aggregate Capital Investment Account, the Gains and Earnings Account, and the Amortization Account.

D. Such other information as in the judgment of the General Partner shall be reasonably necessary for the Partners to be advised of the results of operations of the Partnership.

b. The General Partner may prepare and deliver to the Limited Partners from time to time during each fiscal year, in connection with distributions or otherwise, unaudited statements showing the results of operation of the Partnership to the date of such statement and the balances in the accounts referred to in clause C of subparagraph a(ii) of this paragraph, and shall deliver a statement showing the balances in such accounts and the additional information described in subdivision i of subparagraph 8(b) in connection with any distribution.

21. *Bank accounts*

All funds of the Partnership shall be deposited in the Partnership's name in such bank account or accounts as shall be designated by the General Partner. Withdrawals from such bank account or accounts shall be made upon the signatures of such persons as the General Partner shall designate.

22. *Termination and dissolution*

a. The dissolution of the Partnership shall occur only upon the termination of the Partnership as provided in paragraph 4. Upon the dissolution of the Partnership, the General Partner shall proceed to the liquidation of the Partnership, and the proceeds of such liquidation shall be applied and distributed in the following order of priority:

i. To the payment of debts and liabilities of the Partnership (other than any loans or advances that may have been made by any of the Partners to the Partnership) and the expenses of liquidation.

ii. To the setting up of any reserves that the General Partner may deem reasonably necessary for any contingent or unforeseen liabilities or obligations of the Partnership or of the General Partner, arising out of or in connection with the Partnership. Such reserves shall be paid over by the General Partner to an escrowee designated by the General Partner to be held by him or her for the purpose of disbursing such reserves in payment of any of the aforementioned contingencies, and, at the expiration of such period as the General Partner shall deem advisa-

Limited Partnership Agreement

ble, to distribute the balance thereafter remaining in the manner hereinafter provided.

iii. To the repayment of any loans or advances that may have been made by any of the Partners to the Partnership, but if the amount available for such repayment shall be insufficient, then pro rata on account thereof.

iv. To return to the Partners an amount equal to the capital of the Partnership, to be divided among the Partners in proportion to the number of Units held by them. If the amount available is less than the capital, the distribution shall be pro rata on account thereof.

v. To satisfy the annual distribution preference for the current fiscal year and then to the extent that it has not been satisfied for all preceding fiscal years ending after January 1, 1971, to satisfy the annual distribution preference for all such fiscal years.

vi. Any balance then remaining shall be distributed as follows: 25 percent to the General Partner and 75 percent to all Partners divided among the Partners in proportion to the number of Units held by them.

b. A reasonable time shall be allowed for the orderly liquidation of the assets of the Partnership and the discharge of liabilities to creditors so as to enable the General Partner to minimize the normal losses attendant upon a liquidation.

c. Each Partner shall be furnished with a statement prepared by the General Partner, which shall set forth the assets and liabilities of the Partnership as of the date of complete liquidation. Upon the General Partner complying with the foregoing distribution plan (including payment over to the escrowee if there are sufficient funds therefor), the Limited Partners shall cease to be such, and the General Partner, as the sole remaining Partner of the Partnership, shall execute, acknowledge, and cause to be filed a certificate of cancellation of the Partnership.

d. The General Partner shall not be personally liable for the return of all or any part of the contributions of the Limited Partners to the capital. Any such return shall be made solely from Partnership assets.

23. *Arbitration*

Any dispute or controversy arising under, out of, in connection with, or in relation to this Agreement, and any amendment thereof, or the breach thereof, or in connection with the formation, operation, or termination of the Partnership, shall be determined and settled by arbitration in accordance with the rules of the American Arbitration Association. Any award rendered therein shall be final and binding upon the Partners, and judgment may be entered thereon in any court having jurisdiction thereof.

24. *Power of attorney and amendments*

　　a. Each Limited Partner hereby makes, constitutes, and appoints the General Partner as true and lawful attorney in his or her name, place, and stead to make, execute, sign, acknowledge, and file with respect to the Partnership:

　　　　i. A certificate of Limited Partnership under the laws of the State of _____ or any other state, and including therein all information required by the laws of such state.

　　　　ii. Such amended Certificates of Limited Partnership as may be required by law or pursuant to the provisions of this Agreement.

　　　　iii. All papers that may be deemed necessary or desirable by said attorneys to effect the dissolution of this Partnership after its termination.

　　　　iv. All such other instruments, documents, and certificates that may from time to time be required by the laws of the State of _____, the United States of America, or any other jurisdiction in which the Partnership shall determine to do business, or any political subdivision or agency thereof, to effectuate, implement, continue, and defend the valid and subsisting existence of the Partnership.

　　b. Notwithstanding the provisions of subparagraph a of this paragraph, when acting in a representative capacity, the General Partner shall not have any right, power, or authority to amend or modify this Agreement.

25. *No oral modification*

No modification or waiver of this Agreement, or any part hereof, shall be valid or effective unless in writing signed by the party or parties sought to be changed therewith; and no waiver of any breach or condition of this Agreement shall be deemed to be a waiver of any other subsequent breach or condition, whether of like or different nature.

26. *Copy on file*

Each Partner hereby agrees that one original of this Agreement, or set of original counterparts, shall be held at the office of the Partnership, that a Certificate of Limited Partnership and all amendments thereto shall be filed in the office of the County Clerk of the County of _____, and duplicate originals thereof shall be held at the office of the Partnership, and that there shall be distributed to each Partner a conformed copy of this Agreement.

Limited Partnership Agreement

27. *Notices and addresses*

All notices or other communications given or made under this Agreement shall be in writing. Notices or other communications shall be mailed to a Limited Partner at the address set forth after the signature of such Limited Partner at the foot of this Agreement or at such other address as he or she may specify in a notice to the General Partner and to the General Partner or the Partnership at the office of the Partnership specified in paragraph 2 or at such other address as the General Partner may specify in a notice to all Limited Partners.

28. *Applicable laws*

This Agreement shall be governed by and construed in accordance with the laws of the State of _____.

29. *Counterparts*

This Agreement may be executed in one or more counterparts, and each of such counterparts shall, for all purposes, be deemed to be an original, but all of such counterparts shall constitute one and the same instrument

30. *Variation in pronouns*

All pronouns and any variations thereof shall be deemed to refer to masculine, feminine, neuter, singular, or plural, as the identity of the person or persons may require.

31. *Binding effect*

Except as herein otherwise provided to the contrary, this Agreement shall be binding upon and inure to the benefit of the parties hereto, their personal representatives, successors, and assigns.

In witness whereof, the parties hereto have executed this Agreement.

    As General Partner:

        _____ Corporation

    By _____

    As Limited Partner:

    Name _____ (L.S.)

    Address _____

GENERAL PARTNERSHIP AGREEMENT

In the following pages a general partnership agreement is briefly set forth in which three general partners (called agents) engage in a joint venture to hold property with a leaseback. The entity probably would be construed as a general partnership under the laws of most states.

Of particular interest are the clauses governing the right to sell, mortgage, or transfer (paragraph 4), partial continuity in the event of the death of an agent–partner (paragraph 6), and limited transferability of the partnership interests (paragraphs 7 and 8).

GENERAL PARTNERSHIP AGREEMENT

Agreement made as of _____ among _____, residing at _____ (herein called the "Agent"), and _____, residing at _____, and _____, residing at _____ and (herein called the "Participants").

Witnesseth:

Whereas, Investor's Partnership, a partnership, owns the premises known as _____, and

Whereas, Investor's Partnership has heretofore executed a lease of said premises with Syndicator's Leasehold Partnership, a partnership; and

Whereas, the Agent owns a one-third interest in Investor's Partnership, which partnership interest is herein referred to as "the Property"; and

Whereas, the parties wish to establish the ownership of the Property and to define their rights and obligations with respect thereto;

Now, therefore, in consideration of the mutual covenants herein contained, the parties agree as follows:

General Partnership Agreement

1. A joint venture is hereby formed for the ownership of the Property. It is acknowledged that the contribution of each Participant to the capital of Investor's Partnership and his or her fractional interest in the Property are as set forth below opposite his or her signature.

2. The joint venture shall continue until the Property shall have been disposed of in accordance with paragraph 4 hereof, and shall not be interrupted by the act, bankruptcy, or death of any Participant, the assignment of any interest of any Participant hereunder, the appointment of a successor to the Agent, or any other cause.

3. The Agent shall act, without compensation, as agent for the joint venture in the ownership of the Property. Any action taken by him or her with respect thereto, subject to the terms of this Agreement, shall bind the joint venture. All profits and losses arising from the ownership of the Property shall be shared by the Participants in proportion to their respective fractional interests.

4. The Agent shall not agree to sell, mortgage, or transfer the Property or the premises, nor to make or modify any mortgage or lease of the premises, nor to dispose of any partnership asset, without the consent of all Participants.

If the consents of Participants owning at least 90 percent of the Property have been obtained, the Agent or a designee (herein called "Purchaser") shall have the right to purchase the interest of any Participant in the Property who has not given such consent within 10 days of the mailing by the Agent of a written request therefor, by certified or registered mail, of a certified check for the purchase price, at any time within 90 days of such 10-day period, directed to such nonconsenting Participant at his or her last known address, shall effect the sale and transfer to the purchaser of the interest of such Participant in the Property. The Agent is hereby irrevocably appointed attorney-in-fact for such Participant to execute any papers and to take any other action necessary to evidence such sale and transfer. The Purchaser shall then accept the transfer in writing, and shall thereupon be a member of the joint venture with the same rights and obligations as such Participant. The price shall be the amount of said capital contribution of such Participant, less any repayment thereon to the date of the mailing of the purchase price, but under no circumstances shall such price be less than $100.

5. The Agent shall not be personally liable for any act performed in good faith, nor for anything save willful misconduct, gross negligence, or any liabilities under the Securities Act of 1933. The Participants shall indemnify the Agent in proportion to their interests in the Property against

any liability to which the Agent may be subjected by reason of acting as agent hereunder.

6. (A) If the Agent shall desire to terminate his or her agency, or if the Agent shall be removed as such in the manner provided below, the Agent shall, upon accounting to his or her successor for all funds that have previously come into his or her possession, be discharged from all further liability as Agent.

(B) The Agent may be removed by the written direction of Participants owning at least three-fourths of the Property.

(C) In the event of the resignation, removal, death, incompetency, or other disability of the Agent during the continuance of the joint venture, the following persons shall act as his or her successors in the order stated:

(1) _____.

(2) _____ _____.

(3) _____.

(4) Any person of full age designated in writing by Participants owning at least three-fourths of the Property.

Each successor shall have the same rights and obligations as the Agent named herein. Any person who shall be acting as an agent pursuant to any other agreement relating to a partnership interest in Investor's Partnership shall be disqualified from acting as Agent hereunder.

(D) Simultaneously with the execution of this agreement, the Agent shall execute an assignment of the Property and a quitclaim deed to the premises, leaving blank the names of the assignee and grantee respectively. Such assignment and deed shall be deposited in escrow, together with the original copy of this agreement, with _____, Escrow Agent. Upon the appointment of a successor to the Agent, the name of such successor shall be inserted in the assignment and deed, and the escrow shall be released. The successor shall thereupon similarly execute an assignment and deed for use by his or her successor in the same manner.

7. The sale or transfer of the interest of any Participant hereunder, except pursuant to paragraph 4 hereof, shall not be valid unless the transferee is an individual of full age, unless duplicate originals of appropriate written instruments evidencing such sale and transfer are delivered to the Agent for deposit with the original copy of this agreement, and unless the transferee shall accept the transfer in writing. If the transferee complies with these requirements, he or she shall be a member of the joint venture with the same rights and obligations as the transferor.

General Partnership Agreement

8. Any Participant may designate any individual of full age to succeed him or her, upon his or her death, as a member of the joint venture. Such designation shall be made in the last will and testament of the deceased Participant or, if not so made, the executor or administrator of the deceased Participant's estate shall make and deliver such designation. In either event, the executor or administrator shall also deliver such other instruments as the Agent may require to evidence the transfer of the deceased Participant's interest to the designee. Any individual so designated shall accept such designation in writing, and shall thereupon be a member of the joint venture with the same rights and obligations as the deceased Participant.

In the event that any Participant dies and no successor is qualified within eight months thereafter, the surviving Participants may purchase the interest of the deceased Participant hereunder within 90 days of the expiration of such eight months' period, and the surviving Participants shall share in such purchase in proportion to their respective fractional interests. The price shall be the amount of said capital contribution of the deceased Participant, less any repayment thereon to the date of death, but under no circumstances shall such price be less than $100.

9. Any dispute regarding this Agreement or the Property shall be determined by arbitration in the City of _____, in accordance with the rules of the American Arbitration Association then in effect, and such decision shall be binding upon all parties.

10. This Agreement shall inure to the benefit of and be binding upon the heirs, legal representatives, successors, and assigns of the parties.

11. This Agreement may be executed in any number of counterparts, each of which shall be deemed to be an original, and all such counterparts shall together constitute a single Agreement.

In witness whereof, the parties have hereunto set their hands the day and year first above written.

_____
Investor

_____
Syndicator (agent)

GUIDE 5—SEC REGULATIONS

While the SEC Guide 5 is headed as a guide to the preparation of registration statements, it is also used in private offerings on the theory that you cannot go wrong if you give the investors all of the information they would have been entitled to in a registration.

Your attorney will want to be certain to have the latest amendments to the Guide, which the SEC alters from time to time. You should not rely on the attached material as being strictly up to date, but it will give you an idea of what goes into a Regulation D or a real estate limited partnership that is registered.

SECURITIES ACT GUIDE 5: PREPARATION OF REGISTRATION STATEMENTS RELATING TO INTERESTS IN REAL ESTATE LIMITED PARTNERSHIPS

References to the General Partner and its affiliates, also referred to as sponsors, are intended to include references to the General Partner(s), promoters of the partnership, and all persons that, directly or indirectly, through one or more intermediaries, control or are controlled by, or are under common control with, such General Partner(s) or promoters.

It is suggested that, where appropriate, the information in the prospectus be presented in the same order as the following comments. Where the registrant believes that specific comments are not relevant or are otherwise inappropriate, the registrant should bring this to the staff's attention in a letter indicating the reasons therefor.

1. Cover Page

A. The disclosure on the cover page should be as succinct and brief as possible.

B. The cover page should set forth, in addition to basic information about the offering, the termination date of the offering, any minimum

Guide 5—SEC Regulations

required purchase, and any arrangements to place the funds received in an escrow, trust, or similar arrangement.

C. The cover page should contain a tabular presentation of the total maximum and minimum interests to be offered:

	Price to Public	Selling Commissions	Proceeds to the Partnership
Per limited partnership interest			
Total minimum			
Total maximum			

D. The cover page should also contain brief identification of the material risks involved in the purchase of the securities with cross-reference to further discussion in the prospectus. The most significant risk factors should be identified where applicable, for example:

(i) Tax aspects

For example:

There are material income tax risks associated with the offering.

(ii) Use of proceeds

For example:

The proceeds of the offering are insufficient to meet the requirements for funds as set forth in the partnership's investment objectives.

(iii) Conflicts of interests

For example:

The operation of the partnership involves transactions between the partnership and the General Partner or its affiliates which may involve conflicts of interest. (As amended by Sec. Act Rel. No. 6405, eff. 9–1–82.)

2. Suitability Standards

Standards, if any, to be utilized by the registrant ("suitability standards") in determining the acceptance of subscription agreements should be described immediately following the cover page. Suitability standards should include those established by the registrant, if any, or by any self-regulatory organization or state agency having jurisdiction over the offering of the securities. Registrant should disclose the method(s) it intends to employ to assure adherence to the suitability standards by persons selling the interests and should briefly discuss the factors pertaining to the need for such standards, such as lack of liquidity (resale or assignment of securities), importance of the investor's federal income tax bracket in terms of the tax benefits to be derived, the long-term nature of the investment, and possible adverse tax consequences of premature sale of the interests. If suitability standards apply to resale of the interests, this should be discussed.

3. Summary of the Partnership and Use of Proceeds

A two-part, concise outline summary relating to the partnership and a tabular summary of use of proceeds should follow the suitability section of the prospectus. These summaries may replace the Introductory Statement and Use of Proceeds sections required by the relevant Form if such sections would merely repeat the information in the summaries.

A. *Summary of the Partnership.* The following information should be disclosed in outline form with appropriate cross-references, where applicable:

(i) Give name, address, and telephone number of the General Partner, and names of persons making investment decisions for the partnership.

(ii) Give the intended termination date of the partnership.

(iii) State, if true, that the General Partner and its affiliates will receive substantial fees and profits in connection with the offering.

(iv) If current distributions are an investment objective, state the estimated maximum time from the closing date that the investor might have to wait to receive such distributions.

(v) Describe briefly the properties to be purchased. If a material portion of the minimum net proceeds of the offering (allowing for reserves) is not committed to specific properties, so indicate.

(vi) Describe the depreciation method to be used.

(vii) State the maximum leverage expected to be used by the partnership as a whole and on individual properties, where it may differ.

(viii) Include a cross-reference to the Glossary.

B. *Use of Proceeds.* The use of proceeds tabular summary will vary according to the partnership but should include, where appropriate, estimates of the public offering expenses (both organizational and sales), the amount available for investment, nonrecurring initial investment fees, prepaid items and financing fees, cash down payments, reserves, and acquisitions fees, including those paid by the seller. Estimated amounts to be paid to the General Partner and its affiliates should be identified. The summary should include both dollar amounts and percentages of the maximum and minimum proceeds of the offering. Inclusion of percentages of the estimated maximum and minimum total assets is optional. An example of a summary of Use of Proceeds is in Appendix I, but the summary will vary according to the circumstances. (As amended by Sec. Act Rel. No. 6405, eff. 9-1-82.)

4. Compensation and Fees to the General Partner and Affiliates

A. This section should include a summary tabular presentation, itemizing by category and specifying dollar amounts where possible of all compensation, fees, profits, and other benefits (including reimbursement of out-of-pocket expenses) that the General Partner and its affiliates may earn or receive in connection with the offering or operation of the partnership. If more detailed information is required, it should be located in the Summary of Partnership Agreement section with cross-reference to that summary. The presentation should identify the person, including affiliations with the General Partner, who will receive such compensation, fees, profits, or benefits and the services to be performed by such person.

The summary should be organized so as to indicate clearly whether the compensation relates to the offering and organizational stage, the development or acquisition stage, the operational stage, or the termination and liquidation stage of the partnership. Separate subcaptions are recommended.

The type of compensation, fees, profits, or other benefits that should be disclosed includes, but is not limited to, the following: disbursements incident to the purchase and sale of the limited partnership interests, including sales commissions, reimbursements for expenses, and real estate commissions; finder's fees; fees for property acquisitions, marketing or leasing up of properties, financing or refinancing, management of properties, insurance, and miscellaneous services; commissions and other fees to be paid upon sale of the partnership's properties; participation by the General Partner in cash flow or profits and losses or capital gains and losses arising out of the operation, refinancing, or sale of properties; fees or builder's profits; overhead absorption and/or land write-ups; and all profits on the purchase of investments for the partnership from the General Partner or its affiliates. If the partnership agreement limits the losses the General Partner and its affiliates can sustain, this should be discussed.

B. Maximum aggregate dollar front-end fees to be paid during the first fiscal year of operations should be disclosed based upon the assumption that the partnership's maximum leverage is utilized.

C. Where compensation arrangements are based upon a formula or percentage, the terms of such arrangements should be disclosed and illustrated. The assumptions underlying the dollar figures should be disclosed, and the calculations underlying the figures should be submitted to the staff supplementally with the initial filing. Compensation based upon a given return (percentage of contributed investor capital) to investors should disclose whether such return is cumulative or noncumulative.

D. Where the General Partner or an affiliate receives a disproportionate interest in the partnership in relation to its own contribution, registrant's attention is directed to Item 506 of Regulation S–K. A bar chart comparison of the various interests and contributors should be provided.

5. Conflicts of Interest

A. This section should include a summary of each type of transaction which may result in a conflict between the interests of the public investors and those of the General Partner and its affiliates, and of the proposed method of dealing with such conflict. The types of conflicts of interest which should be disclosed and discussed, if appropriate, include, but are not limited to:

(i) The General Partner is a general partner or an affiliate of the general partner in other investment entities (public and/or private) engaged in making similar investments or otherwise makes or arranges for similar investments.

(ii) The General Partner has the authority to invest the partnership's funds in other partnerships in which the General Partner or an affiliate is the general partner or has an interest.

(iii) Properties in which the General Partner or its affiliates have an interest are bought from partnership properties are sold to the General Partner or its affiliates or entities in which they have an interest. Where appraisals are used in connection with any such transaction, it should be made clear that appraisals are only estimates of value and should not be relied on as measures of realizable value. If the appraiser is named as an expert, a consent to the use of his name should be furnished. If specific appraised values are included in the registration statement, the appraiser should be named as an expert, his consent furnished, and the appraisals filed as exhibits to the registration statement. If a statement that the purchase price of the property does not exceed its appraised value is included and the appraiser is not named and specific values are not cited, there need not be furnished a consent to use the appraiser's name. In that event, a copy of the appraisal should be submitted supplementally with the registration statement. If any relationship exists between the appraiser and the General Partner or its affiliates, this should be stated. If the General Partner intends to buy any properties in which the general partner or any of its affiliates have a material interest, such properties should be appropriately described in the prospectus along with the investment objectives of the partnership (see paragraph 10, Investment Objectives and Policies). If it is disclosed in the prospectus that the partnership may purchase properties in which the General Partner or its affiliates have a material interest, but no properties are described, and such properties are thereafter purchased for the partnership, the General Partner will have the heavy burden of demonstrating that it did not intend to purchase such property at the time the registration statement became effective.

(iv) The General Partner or its affiliates own or have an interest in properties adjacent to those to be purchased and developed by the partnership.

(v) Affiliates of the General Partner who act as underwriters, real estate brokers, or managers for the partnership, act in such capacities for other partnerships or entities.

(vi) An affiliate of the General Partner places mortgages for the partnership or otherwise acts as a finance broker or as insurance agent or broker receiving commissions for such services.

(vii) An affiliate of the General Partner acts (a) as an underwriter for the offering, or (b) as a principal underwriter for the offering, thereby creating conflicts in performance of the underwriter's due diligence inquiries under the Securities Act.

(viii) The compensation plan for the General Partner may create a conflict between the interests of the General Partner and those of the partnership.

B. An organization chart should be included in this section showing the relationship between the various organizations managed or controlled by the General Partner or its affiliate that will do business with the partnership where the relationships are so complex that a graphic display would assist investors in understanding such relationships.

6. Fiduciary Responsibility of the General Partner

A. A discussion of the fiduciary obligation owed by the General Partner to the Limited Partners should be set forth. The following disclosure is suggested with appropriate modification for the laws of the state of organization:

A General Partner is accountable to a limited partnership as a fiduciary and consequently must exercise good faith and integrity in handling partnership affairs. This is a rapidly developing and changing area of the law, and Limited Partners who have questions concerning the duties of the General Partner should consult with their counsel.

B. Where the limited partnership agreement contains an exculpatory provision and/or the right to indemnification, the following disclosure is suggested, as modified to reflect the substance of such provisions:

Exculpation

(i) The General Partner may not be liable to the Partnership or Limited Partners for errors in judgment or other acts or omissions not amounting to willful misconduct or gross negligence, since provision has been made in the Agreement of Limited Partnership for exculpation of the General Partner. Therefore, purchasers of the interests have a more limited right of action than they would have absent the limitation in the Partnership Agreement.

Indemnification

(ii) The Partnership Agreement provides for indemnification of the General Partner by the Partnership for liabilities he incurs in dealings with third parties on behalf of the partnership. To the extent that the indemnification provisions purport to include indemnification for liabilities arising under the Securities Act of 1933, in the opinion of the Securities and Exchange Commission, such indemnification is contrary to public policy and therefore unenforceable.

Registrant's attention is also directed to Items 510 and 512 (i) of Regulations S–K relating to disclosure of indemnification agreements.

7. Risk Factors

A. This section should include a carefully organized series of short, concise, subcaptioned paragraphs, with cross-references to fuller discussion where appropriate, summarizing the principal risk factors applicable to the offering and to the partnership's particular plan of operations. The risk factors section should be brief.

B. This subsection should summarize each material risk of adverse tax consequences with appropriate cross-references to fuller discussions in the federal tax section. For example:

(i) Where no Internal Revenue Service (IRS) ruling as to partnership tax status has been applied for or obtained, the risk that the IRS may on

Guide 5—SEC Regulations

audit determine that for tax purposes the partnership is an association taxable as a corporation, in which case, investors would be deprived of the tax benefits associated with the offering. As part of this disclosure, it should be stated that a material risk of IRS classification as a corporate association may exist even though registrant relies on an opinion of counsel as to partnership tax status as such opinion is not binding on the IRS. It may also be stated that IRS classification of the partnership as a corporate association would deprive investors of the tax benefits of the offering only if the IRS determination is upheld in court or otherwise becomes final. Any such additional disclosure should explain that contesting an IRS determination may impose representation expenses on investors. (See federal tax section.)

(ii) Where the IRS has advised registrant that it proposes not to rule, or to rule adversely, on any tax issue as to which such a ruling was applied for, the risk that investors may lose some or all tax benefits associated with the offering. (See federal tax section.)

(iii) The risk that after some years of partnership operations an investor's tax liabilities may exceed his cash distributions in corresponding years and that to the extent of such excess the payment of such taxes will be out-of-pocket expenses.

(iv) Upon a sale or other disposition (e.g., by gift) of a partnership interest or, upon a sale (including a foreclosure sale) or other disposition of partnership property, the risk that an investor's tax liabilities may exceed the cash he receives and that to the extent of such excess the payment of such taxes will be out-of-pocket expenses. The disclosure should indicate to what extent the gain may be taxed as ordinary income, to what extent as capital gain. (See federal tax section.)

(v) The risk that an audit of the partnership's information return may result in an audit of an investor's own tax return. (See federal tax section.)

C. Risk factors relating to the specific partnership might include, where applicable:

(i) Management's lack of relevant experience, or management's lack of success with similar partnerships or other real estate investments.

(ii) Where the proceeds of the offering will be insufficient to meet the requirements of the partnership's investment objectives, a discussion of the additional sources of capital for the partnership and of the risk of not being able to satisfy the partnership's objectives as a result of not obtaining additional necessary funds.

(iii) Where the partnership has high-risk investment objectives, including high leveraging, these should be explained.

(iv) The risk that no public market for interests is likely to develop and that holders of interests may not be able to liquidate their investment quickly.

(v) Risks associated with contemplated rent stabilization programs, fuel or energy requirements or regulations, and construction in areas that are subject to environmental or other federal, state, or local regulations, actual or pending.

(vi) Where a material portion of the minimum net proceeds of the offering is not committed to specific properties, disclosure of the particular risk associated with an investment in such an offering. Such disclosure should include the increased uncertainty and risk to investors since they are unable to evaluate the manner in which the proceeds are to be invested and the economic merit of the particular real estate projects prior to investment. Also, it should be disclosed that there may be a substantial period of time before the proceeds of the offering are invested and therefore a delay to investors in receiving a return on their investment.

D. Risk factors relating to real estate limited partnership offerings in general should be briefly discussed after those relating to the specific partnership. Such risks might include, where applicable: the risks associated with the ownership of real estate including uncertainty of cash flow to meet fixed and maturing obligations, adverse local market conditions, risks of "leveraging," and uninsured losses.

8. Prior Performance of the General Partner and Affiliates

A narrative summary of the "track record" or prior performance of programs sponsored by the General Partner and its affiliates containing the information set forth below should be included in the text of the prospectus. Tables following the format of those in Appendix II, relating to historical use of proceeds of prior programs, compensation to the sponsors, operations of prior programs, and acquisitions and sales of properties by prior programs, should be included at the back of the prospectus or in Part II of the registration statement as specified in paragraph B, "Prior Performance Tables," hereunder.

Sponsors are urged not to include in the prospectus information about prior performance beyond that required by this Guide except for such further material information as may be necessary to make the required statements, in light of the circumstances under which they are made, not misleading.

Terms used in the Guide. "Public" programs include all offerings registered under the Securities Act of 1933, all programs required to report

Guide 5—SEC Regulations

under Section 15(d) of the Securities Exchange Act of 1934 ("Exchange Act"), all programs with a class of equity securities registered pursuant to Section 12(g) of the Exchange Act, and all other programs with at least 300 security holders of record that initially raised at least $1 million.

Programs with "similar investment objectives" are those with similar objectives as set forth in the prospectus. Generally, the sponsor has the responsibility to determine which previous programs had "similar investment objectives," taking into consideration the materiality of information about the prior programs in analyzing the registrant's proposed activities.

A sponsor would be considered to have a "public track record" if it has sponsored at least three programs with investment objectives similar to those of the registrant that files reports under Section 13(a) or Section 15(d) of the Exchange Act and at least two public programs with investment objectives similar to those of the registrant that had three years of operations after investment of 90 percent of the amount available for investment. In addition, at least two of the public offerings for programs with investment objectives similar to those of the registrant must have closed in the previous three years.

A. *Narrative Summary*

1. The narrative summary in the text of the prospectus should include a description of the sponsor's experience in the last 10 years with all other programs, both public and nonpublic, that have invested primarily in real estate, regardless of the investment objectives of the programs. This summary should include at least (a) the number of programs sponsored, (b) the total amount of money raised from investors, (c) the total number of investors, (d) the number of properties purchased and location by region, (e) the aggregate dollar amount of property purchased, (f) the percentage (based on purchase prices rather than on number) of properties that are commercial (broken out by shopping centers, office buildings, and others) and residential, (g) the percentage (based on purchase prices) of new, used, or construction properties, and (h) the number of properties sold. Aggregate figures should be presented separately for public and nonpublic programs. In addition, the narrative should indicate the approximate percentage of the overall data that represents activities of programs with investment objectives similar to those of the registrant. The summary also should cross-reference the prior performance tables.

2. The narrative summary should include a discussion of those major adverse business developments or conditions experienced by any prior program, either public or nonpublic, that would be material to investors in this program. The narrative summary also should include a cross-refer-

ence to further information that may be found in Appendix II as part of Table III.

3. The narrative summary should include a list of all prior public programs sponsored by the General Partner and its affiliates and an undertaking to provide upon request, for no fee, the most recent Form 10-K Annual Report filed with the Commission by any prior public program that has reported to the Commission within the last 24 months and to provide, for a reasonable fee, the exhibits to each such Form 10-K.

4. The narrative summary should include a summary of acquisitions of properties by programs in the most recent three years as set forth in Table VI of Appendix II. The summary should include the number of properties purchased, the type, location, and method of financing. Reference should be made to the more detailed description of these acquisitions in Part II of the registration statement, and the registrant should undertake to provide the more detailed description from Part II without fee upon request.

B. *Prior Performance Tables.* The information required by the tables set forth in Appendix II should be included in the format shown. Tables should appear at the back of the prospectus except fot Table VI, which should appear only in Part II of the registration statement. The instructions to the tables specify the programs and time periods about which information is required. (As amended by Sec. Act Rel. No. 6405, eff. 9-1-82.)

9. Management

A. If a material portion of the maximum net proceeds (allowing for reserves) is not committed to specific properties, disclosure should be made of the identity of the individuals who will make the investment decisions, with appropriate background information, including that required by Item 401(f) of Regulation S-K.

B. Any substantial reliance on a nonaffiliate in running the operation of the partnership should be disclosed, and any relevant prior experience should be discussed. If material amounts of compensation or fees are to be paid to nonaffiliates, a separate heading should be provided entitled, "Fees and Compensation Arrangements with Nonaffiliates," and a tabular presentation describing such fees should be provided.

C. If there is provision in the partnership agreement or otherwise for a change in the management of the partnership, a description of how such change could be accomplished should be included.

D. The amount of, and reason for, any contingent liabilities of the General Partner and its affiliates with regard to prior programs now in

Guide 5—SEC Regulations

existence should be disclosed. If this information appears in the financial statements it may be incorporated hereunder by reference. (As amended by Sec. Act Rel. No. 6405, eff. 9-1-82—but earlier use permitted.)

10. Investment Objectives and Policies

A. Disclosure should be made of the nature of the property intended to be purchased (e.g., commercial, residential) and the criteria (e.g., method of depreciation, location) to be utilized in evaluating proposed investments.

B. If there is provision in the partnership agreement or otherwise for change in the investment objectives of the partnership, a decription of how such change could be made should be included.

C. Generally, where the net proceeds of the offering will be invested in nonspecified properties or in properties that do not have any significant operating histories, it is not appropriate to make any statement setting forth a rate of return on the investment.

11. Description of Real Estate Investments

A. Risks associated with specified properties, such as competitive factors, environmental regulation, rent control regulation, fuel or energy requirements and regulation, should be noted.

B. If a material portion of the minimum net proceeds (allowing for reasonable reserves) is not committed to specific properties, the issuer should clearly so indicate in the prospectus.

When a reasonable probability exists that a property will be acquired and the funds to be expended represent a material portion of the net proceeds of the minimum offering, the issuer should describe such property in the registration statement at the time of filing. Where after the registration statement has been filed but prior to its effectiveness a reasonable probability arises that a property will be acquired, a description of such property should be included in a preeffective amendment to the registration statement. Where a reasonable probability that a property will be acquired arises after the effectiveness of the registration statement and during the distribution period, a 424(c) supplement or posteffective amendment, as appropriate, should be promptly filed. (See Undertaking D.)* Whether adequate disclosure of properties to be acquired has been timely made can only be determined by an examination of the facts in each case.

---

* It has come to the staff's attention that on a number of occasions issuers have identified properties to be purchased and have delayed proceeding with the purchase in order to avoid the necessary disclosure. In the staff's opinion, such practice is not consistent with the obligation of the issuer to disclose material facts relating to the offering.

This may vary due to different business practices particular to each issuer. Thus, as in all other situations, the burden of making adequate and timely disclosure rests solely with the issuer.

12. Federal Taxes

A. *General Instructions.* This section should summarize under a series of appropriate headings all material federal income tax aspects of the offering. State tax aspects need usually be summarized only to the extent required by Subsection L, below. Proper citations should be used whenever reference is made to sections of the Internal Revenue Code (the "Code"), the Treasury regulations, decided cases, or other sources. An opinion of counsel as to all material tax aspects of the offering should be filed as an exhibit. Such opinion should cite relevant authority for any conclusions expressed. The tax sections of the prospectus should summarize or restate the tax information contained in the opinion.

The function of the tax opinion is to inform investors of the tax consequences they can reasonably expect from an investment in the partnership. If, with respect to an intended tax benefit, counsel is unable to express an opinion that such benefit will be available because of uncertainty in the law or for other reasons, the opinion should so state and also disclose that there is or may be a material tax risk the particular benefit will be disallowed on audit. The tax effect of such disallowance should be explained. Each material risk of disallowance of an intended tax benefit should be disclosed in the tax opinion and under the appropriate heading in the prospectus.

Tax counsel should be aware that its opinion speaks as of the effective date of the registration statement. Such opinion should be updated for any material changes or events occurring subsequent to filing and prior to the effective date. Ruling requests (including amendments) and rulings should also be filed as exhibits with the original filing, or by amendment as soon thereafter as available.

B. *Partnership Status.* This subsection should state whether an IRS ruling has been requested as to the entity's classification as a partnership for federal income tax purposes. The contents of any ruling, including any conditions therein, should be summarized. Where a ruling or opinion of counsel as to partnership status is conditioned on the maintenance of certain net worth or other standards, there should be disclosure as to how these standards will be maintained in the future. If no IRS ruling as to partnership tax status has been requested or obtained, counsel's opinion as to partnership tax status should be summarized, and the risk of IRS classification of the entity as a corporate association, referred to in the Risk Factors section, should be discussed.

C. *Taxation of Limited Partners.* Insofar as necessary to an understanding of the intended tax benefits and any material risks of their disallowance, this subsection should summarize basic rules of partnership taxation, such as that a partnership is not a taxable entity, that a partner will be required to report on his federal tax return his distributive share of partnership income, gain, loss, deductions, or credits, whether or not any actual distribution is made to such partner during his taxable year. The tax treatment of cash distributions to partners should also be explained.

If the partnership agreement provides special allocations among partners of distributive shares of income, gain, loss, deductions, or credits, this subsection should set forth an opinion of counsel on the effect that the principal purpose of the allocations is not tax avoidance or evasion under Code Section 704(b)(2), and/or a risk disclosure to the effect that the IRS may on audit disallow any special allocation which it determines to have tax avoidance or evasion as its principal purpose. The tax consequences to partners of disallowance of a special allocation should be explained. Where applicable, the tax consequences of retroactive allocations to new partners should be discussed.

D. *Basis.* This subsection should explain that a partner may deduct his share of partnership losses only to the extent of the adjusted basis of his interest in the partnership. Inclusion of a partner's share of the partnership's nonrecourse debt in the adjusted basis of his partnership interest should be explained. If there is a question as to whether the partnership's nonrecourse debt will enter into bases of the limited partners' interest, that should be disclosed.

Where appropriate, there should be an explanation of the consequences to a limited partner of a reduction in his share of the partnership's nonrecourse debt as may result, for example, from a change in his profit-sharing ratio.

E. *Depreciation and Recapture.* This subsection should explain the method or methods of depreciation to be used by the partnership on its depreciable property as well as the basis for determining useful lives of such property. Any material risk that the IRS may challenge useful lives chosen by the partnership should be disclosed together with an explanation of the possible tax consequences of applying longer useful lives to partnership property. If methods of depreciation available only to a "first user" are to be utilized, the basis of such "first-user" status should be explained. Depreciation recapture may be explained here with appropriate cross-reference to subsections on Sale or Other Disposition of Partnership Property and Sale or Other Disposition of a Partnership Interest.

F. *Deductibility of Prepaid and Other Expenses.* As to prepaid interest, possible nondeductibility in the year of payment should be discussed. It should be explained that if a partnership takes a large deduction for prepaid interest in its first year of operation, having little or no income in such year, the IRS may determine that the prepayment created a material distortion of income at the partnership level and require that it be allocated over the term of the loan.

As to other material partnership expenses (e.g., interim commitment fees, management fees permanent mortgage fees, etc.), it should be stated which are deductible, which are nondeductible, and as to which deductibility is uncertain. Where applicable, the possible nondeductibility of guaranteed payments under Code Section 707(c) should be discussed.

G. *Tax Liabilities in Later Years.* This subsection should discuss the Risk Factors disclosure that after some years of partnership operations an investor's tax liabilities may exceed cash distributions in corresponding years. The tax problems that will arise after partnership property reaches the point when the partnership's nondeductible mortgage amortization payments exceed its depreciation deductions (the crossover point) should be explained.

It should also be explained that where partnership losses offset an investor's earned income taxable at a 50 percent rate, partnership income in later years may be taxed to the investor at a higher rate.

H. *Sale or Other Disposition of a Partnership Interest.* This subsection should begin with a restatement of the Risk Factors disclosure that an investor may be unable to sell his partnership interest as there may be no market for it. The subsection should then discuss the Risk Factors disclosure that taxes payable on a sale of a partnership interest may exceed cash received. The discussion should explain the tax effect on a partner of being relieved from his share of the partnership's nonrecourse liabilities. The discussion should also state to what extent the gain recognized will be taxed as ordinary income and to what extent as capital gain.

Whether or not the partnership plans to make the Section 754 election should be disclosed together with an explanation of the possible tax consequences on a transferee Limited Partner should the election not be made.

This subsection should also explain that a gift of an interest in a partnership holding leveraged property may result in federal income tax (as well as federal gift tax) liability to the donor. It should be explained that the IRS is likely to consider that a partner who gives away his partnership interest is relieved of his share of the partnership's nonrecourse liabilities and that he may realize a taxable gain on the gift to the extent that his share of such liabilities exceeds his adjusted basis in his partnership interest. It should be stated to what extent the gain will be taxed as ordinary income, to what extent as capital gain.

I. *Sale or Other Disposition of Partnership Property.* This subsection may use cross-reference to, or be combined with, subsection H in order to avoid repetition.

The subsection should discuss the Risk Factors disclosure that upon a sale (including a foreclosure sale) or other disposition of partnership property an investor's tax liability may exceed cash he would receive. The discussion should explain that the amount received by the partnership on sale (including a foreclosure sale) or other disposition of property will include any nonrecourse indebtedness to which the property was subject. It should be stated to what extent the gain will be taxed as ordinary income, to what extent as capital gain.

If appropriate, the tax treatment of dealer property should be explained. Should the sale of condominium units by the partnership be contemplated, it should be pointed out such units may be treated as dealer property.

J. *Section 183.* The possible impact of this Code section on investors lacking a profit objective in investing in any tax shelter program which is expected to generate annual net losses for tax purposes for a period of years should be discussed. The discussion should note that the section may apply to the Limited Partners of a partnership notwithstanding any profit objective the partnership itself may be deemed to have.

K. *Liquidation or Termination of the Partnership.* The tax consequences to a Limited Partner of partnership liquidation or termination should be explained.

L. *State, Local, and Foreign Taxes.* It should be disclosed whether partners will be required to file tax returns and/or be subject to tax in any state or states other than their state of residence, or in any foreign countries. Where applicable, state and foreign tax rates should be noted.

M. *Tax Returns and Tax Information.* It should be disclosed what kind of tax information will be supplied to Limited Partners and when, and whether the same kind of information will also be supplied to assignees who are not substitute Limited Partners.

It should be explained that the information return filed by the partnership may be audited and that such audit may result in adjustments or proposed adjustments. Any adjustment of the partnership information return would normally result in adjustments or proposed adjustments of a partner's own return. Any audit of a partner's return could result in adjustments of nonpartnership as well as partnership income and losses.

N. *Other Headings.* Where applicable, the tax section should also discuss the limitation on deductions of investment interest, the minimum tax on tax preference income, the impact of tax preference items on the maximum tax on earned income, and any other tax information deemed material in the particular offering.

13. Glossary

If terms are used in the prospectus that are technical in nature or are susceptible to varying methods of computation, such as acquisition fees, book value, capital contribution, cash flow, cash available for distribution, construction fees, cost of property, development fee, net worth, organization and offering expenses, profit, partnership management fee, and property management fee, definitions should be provided. For purposes of uniformity, it is suggested that these definitions conform to those that appear in the Statement of Policy Regarding Real Estate Programs of the North American Securities Administrators Association, or that any variations, and the economic effect thereof, be disclosed. (As amended by Sec. Act Rel. No. 6405, eff. 9-1-82.)

14. Summary of Partnership Agreement

A brief summary of the material provisions of the Limited Partnership Agreement should be included.

15. Reports to Limited Partners

The registrant should identify all reports and other documents that will be furnished to Limited Partners as required by the partnership's Limited Partnership Agreement and the undertakings to the registration statement. In particular, registrant should disclose (1) whether the financial information contained in such reports will be prepared on an accrual basis in accordance with generally accepted accounting principles, with a reconciliation with respect to information furnished to limited partners for income tax purposes; (2) whether independent Certified Public Accountants will audit the financial statements to be included in the annual report; (3) whether the annual report will be provided to limited partners within 90 days following the close of the partnership's fiscal year; (4) that a detailed statement of any transactions with the General Partner or its affiliates, and of fees, commissions, compensation, and other benefits paid or accrued to the General Partner or its affiliates for the fiscal year completed, showing

Guide 5—SEC Regulations

the amount paid or accrued to each recipient and the services performed, will be furnished to each limited partner at least on an annual basis pursuant to the registrant's undertaking; (5) that the information specified by Form 10-Q (if such report is required to be filed with the Commission) will be furnished to limited partners within 45 days after the close of each quarterly fiscal period pursuant to the registrant's undertaking; and (6) if the registrant has applied for but not received an IRS ruling as to the tax status at the time of effectiveness of the registration statement, that the registrant will promptly notify each limited partner, in writing, pursuant to its undertaking of the receipt of the ruling or of an adverse ruling or refusal to rule by the IRS.

16. The Offering—Description of the Units

In addition to the disclosure required by the relevant items of Form S–1 or S–11, disclosure should be made of all restrictions on transfer of the interests, including those in the Partnership Agreement, those imposed by state suitability standards or blue-sky laws, and those resulting from the tax laws.

17. Redemption, Repurchase, and Right of Presentment Agreements

There should be a discussion of any provisions in the partnership agreement that allow the General Partner or its affiliates to redeem or repurchase the offered security or that allow the investor to seek redemption or repurchase. The conditions or formulae used such as purchase price less capital returns, should also be disclosed. Registrant should be careful to appropriately describe the investor's right—whether it be redemption, repurchase, or merely a right of presentment. The discussion should include the following factors:

(1) That appraisals are simply estimates of value and may not necessarily correspond to realizable value.

(2) The order in which redemption requests will be honored (postmark or other objective standard).

(3) Whether the General Partner and its affiliates will defer their redemption requests until requests for redemption by the Limited Partner public investors have been met.

(4) The source and amount of funds (together with any legal or practical limitations) available for this purpose.

(5) The circumstances under which a later request will be honored, while an earlier request is still pending.

(6) Tax consequences related to redemption.

(7) The period of time during which a redemption request may be pending prior to its being granted or rejected.

(8) Whether there is to be allocation of funds among partners requesting redemption in circumstances where redemption requests exceed funds available for this purpose. If so, state and briefly describe the allocation process.

(9) Whether Limited Partners must hold an interest in the partnership for a specified period prior to making a redemption request.

(10) A detailed statement of the procedure that must be followed in order to redeem or seek repurchase of the interest, including the forms that must be presented, and whether signature guarantees will be required.

18. Plan of Distribution

A. If there is an understanding or arrangement, whether written or oral, between the registrant and any broker or dealer, relating to the distribution of the interests, which is intended to be finalized after effectiveness of the registration statement, such understanding or arrangement should be disclosed.

B. If, after the registration statement becomes effective, the registrant enters into any selling arrangement which calls for the payment of more than the usual and customary compensation, a sticker supplement, Rule 424(c), describing such arrangement should be filed.

C. If the registrant intends to pay referral or similar fees to any professional or other persons in connection with the distribution of the interests, this fact should be disclosed.

D. If the General Partner or its affiliates intend to purchase interests, and such interests will be included in satisfying the minimum offering requirements, it should be disclosed whether such interests are intended to be resold and, if so, the period of time these interests will be held prior to being resold. Depending on the circumstances, such interests may be considered to be unsold allotments under Section 4(3) of the Act. (See Securities Act Release 4150.) (Amended by Sec. Act Rel. No 6465, Exch. Act Rel. No. 19695, eff. 4-22-83.)

19. Summary of Promotional and Sales Material

A. The sales material should present a balanced discussion of both risk and reward. The contents of the sales material or sales meetings or seminars should be consistent with the representations in the prospectus.

Guide 5—SEC Regulations

B. A section which identifies all written sales material proposed to be transmitted to prospective investors orally or in writing should be included. The sales material should be appropriately identified by title and character and should be separately categorized either as the registrant's material or that of another person. If material provided by the latter is to be used, state the name of the author and publication and the date of prior publication, if any, identifying any persons who are quoted without being identified, and, except in the case of a public official document or statement, state whether or not the consent of the author and publication have been obtained for the use of the material as sales material. Sales materials include memoranda, summary descriptions, graphics, supplemental exhibits, media advertising charts, and pictures relating to the offering of the security and proposed to be transmitted to prospective investors.

C. If any other material is to be used subsequent to the effective date, a "sticker" supplement, 424(c) prospectus, should be filed to describe any such sales material.

D. Any sales material that is intended to be furnished to investors orally or in writing, other than that which is used for internal purposes of the registrant, and including all material described in paragraph B above, should be submitted to the staff supplementally, prior to its use. For purposes of this paragraph only, sales material includes all marketing memoranda that are sent by the General Partner or its affiliates to broker–dealers or other sales personnel and may include material labeled "for broker–dealer use only." Staff comments, if any, will be promptly communicated to the registrant. Registrant should check with the staff before using sales material that has been submitted to the staff.

E. Wherever public sales meetings or seminars are to be employed to discuss the offering, individually or in conjunction with other tax sheltered offerings, the staff should be provided, as supplemental information, copies of any written scripts or outlines which are prepared for use in such meetings a reasonable time prior to their use.

F. Reference in sales material or at such sales meetings or seminars to federal income tax treatment of the partnership and its investors should refer to either a ruling of the IRS or an opinion of counsel. Counsel should be named, his acknowledgment furnished supplementally with respect to such use, and any qualification contained in counsel's opinion should be referred to in such material by cross-referencing to the prospectus. Where the program has not sought a ruling as to the tax status (partnership) from the IRS and is relying on an opinion of counsel, it should be indicated that an opinion of counsel is not binding on the IRS. (Amended by Sec. Act Rel. No. 6465, Exch. Act Rel. No. 19695, eff. 4–22–83.)

20. Undertakings

A. The following undertaking should be included in the registration statement if the securities to be registered are to be offered in a continuous offering over an extended period of time:

The registrant undertakes (a) to file any prospectus required by Section 10(a)(3) as posteffective amendments to the registration statement, (b) that for the purpose of determining any liability under the Act each such posteffective amendment may be deemed to be a new registration statement relating to the securities offered therein and the offering of such securities at that time may be deemed to be the initial bona fide offering thereof, (c) that all posteffective amendments will comply with the application forms, rules, and regulations of the Commission in effect at the time such posteffective amendments are filed, and (d) to remove from registration by means of a posteffective amendment any of the securities being registered which remain at the termination of the offering.

B. The following undertaking should be included in every registration statement:

The registrant undertakes to send to each limited partner at least on an annual basis a detailed statement of any transactions with the General Partner of its affiliates, and of fees, commissions, compensation, and other benefits paid, or accrued to the General Partner or its affiliates for the fiscal year completed, showing the amount paid or accrued to each recipient and the services performed.

C. The following undertakings should be included in every registration statement:

The registrant undertakes to send to the limited partners, within 45 days after the close of each quarterly fiscal period, the information specified by the Form 10–Q, if such report is required to be filed with the Commission.

The registrant undertakes to provide to the limited partners the financial statements required by Form 10–K for the first full fiscal year of operations of the partnership. (Added by Sec. Act Rel. No. 5745, eff. 9–28–76.)

D. The following undertakings relating to investment of the proceeds of an offering in which a material portion of the maximum net proceeds (allowing for reasonable reserves) is not committed (i.e., subject to a binding purchase agreement) to specific properties should be included in the registration statement:

The registrant undertakes to file a sticker supplement pursuant to Rule 424(c) under the Act during the distribution period describing each property not identified in the prospectus at such time as there arises a reasonable probability that such property will be acquired and to consolidate all such stickers into a posteffective amendment filed at least once every three months, with the information contained in such amendment provided simultaneously to the existing Limited Partners. Each sticker supplement should also disclose all compensation and fees received by the General Partner and its affiliates in connection with any such acquisition. The posteffective amendment shall include audited financial statements meeting the requirements of Rule 3–14 of Regulation S–X only for properties acquired during the distribution period.

The registrant also undertakes to file, after the end of the distribution period, a current report on Form 8–K containing the financial statements and any additional information required by Rule 3–14 of Regulation S–X, to reflect each commitment (i.e., the signing of a binding purchase agreement) made after the end of the distribution period involving the use of 10 percent or more (on a cumulative basis) of the net proceeds of the offering and to provide the information contained in such report to the Limited Partners at least once each quarter after the distribution period of the offering has ended.

Note—Offers and sales of the interests may continue after the filing of a posteffective amendment containing information previously disclosed in sticker supplements to the prospectus, as long as the information disclosed in a current sticker supplement accompanying the prospectus is as complete as the information contained in the most recently filed posteffective amendment. (As amended by Sec. Act Rel. No. 6405, eff. 9–1–82.)

E. If the registrant has applied for a ruling from the IRS as to tax status, and has not received it at the time of effectiveness:

The registrant undertakes to promptly notify each limited partner, in writing, of the receipt of the ruling or of an adverse ruling or refusal to rule by the IRS, and undertakes to file with the Commission a Form 8–K describing such event. (Amended by Sec. Act Rel. No. 6465, Exch. Act Rel. No. 19695, eff. 4–22–83.)

APPENDIX I
EXAMPLE OF SUMMARY OF THE USE OF PROCEEDS SECTION
Estimated Application of Proceeds of This Offering

	Minimum Dollar Amount	Percent	Maximum Dollar Amount	Percent
Gross Offering Proceeds	$	100.00%	$	100.00%
Public Offering Expenses: Underwriting Discount and Commissions Paid to Affiliate Organizational Expenses (1)	_____	_____	_____	_____
Amount Available for Investment	$_____	%_____	$_____	%_____
Prepaid Terms and Fees Related to Purchase of Property (2)				
Cash Down Payment (Equity)				
Acquisition Fees (Real Estate Commissions) (3)				
Working Capital Reserve	_____	_____	_____	_____
Proceeds Invested Public Offering Expenses	_____	_____	_____	_____
Total Application of Proceeds	$_____	%_____	$_____	100.00%

The Corporate General Partner and its affiliates may receive a maximum of $__ (__ percent) if the minimum dollar amount is sold and $__ (__ percent) if the maximum dollar amount is sold from the sellers of the properties as real estate commissions on purchases of properties. Real estate commissions are normally paid by the seller of a property rather

Guide 5—SEC Regulations

than the buyer. However, the price of a property will generally be adjusted upward to take into account this obligation of the seller so that in effect the Partnership, as purchaser, will bear all or a portion of the commission in the purchase price of the property. The partnership also expects to pay commissions in connection with the sale of properties which will reduce the net proceeds to the Partnership of any such sales.

(1) Includes a $___ nonrecurring organization fee to be received by the corporate General Partner and legal, accounting, printing, and other expenses of this offering. To the extent, if any, that expenses of the offering exceed $___ per interest, the excess will be paid by _____.

(2) Includes prepaid interest, points, loan commitment fees, and legal and other costs of acquisition. The percentage of such items to be capitalized is _____ percent.

(3) "Real estate commission" is defined as the total of all fees and commissions paid by any person to any person, including the corporate General Partner or affiliates in connection with the selection, purchase, construction, or development of any property by the Partnership, whether designated as real estate commission, acquisition fees, finder's fees, selection fees, development fees, construction fees, nonrecurring management fees, consulting fees, or any other similar fees or commissions howsoever treated for tax or accounting purposes.

APPENDIX II
PRIOR PERFORMANCE TABLES

Instructions to Appendix II

1. The prior performance tables should be preceded by a narrative introduction that cross-references the narrative summary in the text, explains the significance of the track record and the tables, explains where additional information (Part II of the registration statement or Form 10–K annual reports for prior programs) can be obtained on request, and includes a glossary of terms used in the tables.

This introduction also should include a discussion of the factors the sponsor considered in determining which previous programs had "similar investment objectives" to those of the registrant.

2. Each of the tables should be introduced by a brief narrative explaining the objective of the table and what it covers so that the investor will be able to understand the significance of the information presented. There also should be set forth with or in each table any further material information that may be necessary to make the required tabular data, in light of the circumstances under which it is presented, not misleading.

Table I. Experience in Raising and Investing Funds (*on a percentage basis*)

Instructions:

1. Include information only for programs the offering of which closed in the most recent three years.

2. Sponsors with a "public track record" should include information relating only to public programs with investment objectives similar to those of the registrant.

3. If the sponsor does not have a "public track record," information must be given for each prior program, public or nonpublic, with investment objectives similar to those of the registrant. If the sponsor has not sponsored at least five such programs, then information must be given for each prior program, public or nonpublic, even if the investment objectives for those

Guide 5—SEC Regulations

programs are not similar to those of the registrant. In that case, nonpublic programs with investment objectives that are not similar to those of the registrant should be grouped together according to investment objective and information about these programs presented on an aggregate basis by year. If so presented, the number of programs that have been aggregated should be disclosed. The sponsor also should indicate by note if the investment objectives of any program are not similar to those of the registrant and should briefly describe those investment objectives.

	Program X	Program Y
Dollar amount offered		
Dollar amount raised (100%)		
Less offering expenses:		
Selling commissions and discounts		
Retained by affiliates		
Organizational expenses		
Other (explain)		
Reserves		
Percent available for investment		
Acquisition costs:		
Prepaid items and fees related to purchase of property		
Cash down payment		
Acquisition fees		
Other (explain)		
Total acquisition cost		
Percent leverage (mortgage financing divided by total acquisition cost)		
Date offering began		
Length of offering (in months)		
Months to invest 90% of amount available for investment (measured from beginning of offering)		

Table II. Compensation to Sponsor

Instructions:

    1. Include in a separate column for each program aggregated payments made to the sponsor only by real estate programs the offering of which closed in the most recent three years. Include in another separate column aggregate payments to the sponsor in the most recent three years from all other programs and indicate the number of programs involved.

2. Sponsors with a "public track record" should include information relating only to public programs with investment objectives similar to those of the registrant.

3. If the sponsor does not have a "public track record," information must be given for each prior program, public or nonpublic, with investment objectives similar to those of the registrant. If the sponsor has not sponsored at least five such programs, then information must be given for each prior program, public or nonpublic, even if the investment objectives for those programs are not similar to those of the registrant. In that case, nonpublic programs with investment objectives that are similar to those of the registrant should be grouped together according to investment objective and information about those programs presented on an aggregate basis by year. If so presented, the number of programs that have been aggregated should be disclosed. The sponsor also should indicate by note if the investment objectives of any program are not similar to those of the registrant and should briefly describe those investment objectives.

4. The table should include any real estate commissions and other fees paid to the sponsor in connection with the acquisition or disposition of any properties by the program by entities other than the program itself.

Type of Compensation	Program X	Program Y	Other Programs
Date offering commenced			
Dollar amount raised			
Amount paid to sponsor from proceeds of offering:			
Underwriting fees			
Acquisition fees:			
Real estate commissions			
Advisory fees			
Other (identify and quantify)			
Other			
Dollar amount of cash generated from operations before deducting payments to sponsor			
Amount paid to sponsor from operations:			
Property management fees			
Partnership management fees			
Reimbursements			
Leasing commissions			
Other (identify and quantify)			

Guide 5—SEC Regulations

Type of Compensation	Program X	Program Y	Other Programs

Dollar amount of property sales and
  refinancing before deducting payments
  to sponsor:
  Cash
  Notes
Amount paid to sponsor
  from property sales and refinancing:
  Incentive fees[1]
  Other (identify and quantify)

Table III. Operating Results of Prior Programs

Instructions:

    1. Include information only for programs the offerings of which closed in the most recent five years. Financial data for each program should be presented separately for each year.

    2. Sponsors with a "public track record" should include information relating only to public programs with investment objectives similar to those of the registrant.

    3. If the sponsor does not have a "public track record," information must be given for each program, public or nonpublic, with investment objectives similar to those of the registrant. If the sponsor has not sponsored at least five such programs, then information must be given for each prior program, public or nonpublic, even if the investment objectives for those programs are not similar to those of the registrant. In that case, nonpublic programs with investment objectives that are not similar to those of the registrant should be grouped together according to investment objective and information about those programs presented on an aggregate basis by year. If so presented, the number of programs that have been aggregated should be disclosed. The sponsor also should indicate by note if the investment objectives of any program are not similar to those of the registrant and should briefly describe those investment objectives.

    4. Information should be presented on the basis of generally accepted accounting principles (GAAP) where indicated. However, where information about nonpublic programs is required to be included, such information may be presented on a tax basis if the program's books have not been kept on a GAAP basis. If there are any significant differences in operating results between accounting on a tax and GAAP basis, they should be

---

[1] Explain subordinated commissions in a note.

explained. This explanation should provide the reader with any additional information about the particular programs presented that may be necessary to make the information contained in the table not materially misleading in light of the circumstances under which the information is given.

	Program X		
	Year 1	Year 2	Year 3
Gross revenues			
Profit on sale of properties			
Less:			
Operating expenses			
Interest expense			
Depreciation			
Net income—GAAP basis			
Taxable income			
From operations			
From gain on sale			
Cash generated from operations[2]			
Cash generated from sales			
Cash generated from refinancing			
Cash generated from operations, sales, and refinancing			
Less: Cash distributions to investors			
From operating cash flow			
From sales and refinancing			
From other			
Cash generated (deficiency) after cash distributions			
Less: Special items, not including sales and refinancing (identify and quantify)			
Cash generated (deficiency) after cash distributions and special items			

Tax and Distribution Data per $1000 Invested

Federal income tax results:
  Ordinary income (loss)
    From operations

---

[2] Indicate in a note what amount is from sources other than operations, such as guaranteed rents or interest.

Guide 5—SEC Regulations

	Program X		
	Year 1	Year 2	Year 3

From recapture
Capital gain (loss)
Cash distributions to investors
   Source (on GAAP basis)
   Investment income
   Return of capital
   Source (on cash basis)
   Sales
   Refinancing
   Operations
   Other
Amount (in percentage terms) remaining invested in program properties at the end of the last year reported in the table (original total acquisition cost of properties retained divided by original total acquisition cost of all properties in program).

Table IV. Results of Completed Programs

Instructions:

    1. Include programs that have completed operations (no longer hold properties) in the most recent five years, even if they still hold notes.

    2. Sponsors with a "public track record" should include information relating only to public programs with investment objectives similar to those of the registrant.

    3. If the sponsor does not have a "public track record," information must be given for each prior program, public or nonpublic, with investment objectives similar to those of the registrant. If the sponsor has not sponsored at least five such programs, then information must be given for each prior program, public or nonpublic, even if the investment objectives for those programs are not similar to those of the registrant. In that case, nonpublic programs with investment objectives that are not similar to those of the registrant should be grouped together according to investment objective and information about those programs presented on an aggregate basis by year. If so presented, the number of programs that have been aggregated should be disclosed. The sponsor also should indicate by note if the invest-

ment objectives of any program are not similar to those of the registrant and should briefly describe those investment objectives.

Program Name

    Dollar amount raised
    Number of properties purchased
    Date of closing of offering
    Date of first sale of property
    Date of final sale of property

Tax and Distribution Data per $1,000 Through

Federal income tax results:
    Ordinary income (loss)
        From operations
        From recapture
    Capital gain (loss)[1]
    Deferred gain[2]

        Capital
        Ordinary

Cash distributions to investors
    Source (on GAAP basis)
        Investment income
        Return of capital

    Source (on cash basis)
        Sales
        Refinancing
        Operations
        Other

    Receivable on net purchase money financing[3]

Table V. Sales or Disposals of Properties

Instructions:

    1. Include all sales or disposals of property by programs with similar investment objectives within the most recent three years.

---

[1] Note 60 percent capital gain exclusion.
[2] Explain in a note deferred capital gain.
[3] Explain in a note the terms of notes taken back and annual payments, and the fact that the amounts presented are face amounts and do not represent discounted current value.

Property	Date acquired	Date of sale[1]	Selling price, net of closing costs and GAAP adjustments					Cost of properties including closing and soft costs			Excess (deficiency) of property operating cash receipts over cash expenditures[6]
			Cash received net of closing costs	Mortgage balance at time of sale	Purchase money mortgage taken back by program[2]	Adjustments resulting from application of GAAP[3]	Total[4]	Original mortgage financing	Total acquisition cost, capital improvement, closing and soft costs[5]	Total	

[1] Note if sales of properties are to related parties.

[2] Indicate in a note that the amounts shown are face amounts and do not represent discounted current value. In addition, describe the terms of purchase money mortgages taken back by the partnerships, including the interest rate, any balloon payment requirements, and other special provisions. Also, describe those sales made with a leaseback or any other guarantees which require continued seller involvement.

[3] Include an explanation of any GAAP adjustments.

[4] Note the allocation of the taxable gain between ordinary and capital, and identify those sales that are being reported for tax purposes on the installment basis.

[5] Identify real estate commissions carried but not taken. Indicate that the amounts shown do not include pro rata share of original offering costs.

[6] Do not include amounts otherwise included under "Selling Price, Net of Closing Costs and GAAP Adjustments" or "Cost of Properties Including Closing and Soft Costs." Costs incurred in the administration of the partnership not related to the operation of properties need not be included if so indicated in a note to the table.

2. Sponsors with a "public track record" should only include information relating to public programs. If the sponsor does not have a "public track record," then information should be given about sales or disposals of properties by public and nonpublic programs. Where properties held by nonpublic programs are included, information should be on a GAAP basis where feasible without undue effort of expense.

Table VI. Acquisition of Properties by Programs

Instructions:

1. Include the following table only in Part II of the registration statement.

2. Include all properties acquired by any prior programs with similar investment objectives in the most recent three years.

3. Sponsors with a "public track record" should only include information relating to public programs. If the sponsor does not have a "public track record," then information should be given about properties acquired by public and nonpublic programs.

Program X

Name, location, type of property

Gross leasehold space (sq. ft.) or number of units and total square feet of units

Date of purchase

Mortgage financing at date of purchase

Cash down payment

Contract purchase price plus acquisition fee

Other cash expenditures expensed

Other cash expenditures capitalized

Total acquisition cost

(Appendix II added by Sec. Act Rel. No. 6405, eff. 9–1–82.)

REGULATION D PRIVATE OFFERING
SAMPLE TABLE OF CONTENTS

The table of contents set forth in the next few pages comprises the table of contents of a prospectus prepared pursuant to Guide 5 to give you an idea of what goes into such a prospectus.

The typical Regulation D or fully registered statement runs 200 or more pages when all documents are included (labeled Exhibits).

TABLE OF CONTENTS
(of prospectus prepared pursuant to Guide 5)

Cover page

Glossary

Suitability Standards

Summary of Offering

    Partnership
    General Partner of the Partnership
    Purpose of Offering; Nature of Business of Partnership
    Securities Offered
    Subscription Procedure
    Termination of Offering
    Purchase of Property and Mortgage Debt Affecting the Property
    Order of Distribution of Profits, Losses, Cash Flow, and Other Distributions
    Management of the Property; Compensation of Manager
    Tax Consequences of the Offering
    Cancellation of Subscription
    Risk Factors
    Conflicts of Interest
    Additional Information; Documents for Inspection

The Offering

    General
      Purpose of the Offering
      Priority Cash Flow Return
    Subscription Procedure
    Admission of Limited Partners
    Rescission of Sale of Unit
    Withdrawal of Offering
    Schedule of Payments for Interests
    Failure to Make Payment on Investor Note
    Compensation of Purchaser Representatives

Source and Use of Proceeds and Projected Working Capital (1982–1986)

Operating Deficit

Compensation of the General Partner and the Manager

Conflicts of Interest

Dilution

Risk Factors

    Acquisition Risks
    Transfer of Property
    Nova Consent
    Operating Risks
    Projections—Operating Results
    Lack of Prior Experience of General Partner
    Continuity of Partnership
    Default under Mortgages
    Payment of Priority Cash Flow
    Sale of the Property—Refinancing Existing Mortgages
    Investment Risks
      Restrictions on Transfer of Interests
      Payment of Fees and Other Compensation to General Partner and the Manager
      Absence of Effective Remedy against the General Partner
      Lack of Marketability of (1) the Property and (2) the Limited Partnership Interests
        The Property
        Limited Partnership Interests

Regulation D Private Offering Sample Table of Contents

    Additional Income of Investors
    Conflicts of Interest
    Default by Investors of Payment of Installment
    Tax Risks
    Partnership Status
    Risk of Audit, Disallowance of Partnership Deductions, and Reallocation of Partnership Allocations
    Disposition of Property or Interests
    Suitability of Investment; Changes in Tax Laws
    Repair Fund

Description of the Property

    General
    Location, Access, and Area Data
    Property Description
        Construction
        Utility System
        Unit Features
        Amenities
        Repairs and Upgrades
        Apartments
        Comparison of Competing Apartment Complexes, Facilities, and Rental Charges

Acquisition of the Property

    The Purchase Agreement
    The Assignment
    The Partnership Assignment

Mortgage Debt Affecting the Property

    First and Second Notes and Mortgages
    Purchase Wrap Note and Mortgage
    Partnership Wrap Note and Mortgage

Prior Experience of the General Partner and the Manager

    The General Partner
    The Manager

Income Tax Aspects

    Federal Income Tax Aspects
    General

Classification as a Partnership
Partners Not Partnership Subject to Tax
Allocation of Partnership Profits and Losses for Tax
  Purposes
Activities Not Engaged in for Profit
Calculation of Limited Partner's Adjusted Tax Basis
Valuation of the Property
Interest on Wraparound Mortgage
Rule of 78s
Deductibility of Payments and Fees
Accelerated Cost Recovery System
ACRS Allowance Recapture
Cash Distributions from the Partnership
Gain or Loss on Sale of Partnership Interest
Sale or Foreclosure of the Property
Investment Interest
Minimum Tax for Tax Preferences
Gifts of Interest
Partnership Elections
Risk of Audit
Possible Further Changes in Tax Laws
State and Local Taxes

*Projections—Projected Financial Statements
(1982–1986)*

Accountant's Letter
Statement of Projected Cash Flow
Projected Results of $102,750 Unit Investment
Projected Results of Limited Partners' Investment
Projection of Taxable Income (Loss)
Notes and Assumptions to the Projections

Fiduciary Responsibility of the General Partner

Summary of Partnership Agreement

Formation and Power of General Partner
Powers of Limited Partners
Purpose—Investment Objectives
Term
Capital Contributions
Profits and Losses
Allocation of Taxable Net Income and Losses Resulting from

Regulation D Private Offering Sample Table of Contents

      Capital Transactions
    Cash Flow
    Capital Distributions
    Compensation of the General Partner
    Power of Attorney
    Assignment of Interest—Substituted Limited Partners
    Distributions on Dissolution
    Exculpation and Indemnification of the General Partner
    Investment Representation
    Sale of the Property
    Amendment of Agreement of Limited Partnership

Summary of the Management Agreement

    Agent's Compensation
    Surety Bond
    Term

Reports to Partners—Tax Return

Additional Information—Documents for Inspection

Private Placement Memorandum

Exhibits

      Exhibit A—Description of Property
      Exhibit B—Maintenance Items Inventory and Clubhouse
          and Office Equipment List
      Exhibit C—Mortgage Note (See Exhibit VIII)
      Exhibit D—Mortgage (See Exhibit VIII)
      Exhibit E—Rent Roll

III. PAA Assignment

    Exhibit A—Description of Property
    Exhibit B—Note

IV. Partnership Assignment

    Exhibit A—Description of Premises
    Exhibit B—Promissory Note (See Exhibit IX)

V. Subscription Agreement

VI. Management Agreement

VII. First and Second Notes and Mortgages

VIII. Purchase Wrap Note and Mortgage

IX. Partnership Wrap Note and Mortgage
X. Option Agreement
XI. Loan Commitment Agreement
XII. Collection Agency Agreement
XIII. Funding Commitment Agreement
XIV. Appraisal of Property
XV Tax Opinion

JOINT VENTURE CHECKLIST

This document is similar to the syndication checklist presented earlier. Similarly, it is an outline of opportunities and trouble spots. It is based on the experience of myself, my law partners, and our clients in many transactions.

It asks questions; it does not offer solutions. It is an agenda of opportunities and trouble spots that you will have to think through before you start negotiating with your joint venture partner and that will become the subject of your joint venture partnership agreement.

As you go through the remaining forms of joint venture agreement that immediately follow the checklist, you will see how a developer resolves some of the problems in his or her favor in the developer's agreement and how an institution resolves almost the identical problems in their favor in the institutional investor agreement form. Your deal will probably come out somewhere in the middle.

JOINT VENTURE CHECKLIST

I. *Why Joint Venture?*

   a. One-half of three loaves is better than no loaves.
   b. A well-funded partner supplies staying power, and staying power is the key element in the larger deals. Compare Reston with Columbia.
   c. Joint ventures offer the opportunity of ever-widening pools of deals. Nothing succeeds like success.
   d. The joint venture is the only way the smaller local builder can compete with the giants.

II. *Some Joint Venture Traps*

   a. *Tax treatment:* Who gets tax benefits? Will tax benefits match cash flow? Will you pay tax on money you don't get? Will you

get tax benefits you can't use? Shall tax benefits be sold to third parties for the account of the venture?
   b. *Capital requirements:* What happens if capital requirements exceed budget? Who is responsible for raising those funds? Will they be treated as loans or additional contributions? Will they come from third parties or one of the venturers? Will the over-budget capital get a special premium because it is at special risk?
   c. *Default:* What happens if the cash requirements do not come in on time? What are the rights of the innocent venturer on default of his or her partner? What penalty clauses? What rights to raise money from third parties? What forfeitures or rights to buy out?
   d. *Turnkey costs:* Responsibilities of the developer, timetable, risk of cost overrun, acts of God, rent-up, break-even point, cash flow.
   e. *Dissolution or Buyout:* Who can dissolve the venture? Walk away from it? Close out a loser? What happens in case of disagreement? Right to sell, liquidate, buy out, or walk away?

III. *Legal Format*
   a. *Entity:* Corporation, general partnership, limited partnership, joint venture or loan agreement?
   b. *Financial provisions:* Priority of return of capital contributions, priority of distribution of cash flow, allocation of tax benefits, defining cash flow and tax benefits. Priority and amount of builder's fees and management fees. What is covered? What is excluded and separately billable?
   c. *Cash distributions:* Timing mandatory or optional? Failure to cover can result in money man squeezing out partner.
   d. *Transferability:* The business problem: Can you get stuck with a new partner without your consent? If you are an institution, do you want to hide behind a shell? Are you ashamed to have people identify you with your developer partner? If you are a developer, do you insist (for prestige and local banking and leasing purposes) that the moneyed partner be identified?
   e. *Admission of new partners:* Transferability of partnership interests. What happens in case of death? Bankruptcy? Insanity? Disability? Etc.?

IV *Management and Capital: Decision Making*
   a. *Leasing:* Who makes decisions? Sale or refinancing? Minor leases, plans and specifications, substitution of materials, hiring

professional consultants (lawyers, architects, accountants, etc.), major repairs, improvements, insurance, accounting methods (cash versus accrual), depreciation (maximize or minimize).
   b. *Disputes:* What happens if there is a dispute? What are your rights as developer? As investor? Know your strengths and the investor's, and be sure you protect them. Bear in mind that the institution has been brought into the deal for its money. If you are thinly financed, many of the rights you get may be academic.

V. *Financing*
   a. Exculpatory clauses; personality liability.
   b. Self-dealing and breach of fiduciary duty.
   c. Budget in form satisfactory to investor; regular comparison of budget with operating results.

VI. *Competition*
   a. Developer's right to make any other deals with the same tenants, in the same area, with the same personnel.
   b. Developer's depth of staff versus dividing itself too thin.
   c. Rights of first refusal.

VII. *Fees to Developer*
   a. What do fees cover? (Internal overhead, rent of developer's office space, direct labor, secretarial services, advertising budget, etc.)
   b. Rights of investors to substitute new management in lieu of developer; objective criteria or sole discretion?
   c. Is right of first refusal or buyout suitable? Remember, an institution has money; a developer may not have. A right of first refusal is not always helpful.

VIII. *Tax Aspects*
   a. *Developer objectives:* Tax-free going in; share of mortgage proceeds versus ordinary income or capital gain (see Section 721, Internal Revenue Code).
   b. *Investor objectives:* Maximizing tax shelter and construction write-offs.
   c. Conflicts of the two positions.
   d. Advance decisions on depreciation, interest, prepayment, and so on.
   e. *Dissolution:* All cash, cash and paper, cash and kind.

f. Basis and recognition of gain (Sections 707 and 722, Internal Revenue Code).
g. Allocation of losses versus allocation of cash flow.
h. Prepaid interest (Revenue Ruling 68–643).
i. *Limited partnership:* Safe harbor rules, two out of four, 10 or 15 percent net worth test for corprate general partners.
j. Tax problem on disposition; tax on money never received.
k. Depreciation recapture.
l. Section 754 election for transfers of partnership.
m. *Nominee problem:* Loss of deduction, usury problem, collapsible corporation.

JOINT VENTURE AGREEMENTS

Presented here are two forms of joint venture agreement. One favors the developer; the other favors an institutional investor. In each case, before getting to the forms themselves, you will read what should be covered by the agreement.

Of course, these agreements were tailored to specific transactions and cannot be followed slavishly. But they will give you an idea of some of the problems involved and how other venturers treated the problems.

A JOINT VENTURE AGREEMENT FAVORING THE DEVELOPER

What the Agreement Should Cover

1. *Basics and formation*

The agreement, of course, will list the names and addresses of the general and limited partners. Here the general partner will be the developer. The limited partners are assumed to be private investors—not as hard in driving a bargain as an institutional investor. On pages 254 to 282, you will find an agreement drafted to favor an institutional investor. Compare the two.

The name of the venture or partnership will be listed along with its address. The agreement will state under what partnership law it is being formed (whether in the state where the partners reside or where the property is located). The life of the partnership will be covered (generally until the expiration of the major mortgage or lease, although some other fixed period may be chosen).

Most joint venture agreements are cast in the form of a partnership, either limited or general. In some cases, they may be set up in the form of tenancies in common. Your choice will depend on such business considerations as liability exposure, as well as tax considerations.

2. Money

Money involves two problems: how it goes in and how it comes out.

For money going in (capital contributions), there are two different phases:

(1) Initial capital contributions (the money going in).

(2) Additional contributions or loans (should the partnership suffer operational deficits or have capital requirements over and above those budgeted for initially).

Both sets of problems must be covered. If one partner is to make a contribution of property rather than cash, the property should be valued either as a percentage of the total partnership or with a dollar figure (but beware of tax considerations). If the contributed property has any restrictions or liens, they should be specifically set forth in the agreement.

For additional contributions for the future, if they are to be required, they should be specifically listed with who will make them and under what circumstances. Also, there should be a specific discussion of whether additional capital contributions are paid interest, whether they are to be made in the form of loans, and whether, if they are to be made, they dilute the interests of noncontributing partners.

Finally, if additional contributions or loans are required, any preferential treatment they are to get on repayment should be specifically discussed.

3. Capital withdrawals

Any preferential rights on distribution regarding both initial capital contributions and additional contributions should be specifically covered. In other words, is capital to be returned before profits are shared? If so, who gets preference?

4. Cash flow distributions

These are to be spelled out specifically. First you have to define cash flow. Are mortgage amortization and depreciation to be taken into consideration? Are reserves to be subtracted before cash flow comes out? How are cash flow distributions to be divided? Shall preference be given to partners to cover the expense of management services? Is there to be any flip-flop or turnaround of preferences? Often, limited partners who make cash contributions get their money out first or in some kind of preferential ratio. However, once the preferential partners receive a certain

Joint Venture Agreements

sum of money, cash flow may begin to be divided in different percentages.

5. *Duties of general partner–developer*

Generally, the developer–partner is required to do certain work on behalf of the partnership. If property is to be built, exactly what is being built should be described, and often a set of plans is annexed. If certain mortgages or liens are to be put on the property, they should be specified, and the problem of who pays them off and out of what proceeds should be discussed.

If a maximum mortgage is to be sought by the general partner, it should be clear whether this is being done on a "best efforts" basis or the procuring of such a mortgage is a condition precedent to limited partner investors' liabilities.

What are the developer's obligations to lease the property or produce some kind of rent roll? If the property is to be built on speculation, are the limited partners to put their money in before there is a rent roll?

6. *Tax aspects*

If there is going to be a difference between distributions of cash flow and distributions of taxable profits and losses, the agreement should clarify what will happen on disposition of the property. If one partner is going to get taxable income and the other is going to get cash, the partner who gets taxable income and no cash must fund the payment of his or her own personal income tax out of his or her own pocket.

Similarly, the tax aspects of allocating one partner more basis than the other (on mortgages) and the tax aspects of disparity of capital accounts at the time of sale (one partner may have gotten all the write-offs and have a lower tax base than the other) should be considered in the agreement.

7. *Management duties and responsibilities*

Generally, under most uniform partnership laws, the general partners have sole management responsibilities and duties. However, you may want to limit those rights and duties. Shall the general partner–developer retain outside management to run the property? If so, at whose expense and under what circumstances can the general partner's decisions be vetoed? What happens if the project goes into default? Who gets the fees (if anyone) for management, mortgage procurement, leasing, sale, and so on, and what shall those fees be? Will the general partner still be rewarded if the project goes into default or if it comes in above budget?

8. *Miscellaneous*

What happens on dissolution? On liquidation? On sale or refinancing? What preferences? What happens in case of death or bankruptcy of either the general or limited partners? Are the units to be transferable? What are the restrictions on transferability, particularly in view of the tax law?

9. *Other details*

Finally, see the more detailed joint venture checklist (page 229) before drafting your own agreement, and take a look at the joint venture agreement favoring an institutional investor (page 254) so that you can see what the other side may be asking for.

AGREEMENT

Agreement made as of this __ day of _____, 19__, among _____, residing at _____; _____, residing at _____; and _____, residing at _____, who shall be the general partners; and each of the persons set forth in Exhibit A annexed hereto and incorporated herein by reference who shall be the limited partners, as well as all other persons who shall hereafter become parties to this Agreement in accordance with the provisions hereof and the provisions of the Uniform Limited Partnership Act of the State of _____.

WITNESSETH:

Whereas, the parties hereto desire to form a limited partnership (the "Partnership") to own, improve, and operate approximately __ acres of land located _____ (the "Property") and more particularly described in Exhibit B hereto.

It is therefore agreed:

1. *Format*

The parties hereto hereby form a limited partnership pursuant to the provisions of the Uniform Limited Partnership Act of the State of _____.

2. Name

The Partnership shall be conducted under the firm name and style of _____, and its principal place of business (unless changed by the general partners upon notice to the limited partners) shall be _____.

3. Business

The character of the business of the Partnership is to acquire, own, hold, improve, develop, operate, and manage the Property and to do all things reasonably incident thereto, including mortgaging, selling, leasing and subleasing, or otherwise disposing of the Property and the improvements thereon at any time.

4. Term

The term of the Partnership shall be deemed to commence on the date of filing the Certificate of Limited Partnership, as required by the Uniform Limited Partnership Act of the State of _____ and shall expire on _____ unless sooner terminated by agreement of all partners or pursuant to the provisions hereof.

5. Capital

The initial capital of the Partnership shall be $_____ cash and the Property. The $_____ cash contribution to the partnership capital has been or will be made prior to _____ by the limited partners. The Property will be contributed prior to _____ by the general partners subject to a mortgage dated _____ ("Mortgage") in favor of _____ (the "Bank"), securing a note in the principal amount of $_____. Concurrently with the conveyance to the Partnership of the Property, the following shall also occur:

  a. The general partners will cause to be assigned to the Partnership all of the rights and benefits of _____ in, to, and/or under the following:

   i. The Construction Loan Agreement.
   ii. That certain Note Purchase Agreement dated __ between the Bank __ and __ ("Note Purchase Agreement").
   iii. The Contract for Construction Work dated _____ between _____ and _____ ("Construction Contract").

  b. The Partnership will assume and agree to keep and perform all of the obligations and liabilities of _____ in, to, and/or under:

i. The Construction Loan Agreement.
   ii. The Note Purchase Agreement.
   iii. The Construction Contract.

6. *Duties of general partners*

   The general partners especially covenant and agree as follows:

   a. The general partners will complete or cause to be completed on the Property by _____ the improvements ("Improvements") contemplated by and in accordance with the plans and specifications prepared by _____, Architects, which have been identified and approved by _____ and by the Bank and are described in Exhibit C to the Note Purchase Agreement.

   b. By _____ the Property will be free and clear of all liens and encumbrances other than those set forth in Schedule _____.

   c. The general partners will not permit the aggregate amount of the principal of indebtedness outstanding under the Mortgage to exceed at any time the sum of _____.

   d. By _____ the general partners will perform or cause to be performed, to the extent that it is within their power to do so, all the conditions and requirements of the Note Purchase Agreement necessary or appropriate to cause _____ to purchase from the Bank the _____ note secured by the Mortgage.

   e. The general partners will use their best efforts to cause, by _____, the aggregate annual gross rental payable under valid and enforceable leases covering apartments on the Property with an original term of not less than one year, free of concessions, allowances, or offsets, to be equal to _____ from not more than _____ percent of the number of units, and in the event that such rental has not attained such level by _____, the general partners shall use their best efforts to attain such level prior to _____.

   f. It is understood and agreed that if _____ does not purchase from the Bank by _____ the _____ note secured by the Mortgage, then the general partners will promptly obtain for and on behalf of the Partnership a long-term loan (or loans) in the aggregate principal amount of _____ secured by one or more mortgages on the Property, on such terms and conditions as in the discretion of the general partners may be in the best interests of the Partnership and shall give written notice of the terms of such replacement loan(s) to the limited partners, who will have 30 days to accept or reject the terms of the

Joint Venture Agreements

replacement loan(s); if for any reason such terms are not acceptable to a majority in interest of the limited partners, then within 30 days after written notice of such lack of acceptance, the general partners shall redeem the interests of the limited partners by returning their initial capital contributions.

g. It is understood and agreed that the term "final closing date," as used in this Agreement, shall mean the sooner of _____ or the date on which the aggregate amount of money advanced or disbursed by_____ pursuant to the Note Purchase Agreement or by substitute mortgage or mortgages equals the sum of _____.

7. Additional capital contributions or loans

Additional contributions to capital or advances to the Partnership shall be governed by the following provisions.

a. No additional contributions, as such, to the Partnership shall be made by any limited partner, except upon the happening of the following event or events. At any time and from time to time subsequent to the date the limited partners shall have received from the Partnership distributions of an amount in cash equal to their respective initial capital contributions (whether such distributions shall have been out of profits of the Partnership or out of other available cash funds of the Partnership), the general partners may (but shall not be obligated to and no creditor of the Partnership shall be entitled to require such advance if the general partners shall not have voluntarily elected to do so) require the limited partners to make an advance or advances to the Partnership in order to meet the then current cash requirements of the Partnership, provided there are no other available funds. In such event each limited partner shall advance his or her pro rata share of any such advances required of the limited partners within 20 days after he or she shall have received a written request from the general partners stating the total amount required, the reason therefor, and the respective share thereof to be advanced by him or her. Notwithstanding the foregoing, the limited partners shall only be required to contribute 50 percent of the total amount required to be advanced as set forth in the general partners' notice, and the general partners agree that they shall advance the other 50 percent. Notwithstanding the foregoing, no limited partner shall be obligated to make an advance whatsoever to the Partnership, but if he or she is called upon to do so pursuant to the provisions of this subparagraph and elects not to do so, he or she must, within 10 days after the general partners' written request for an advance, give written notice of his or her refusal to do so to the general partners and all other limited partners; if any one or more of the other limited partners elects to advance the amount of such limited partner, then such other limited partner(s) must give written notice within 10 days after notice by the limited partner electing not to make the advance, to the general partners and all other limited partners of such election, and then any limited partner who has refused to advance the required amount shall promptly transfer and assign his or her limited partner's interest pro rata to the limited partner(s) who make his or her required advance. If any limited partner's required advance is not made within the required 20-day period (by such limited partner or by some other limited partner electing to do so), the advance shall be made by the general partners, and the defaulting limited partner's interest shall be transferred and assigned to the general partners.

b. If, at any time prior to the date the limited partners shall have received from the Partnership distributions of an amount in cash equal to their respective initial capital contributions, funds are needed to meet the current cash requirements of the Partnership, the general partners shall from time to time provide such funds in the following manner:

i. If the general partners have received any cash distributions pursuant to the provisions of subparagraph 8(a)(i) hereof, then the general partners shall provide the needed funds by making a cash contribution to capital to the extent of the lesser of the amount of funds needed or the amount of cash distributions previously received by the general partners pursuant to the provisions of subparagraph 8(a)(i) hereof, reduced by the amount of any such cash capital contributions previously made by the general partners pursuant to this subparagraph.

ii. If the general partners have not received any cash distributions pursuant to the provisions of subparagraph 8(a)(i) hereof, or if the general partners shall have already contributed pursuant to subparagraph 7(b)(ii) to the capital of the Partnership an amount equal to all of such cash distributions, then the general partners shall advance to the Partnership the needed funds, and the provisions of subparagraph c hereinafter shall apply to such advances.

c. If any partner (general or limited) shall, in excess of his or her contribution to the capital of the Partnership, advance any funds to the Partnership, the amount of any such advance shall not be an increase of his or her capital contribution or entitle him or her to any increase in the share of the distributions of the Partnership; but the amount of any such advance, except if made pursuant to subparagraph 7(b)(i), which shall be deemed a capital contribution and not an advance, shall be an obligation of the Partnership to such partner and shall be repaid without interest pursuant to subparagraph 8(a)(ii) hereof.

Joint Venture Agreements

d. No limited partner shall be personally liable for any debts of the Partnership or for any loss beyond the amount of his or her capital contributions as a limited partner.

8. *Cash distributions*

No limited partner shall be entitled to a return of his or her contribution to capital, as such, but the partners (general and limited) shall be entitled to distributions of the cash flow of the Partnership in accordance with the following provisions:

a. Cash flow (as hereinafter defined) of the Partnership shall be distributed to the general and limited partners in the following manner.

i. Until the "final closing date," as defined elsewhere herein, the general partners shall be entitled to distribute to themselves all cash flow of the Partnership. From and after the "final closing date" until the limited partners shall have received cash distributions aggregating an amount equal to their initial capital contributions (whether such distributions shall have been out of profits or otherwise), the limited partners shall be entitled to all cash flow of the Partnership.

ii. Thereafter, all cash flow shall be distributed pro rata to partners who may have advanced money to the Partnership, to the extent of such advances but without interest thereon.

iii. Thereafter, all cash flow of the Partnership shall be distributed 50 percent to the general partners and 50 percent to the limited partners.

b. For the purposes hereof, the term "cash flow" shall mean Partnership cash in hand or in banks at the end of each quarter, including reserves remaining from the immediately preceding quarter, less "cash reserves" as hereinafter defined. For purposes hereof, the term "cash reserves" shall mean the amount deemed reasonably necessary by the general partners to pay taxes, insurance, and/or other costs and expenses incident to the ownership or operation of the Property which shall become due and payable within the succeeding calendar quarter and for which the cash to make such payment(s) may not be generated by operations during such quarter.

c. Each limited partner shall share the cash flow of the Partnership to which the limited partners shall be entitled in the proportion that his or her capital contribution as a limited partner bears to the total capital contributions of all limited partners.

d. As among themselves, the general partners shall share equally in the cash flow of the Partnership to which the general partners shall be entitled.

e. Cash flow distributions shall be made to the partners entitled thereto within 35 days after the end of each calendar quarter of each year and at such additional times as the general partners may deem appropriate.

9. *Tax aspects*

The only share of the profits or other compensation by way of income that each partner (whether general or limited) shall receive by reason of his or her contribution to the Partnership shall be his or her share of the cash flow as set forth in paragraph 8 hereof; provided, however, that profits and losses of the Partnership shall be allocated, for federal income tax purposes, to the general and limited partners in the following manner:

a. Until the accumulated taxable income of the Partnership equals the accumulated tax losses, all taxable income and losses of the Partnership shall be allocated to the limited partners.

b. Thereafter, all taxable income and losses of the Partnership shall be allocated 50 percent to the limited partners and 50 percent to the general partners. Each limited partner shall share the taxable income and losses of the Partnership to which the limited partners shall be entitled in the proportion that his or her capital contribution as a limited partner bears to the total capital contributions of all limited partners. As among themselves, the general partners shall share equally in the taxable income and losses of the Partnership to which the general partners shall be entitled.

10. *Management*

The management of the Partnership shall be vested solely in the general partners except to the extent, if any, that such management power may be expressly limited herein below or elsewhere in this Partnership Agreement.

a. The general partners shall contribute their personal services to the Partnership and shall devote thereto such time as they in their discretion deem appropriate, without salary or other compensation except for their share of the cash flow as set forth in paragraph 8 hereof. Notwithstanding the foregoing, in the event the general partners shall personally supervise the day-to-day operations of the Property and shall not have hired any other person or entity for such purpose, the general partners shall be entitled, as their sole compensation for the rendering of such supervisory management services, an amount equivalent to 6 percent of the annual gross receipts derived from the operation of the Property (as distinguished from any sale, mortgage, or other disposition). It is understood and agreed that the general partners may hire to provide the supervisory management of the Property _____, a corporation ("Company"), the capital stock of which is owned by the general partners.

Any contracts for outside management shall be cancelable upon 30 days' written notice by the Partnership. It is understood and agreed that all direct costs of operating the Property shall be paid by the Partnership and that such direct costs shall include, without limitation, compensation of resident managers and leasing agents, maintenance and repair of buildings, grounds and facilities, utilities, supplies, insurance premiums, taxes, advertising expenses, bookkeeping and accounting expenses paid to third parties, as well as all other fees, costs, and expenses directly attributable to the ownership or operation of the Property.

b. Any of the partners, general or limited, may engage in other business ventures of every nature and description, independently or with others, including but not limited to the real estate business in all its phases, which shall include, without limitation, ownership, operation, management, syndication, and development of real property; and neither the Partnership nor the other partners thereof shall have any rights in and to such independent ventures or the income or profits derived therefrom.

c. The management decisions of the Partnership shall be determined by the consent or vote of a majority of the general partners. In order to expedite the handling of the Partnership's business, it is understood and agreed that any document executed by any two of the general partners while acting in the name and on behalf of the Partnership shall be deemed to be the action of the Partnership.

d. The general partners shall have the right and power to:

i. Sell and convey all or any part of the property owned by the Partnership, real and personal.

ii. Execute leases or modify leases of any real estate or any part thereof owned by the Partnership.

iii. Borrow money and as security therefor mortgage or otherwise encumber all or any part of the property owned by the Partnership, real or personal.

iv. Prepay in whole or in part, refinance, recast, increase, modify, consolidate, or extend any mortgage or other encumbrances that may affect any of the property owned by the Partnership, and, in connection therewith, to execute or cause to be executed for and on behalf of the Partnership any extensions, renewals, consolidations, or modifications of such mortgages in lieu of the existing mortgages.

v. Manage, improve, alter, and further develop the assets of the Partnership.

vi. Execute any and all other instruments to carry out the intention and purpose hereof, provided, however, that nothing contained herein shall increase the liability of the limited partners as herein stipulated.

e. i. Nothwithstanding the powers of the general partners set forth in subparagraph 10(d), without the prior written consent of the limited partners who shall have made not less than a majority of the total capital contributions of all limited partners, the general partners shall not have the right or the power to do any of the following:

A. Exercise the powers set forth in subsections i, iii, and iv of subparagraph 10(d), except that the general partners shall have the power to consummate the loan transaction with _____ in accordance with the Note Purchase Agreement and/or any loans up to the aggregate principal amount of _____, supplanting or supplementing such loan as provided in subparagraph 6(f) hereof.

B. Notwithstanding subsection 10(d)(ii), execute a lease of the Property other than for the occupancy of the individual apartment units in or on the Property.

C. Engage any person or entity to provide supervisory management of the Property for a fee in excess of 6 percent of the gross receipts derived from the operation of the Property.

D. Borrow money except as permitted by subparagraph A above and except for funds reasonably necessary for capital expenditures not in excess of $10,000, which loans must be on commercially reasonable terms.

ii. In the event that the general partners desire to consummate any of the transactions set forth in subjection i of this subparagraph, the general partners shall notify the limited partners in writing of such desire and shall set forth the terms and conditions of the particular transaction. A transfer of the Property or any part thereof to a nominee for the purpose of mortgage refinancing or other transactions described in subparagraph 10(d) shall not be construed as a sale or conveyance within the meaning of this or any other provision of this Partnership Agreement, provided that immediately after such transaction the Property be reassigned to the Partnership.

f. The general partners may employ, in behalf of the Partnership, such persons, firms, or corporations as they shall deem advisable for the operation and management of the Partnership or sale of any Partnership property, including such supervisory management agents, resident managers, leasing agents, brokers, accountants, and lawyers, and, subject to the provisions of subparagraph 10(e)(i)(C), on such terms and for such

Joint Venture Agreements

compensation as they shall determine, provided such terms are reasonable, and provided further that such services are reasonably necessary and customary.

g. The general partners shall also possess and enjoy, subject to any express limitations contained in this Partnership Agreement, all the rights and powers of partners in a partnership without limited partners, as provided in the Partnership Law of the State of _____.

h. No general partner shall be liable, responsible, or accountable in damages or otherwise to any of the partners, general or limited, for any acts performed by him or her in good faith within the scope of this Partnership Agreement.

i. The general partners shall determine the fiscal year of the Partnership.

j. At all times during the continuance of the Partnership the general partners shall keep or cause to be kept full and true books of account, which shall fully and accurately record each transaction of the Partnership. All of such books of account, together with a certified copy of the Certificate of Limited Partnership and any amendments thereto, shall at all times be maintained at the principal office of the Partnership and shall be open to the reasonable inspection and examination of the general partners and the limited partners and/or their representatives.

k. All funds of the Partnership are to be deposited in the Partnership name in such bank account or accounts as shall be designated by the general partners. Withdrawals from any such bank account or accounts shall be made upon such signature or signatures as the general partners may designate.

11. *Limitations on limited partners*

The limited partners shall take no part in the conduct or control of the Partnership business and shall have no right or authority to act for or bind the Partnership. Limited partners shall have no right to withdraw from the Partnership. Limited partners shall have no right to demand and receive property other than cash in return for their contributions, and their right to cash shall be limited to the rights set forth in paragraph 8 hereof.

12. *Transferability of limited partners' interests*

The power or right of a limited partner to assign or transfer his or her interest in the Partnership shall be governed by the following provisions:

a. Any limited partner may sell or transfer all or any part of his or her interest in the Partnership to any person who is a member of his or her immediate family (i.e., spouse, children, including those adopted and their direct descendants) or to another limited partner or to a corporation 51 percent or more of the issued and outstanding voting stock of which is owned by a limited partner or a member of his or her immediate family.

b. In the event a limited partner desires to sell or transfer all or any part of his or her limited partnership interest in the Partnership to any person(s) other than any of the foregoing pursuant to a bona fide offer therefor which he or she wishes to accept, such limited partner shall give notice in writing to the general partners, who shall, within 10 days of the receipt thereof, cause a similar notice to be sent to each of the limited partners. Said notice shall contain a statement setting forth the price and other conditions of such offer, and the name and address of the maker thereof. For a period of 30 days following such notice to the limited partners, the limited partners shall have the right pro rata to purchase the interest proposed to be sold on the same terms and conditions as the offer set forth in such notice. Any limited partner who desires to purchase such interest shall give notice in writing of such desire to the general partners within 30 days of the date that the general partners give notice. If no limited partner gives notice of his or her desire to purchase such interest, the selling limited partner may sell such interest to the person whose offer was set forth in such notice at any time during the six months following such 30-day period at the price and on the other conditions of such offer.

c. No assignee, legatee, transferee, or distributee of the whole or any portion of a limited partner's interest in the Partnership shall have the right to become a substitute limited partner in place of his or her predecessor in interest with respect to such limited partner's interest without the written consent of the general partners, whose consent shall be binding and conclusive without requiring the consent or approval of any of the other limited partners.

d. If a limited partner shall die, his or her executor, administrator, or trustee, or, if he or she shall be adjudicated insane or incompetent, his or her committee or representative, shall have the same rights and obligations that such limited partner would have had if he or she had not died or had not become insane or incompetent, except that the executor, administrator, trustee, committee, or representative (herein called "successor") shall not become a substitute limited partner without the written consent of the general partners.

e. As a condition of admission as a substitute limited partner with respect to the whole or any portion of the interest of his or her predecessor

Joint Venture Agreements

in interest, such assignee, legatee, transferee, distributee, or successor shall execute and acknowledge such instruments in form and substance reasonably satisfactory to the general partners, as the general partners shall deem necessary or desirable to effectuate such admission and to confirm the agreement of the person being admitted as such substitute limited partner to be bound by all of the terms and provisions of this Partnership Agreement, as the same may have been amended, with respect to the interest or portion of interest acquired from or through such predecessor in interest; and such assignee, legatee, transferee, distributee, or successor shall pay all reasonable expenses in connection with such admission as a substitute limited partner, including but not limited to the cost of preparation, filing, and publishing any amendment of the Certificate of Limited Partnership necessary or desirable in connection therewith.

f. If one or more limited partners purchases the interest of a limited partner in the Partnership, unless they agree among themselves upon a different method of paying the purchase price, each purchasing partner shall contribute a proportionate interest of such purchase price bearing the same relation to the whole purchase price as such partner's interest bears to the sum of the interests in the Partnership owned by the purchasing partners, and the interest so purchased shall be apportioned among the purchasing partners in the proportion that the interest in the Partnership owned by each purchasing partner bears to the total of the interests in the Partnership owned by all such purchasing partners.

g. No sale, assignment, or transfer of a limited partnership interest or portion thereof shall be made to a person who is not a citizen and resident of the United States.

h. No transfer, sale, or assignment shall be valid or effective unless it shall comply with the foregoing conditions.

13. *Dissolution of partnership*

The Partnership shall be dissolved and terminated before the expiration of the term fixed in paragraph 4 of this Partnership Agreement, upon the happening of any of the following events:

a. The sale of the Property or any major portion thereof.

b. The death, bankruptcy, or adjudication of insanity or incompetency of a general partner.

c. The retirement of one or the mutual agreement of all the general partners, provided, however, that the Partnership shall not be dissolved by such retirement or agreement during the first 10 years of the term thereof; provided, however, that in the event of the death, bankruptcy, or adjudication of insanity or incompetency of a general partner or the retirement of a general partner, the general partners may elect at their sole discretion not to dissolve and terminate the Partnership but to continue the same on the same terms and conditions, but with the deletion of the deceased, bankrupt, insane, incompetent, or retired general partner; subject, however, to the ability of the remaining or surviving general partners to effect the redemption or cancellation of the interest in the Partnership of such deceased, bankrupt, insane, incompetent, or retired general partner.

14. a. Upon the dissolution and termination of the Partnership at the death, bankruptcy, retirement, or adjudication of insanity or incompetency of any general partner, the remaining or surviving general partner(s) (hereinafter called the "dissolving general partners") shall have the right but not the obligation to form a new limited partnership upon substantially the same terms and conditions as those herein contained within 60 days of receiving notice of such death, bankruptcy, retirement, or adjudication of insanity or incompetency. Such new limited partnership (hereinafter called the New Partnership) shall be organized under the Uniform Limited Partnership Act of the State of _____.

b. In the event that the dissolving general partners shall determine to form the New Partnership, the limited partners shall become limited partners of the New Partnership. Each Limited Partner, including additional limited partners who shall become parties to this Partnership Agreement after the date hereof, hereby constitutes and appoints each general partner his or her true and lawful attorney for the following acts in the name, place, and stead of the limited partners after the dissolution of this Partnership and the filing of a certificate of cancellation of its Certificate of Limited Partnership: (i) to assign the then respective share of the limited partners in the capital of this Partnership to the New Partnership by way of capital contributions; (ii) to make, execute, sign, acknowledge, and file a new Certificate of Limited Partnership under the Partnership Law of the State of _____, containing provisions substantially the same as those appearing in the Certificate of Limited Partnership filed for this Partnership, as amended from time to time, except that the term of the New Partnership shall be for a period determined by the dissolving general partners, to be not less than the unexpired term of the present Partnership and not more than 25 years after the date of filing the Certificate of Limited Partnership of the New Partnership; and (iii) to do such other things as shall be necessary for the formation of the New Partnership under the laws of the State of _____.

c. In the event that the dissolving general partners decide to form the New Partnership, they shall give written notice of this determination to all limited partners of this Partnership at their respective addresses appearing in the records of this Partnership. Such notice shall also advise the limited partners that they have previously appointed the dissolving general partners attorney-in-fact to form a new limited partnership in their name.

d. If the dissolving general partners shall have determined to form the New Partnership, they shall convey the assets of this Partnership to the New Partnership, subject to liabilities of creditors, and shall establish capital accounts in the New Partnership in favor of the limited partners of this Partnership for whom they are authorized to act as attorney-in-fact, in the amount of their then respective shares of the capital of this Partnership, and shall cause to be prepared and shall execute, sign, and acknowledge in the name of the dissolving general partners and the limited partners for whom they are authorized to act as attorney-in-fact, and any additional persons who may be admitted as limited partners, a Certificate of Limited Partnership under the Uniform Limited Partnership Act of the State of _____, containing provisions substantially the same as those appearing in the Certificate of Limited Partnership filed for this Partnership, as amended from time to time, except for the term of the Partnership, and shall cause the same to be filed and shall cause such other things to be done as shall be necessary or proper for the formation of a limited partnership under the laws of the State of _____.

e. After the formation of the New Partnership, this Partnership Agreement, as amended from time to time, shall be deemed to conform to the changes reflected in the Certificate of Limited Partnership filed for the New Partnership, and so amended shall govern the rights of the partners of the New Partnership.

f. In the event of the death or adjudication of insanity or incompetency of any limited partner, if his or her legatee, distributee, transferee, or successor shall not have become a substitute limited partner before the dissolving general partners shall have given the notice referred to in subparagraph c of this paragraph of their determination with respect to the formation of the New Partnership, such limited partner or his or her legatee, transferee, distributee, or successor shall not become a limited partner of the New Partnership; provided, however, that the legatee, transferee, distributee, or successor of a decreased limited partner or the successor of an incompetent limited partner shall have the right to become a limited partner of the New Partnership in place of his or her predecessor in interest, with the consent of the dissolving general partners, upon executing and acknowledging such instruments in form and substance reasonably satisfactory or desirable to effectuate the admission of such person as a limited partner of the New Partnership.

g. In the event that this Partnership shall have been dissolved by reason of the bankruptcy or adjudication of insanity or incompetency of a general partner, he or she shall be deemed to have retired as a general partner of this Partnership as of the time of its dissolution for all purposes of this Partnership Agreement.

h. If the dissolving general patterns fail to continue the Partnership pursuant to paragraph 14(a) or upon the mutual agreement of the general partners to dissolve the Partnership, or upon the expiration of the Partnership term, the Partnership shall forthwith be dissolved and terminated, and any certificates or notice thereof required by law shall be filed. The general partners or the dissolving general partners, as the case may be, shall wind up and liquidate the Partnership by selling the Partnership property and, after paying the Partnership debts, by distributing the funds remaining in the manner provided in paragraph 8 hereof.

i. A reasonable time shall be allowed for the orderly liquidation of the assets of the Partnership, the discharge of liabilities to creditors, and the distribution of any remaining funds to the partners.

j. Each Partner shall be furnished with a statement prepared by the Partnership's accountants, which shall set forth the assets and liabilities of the Partnerhip as of the date of complete liquidation. Upon completion of distributions, the limited partners shall cease to be such, and the general partners or the dissolving general partners, as the sole remaining partners of the Partnership, shall execute, acknowledge, and cause to be filed a certificate of cancellation of the Partnership.

15. Anything in this Partnership Agreement to the contrary notwithstanding, it is understood and agreed that the general partners:

a. Except as provided in subparagraph 15(b)(y), shall not be personally liable for the return of the capital contribution of or the repayment of any advances or loans by the limited partners, or any portion thereof, it being expressly understood that any such return of contribution or repayment of advances and/or loans shall be made solely from the Partnership assets.

b. Shall not be obligated, from and after _____, (i) to contribute any money or property or advance any funds to the Partnership for any purpose whatsoever, or (ii) to borrow any funds on behalf of the Partnership as to which the general partners would be personally liable either as a partner of the Partnership or individually as maker, endorser, guarantor, surety or otherwise; provided, however, that notwithstanding the provisions of this subparagraph b, the following provisions shall be deemed controlling:

A. If at any time subsequent to the date the limited partners shall have received from the Partnership distributions of an amount in cash equal to their respective initial capital contributions and the general partners require the limited partners to make any advances to the Partnership pursuant to the terms of paragraph 7 hereof, then, of course, the general partners shall be obligated to advance to the Partnership their matching 50 percent of the total amount required to be advanced.

B. If at any time after _____ and before the date the limited partners shall have received from the Partnership distributions of an amount of cash equal to their respective capital contributions, additional funds would be required to meet the current obligations of the Partnership, but the general partners elect not to contribute any money or property or advance any funds to the Partnership or to otherwise obligate themselves so as to be or become personally liable for any indebtedness of the Partnership in order to raise the additional funds, then the general patterns shall properly give notice of such election to the limited partners. If, within 60 days of such notice, limited partners owning not less than 50 percent of limited partnership interests shall have agreed to continue the affairs of the Partnership with a new general partner or partners and shall have formed a successor Partnership by entering into an agreement for that purpose, then the general partners shall transfer and assign to the New Partnership, without cost, all of their right, title, and interest in this Partnership, which transfer and assignment the general partners hereby covenant and agree to do upon receipt of notice from a general partner of the Partnership, and such New Partnership shall be entitled to continue the business of the Partnership under its present name. Such successor Partnership shall have the right and obligation to buy from the limited partners of this Partnership all interest of such partners herein. A limited partner of this Partnership not contributing his or her entire interest to the New Partnership shall be obligated to sell to the successor partnership his or her remaining interest in this Partnership. The purchase price for any such interest shall be an amount equal to the excess of such limited partner's capital contribution over the aggregate amount of cash distributions he or she shall have received pursuant hereto. If at the expiration of such 60-day period the general partners shall not have received notice from a general partner of the New Partnership requesting such assignment and transfer, then the Partnership shall be dissolved and its assets liquidated in accordance with the provisions of subparagraphs h, i, and j of paragraph 14 hereof. In the event that the proceeds from liquidation are insufficient to effect a return to the limited partners of an amount equal to the excess of the limited partners' cash contributions over the amount of cash flow previously distributed to the limited partners, general partners shall be personally liable, jointly and severally, to the limited partners to pay to the limited partners within 30 days of the final liquidation of the Partnership an amount equal to such difference.

16. *Power of attorney*

Each limited partner constitutes and appoints the general partners, and each of them, his or her true and lawful attorney and in his or her name, place, and stead to make, execute, sign, acknowledge and deliver, and file:

   a. The Certificates of Limited Partnership and any amended Certificates or Certificates of Limited Partnership under the laws of the State of _____.

   b. Any certificate or other instrument that may be required to be filed by the Partnership under the laws of the State of _____ or the federal government.

   c. Any and all amendments or modifications of the instruments described in the preceding subparagraphs a and b.

   d. All documents that may be required to effectuate the dissolution and termination of the Partnership and cancellation of its Certificate of Limited Partnership, as amended from time to time.

   e. The Certificate of Limited Partnership and any amended Certificate or Certificates of Limited Partnership of the New Partnership.

   f. The foregoing power of attorney shall survive the delivery of any purported assignment by any of the limited partners of the whole or any portion of that partner's limited partnership interest.

17. *Notices*

   a. All notices given to the Partnership or to the general partners shall be in writing by registered or certified mail, addressed to the Partnership at its principal office.

   b. All notices given by the Partnership or by the general partners to any limited partner shall be in writing by registered or certified mail addressed to the address set opposite his or her signature at the end of this Partnership Agreement or to such address as such limited partner may hereafter designate in writing.

18. *Arbitration*

Any dispute or controversy arising under, out of, in connection with, or in relation to this Partnership Agreement and any amendments or proposed amendements thereto or any breach thereof or in connection with

Joint Venture Agreements

the dissolution of the Partnership shall be determined and settled by arbitration in the City of _____, pursuant to the rules of the American Arbitration Association. Any award rendered therein shall be final and binding on each and all of the partners, and judgment may be entered thereon in any court of competent jurisdiction.

19. *Amendments*

The Partnership Agreement may be amended from time to time with the written consent of all general partners and limited partners owning not less than 52 percent of the total capital contribution of all limited partners.

20. *Governing law*

This Partnership Agreement shall be governed by and construed in accordance with the laws of the State of _____.

21. *Successors and assigns*

Except as otherwise provided herein, this Partnership Agreement shall be binding upon and shall inure to the benefit of the parties, their successors, and their assigns.

22. *Counterpart execution*

This Partnership Agreement may be executed in counterparts, all of which taken together shall be deemed one original.

23. *Merger*

This Partnership Agreement contains the entire understanding between the parties and supersedes any prior understandings and agreements between them respecting the within subject matter.

In witness whereof, the parties hereto have executed this Partnership Agreement as of the day and year first above written.

General Partners:

_____

_____

_____

Limited Partners:

_____

_____

_____

A JOINT VENTURE AGREEMENT FAVORING AN INSTITUTIONAL INVESTOR

What the Agreement Should Cover

1. *Formation of venture*

   Here will be discussed the nature of the venture, whether a limited partnership or a general partnership, the purposes of the venture (one or more projects), and the location of the principal place of business of the venture.

2. *Management*

   The duties and responsibilities of the manager–developer will be delineated; his or her compensation will be laid out; his or her responsibilities, particularly for budget approval, and his or her contractual limitations in giving out work on behalf of the development will be laid out, as well as the specifics of what he or she must get consent to and what can be taken on on his or her own. There is a discussion here of the circumstances under which the general manager–developer may be replaced by the institutional investor.

3. *The development package*

   Here is delineated what is to be done, who is to do it, what it is to cost, and what will happen in case of cost or interest overruns.

4. *Financing*

   The obligations of the institutional investor to supply financial support are laid out here, and a discussion of the various financing stages, beginning with the development loan, running through the construction loan, and followed by the permanent loan, and any subsequent financing are all spelled out. Similarly, the obligations of the various venturers as to who will do what and what it will cost should be laid out here.

5. *Cash distributions and tax aspects*

   Here there should be a discussion of the profit-and-loss ratios, how cash distributions are to be made both out of current operations and out of sales and refinancing. The specifics of the tax treatment of the venture—what will happen to the tax aspects during the construction period, during the operational period, and on sale or refinancing—should be laid out here for each of the three major phases.

6. Dissolution and termination

Here will be discussed the term of the agreement, what happens if one party voluntarily wants to terminate it, what happens if there is a default on the part of one of the parties, what happens if one of the parties wants out, and, finally, what happens on liquidation and dissolution.

7. Assignments

Here is discussed the subject of whether either the developer or the institution can assign its interests to third parties.

8. Miscellaneous

Here will be a discussion of such items as notice clauses, governing laws, arbitration, and other boiler plate.

For other information in analyzing a joint venture agreement, see the Joint Venture Checklist and the Joint Venture Agreement, which is more developer-oriented, to see the other side of the coin and the questions to be raised in negotiations.

AGREEMENT

This Agreement, made and entered into this _____ day of _____, 19__, by and between _____, hereinafter referred to as the "Developer," and _____, a corporation having its principal office at _____, hereinafter referred to as the "Company."

WITNESSETH:

In consideration of the mutual covenants set forth herein and for other good and valuable consideration each party to the other in hand paid, receipt of which is hereby acknowledged, the parties hereto hereby agree as follows:

ARTICLE I
THE PARTNERSHIP

Section 1.01 *Formation*

a. Developer and Company hereby enter into and form a general partnership (herein called the "Venture") for the limited purposes and scope set forth herein. The business and affairs of the Venture shall be conducted solely under the name of "_____, A Joint Venture," and such name shall be used at all times in connection with the Venture's business and affairs. Developer and Company sometimes are referred to hereinafter collectively as "Venturers" and individually as "Venturer."

b. Except as expressly provided herein to the contrary, the rights and obligations of the Ventures and the administration and termination of the Venture shall be governed by the Uniform Partnership Act of the State of _____. A Venturer's interest in the Venture shall be personal property for all purposes. All real and other property owned by the Venture shall be deemed owned by the Venture as an entity, and no Venturer individually shall have any ownership of such property.

Section 1.02 *Purposes and scope of the venture*

a. Contemporaneously with the execution of this Agreement, Developer has transferred to the Venture certain property described in Exhibit A attached hereto and made a part hereof (hereinafter called the "Property") together with all buildings and other improvements located thereon, and described in Exhibit B attached hereto and made a part hereof (such buildings and improvements, together with any other buildings and improvements from time to time constructed or to be constructed on the Property, shall be hereinafter collectively called the "Improvements").

b. The Venture shall be limited strictly to the acquisition, development, and management of the Property and Improvements and land acquired by the Venture pursuant hereto within the area of interest, as defined in Section 7.02 hereof, for the production of income and profit, and shall not be extended by implication or otherwise unless approved by the Venturers.

c. Except for the rights of the Venturers set forth in Section 7.02 hereof, nothing in this Agreement shall be deemed to restrict in any way the freedom of any party hereto to conduct any other business or activity whatsoever (including the acquisition, development, and exploitation of real property) without any accountability to the Venture of any party hereto, even if such business or activity competes with the business of the Venture.

Section 1.03 *Assumed name certificate*

The Venturers shall execute any assumed or fictitious name certificate or certificate required by law to be filed in connection with the formation of the Venture and shall cause such certificate or certificates to be filed in the appropriate records.

Joint Venture Agreements

Section 1.4 *Scope of venturers' authority*

Except as otherwise expressly and specifically provided in this Agreement, no Venturer shall have any authority to act for, or assume any obligations or responsibility on behalf of, any other Venturer or the Venture.

ARTICLE II
MANAGEMENT

Section 2.01 *Management of the venture*

a. The overall management and control of the business and affairs of the Venture shall be vested in the Venturers, collectively. Except where herein expressly provided to the contrary, all decisions with respect to the management and control of the Venture approved by the Venturers shall be binding on the Joint Venture and all Venturers. When the phrase "approved by the Venturers" is used in this Agreement, such phrase shall mean approved in writing by both Venturers. The Venture shall have a manager (hereinafter called the "Manager"), who shall be designated pursuant to Section 2.03 hereof. The Manager shall be responsible for the implementation of the decisions of the Venturers and for conducting the ordinary and usual business and affairs of the Venture as more fully set forth in Section 2.03 hereof and as limited by this Agreement.

b. No act shall be taken, sum expended, decision made, or obligation incurred by the Venture, Manager, or any Venturer with respect to a matter within the scope of any of the major decisions (hereinafter called "Major Decisions") as enumerated below, unless each of the Major Decisions has been approved by the Venturers. The Major Decisions shall include:

1. Acquisition of any land or interest therein.
2. Financing of the Venture, including but not limited to the financing of the acquisition of the Property, interim and permanent financing of the Improvements, and financing operations of the Venture.
3. Sale, or other transfer, or mortgaging or the placing or suffering of any other encumbrance on any of the Property or the Improvements or any part or parts thereof.
4. Lease or other arrangement involving space in any Improvement, if such lease or other arrangement (i) covers more than _____, or (ii) provides for a term of more than _____ years, including all options to renew or otherwise extend the term, or (iii) provides for an annual rental in excess

of _____, or (iv) provides for annual rental or other terms less favorable to the Venture and the rental and other terms, if any, set forth in guidelines approved by the Venturers or which otherwise varies in any material respect from lease forms previously approved by the Venturers.

5. Terminating or modifying any lease or other arrangement involving space in any of the Improvements if such lease or other arrangement was required to be approved by the Venturers pursuant hereto or if such modification would result in a modified lease or other arrangement which, if it were a new lease, would be required to be approved by the Venturers pursuant hereto.

6. Construction of any Improvements or making any capital improvements, repairs, alterations, or changes. The decision on whether an improvement, repair, alteration, or change is or is not capital in nature shall be approved by the Venturers, and, if the Venturers cannot agree, such designation shall be made by arbitration in accordance with Article _____ hereof, in which arbitration the arbitrators shall make their determination on the basis of sound accounting practices.

7. Selecting or varying depreciation and accounting methods and making other decisions with respect to treatment of various transactions for federal income tax purposes, consistent with the other provisions of this Agreement.

8. Approval of all construction and architectural contracts and all architectural plans, specifications, and drawings before the construction of any improvements contemplated thereby.

9. Varying or changing any portion of the insurance program required by Company in accordance with Article III hereof.

10. Determining whether or not distributions should be made to the Venturers, except as set forth in Section 4.03 hereof.

11. Approving each budget pursuant to Section 2.04 hereof.

12. Making any expenditure or incurring any obligation by or of the Venture involving a sume in excess of _____ for any transaction or group of similar transactions except for expenditures made and obligations incurred pursuant to and specifically set forth in a budget theretofore approved by the Venturers; making any expenditure or incurring any obligation that when added to any other expenditure for the fiscal year of the Venture exceeds the budget by _____ percent; or making any

expenditure or incurring any obligation that falls into any category or categories of expenditures which in the opinion of Company and its counsel is required by law to have the prior approval of Company or its board of directors.
13. Determination of the maximum and minimum working capital requirements of the Venture.
14. Any other decision or action that by any provision of this Agreement is required to be approved by the Venture or that materially affects the Venture or the assets or operations thereof.

Section 2.02 *Appointment and replacement of manager*

   a. Company hereby approved the appointment of Developer as the Manager of the Joint Venture, and Developer shall discharge or cause the discharge of the duties thereof unless and until replaced pursuant to Section 2.02(b) hereof.

   b. Company may at any time at its option withdraw its approval of Developer as Manager and thereby terminate the appointment of Developer or any other person or entity herein or hereinafter named as Manager. Within 30 days of the withdrawal of approval by Company of the appointment of Developer or any other person or entity as Manager pursuant to the foregoing provisions of this Section 2.02(b), Company shall deliver to Developer a written statement setting forth the names of three responsible parties experienced in the management of real estate who would be acceptable to Company as Manager and the terms and conditions under which such parties would act as Manager. Within 10 days of receipt of such statement, Developer shall give Company a written notice setting forth the name of the party out of such three parties which Developer selects to act as Manager. In the event that Developer does not give the notice setting forth the name of the party selected to act as Manager within the 10 days, Company shall select the Manager from the list and give Developer notice of its selection. Upon receipt of notice from Developer, Company and Developer shall execute such documents and do such other acts as may be required to appoint such party as Manager.

Section 2.03 *Duties of manager*

   a. The original Manager or any replacement, at the expense of and on behalf of the Venture, shall implement or cause to be implemented all Major Decisions approved by the Venture and shall conduct or cause to be conducted the ordinary and usual business and affairs of the Venture in accordance with and as limited by this Agreement, including the following:

   1. Protect and preserve the title and interests of the Venture with respect to the Property and Improvements and other assets owned by the Venture.

   2. Pay all taxes, assessments, rents, and other impositions applicable to the Property and Improvements and other assets owned by the Venture.

   3. Negotiate and, when approved by the Venturers, enter into and supervise the performance of contracts covering the construction of any Improvements or any repairs or alterations.

   4. Lease to third parties space in the Improvements, provided, however, that where required by the Agreement such lease shall have been approved by the Venturers. In no event shall Manager collect more than one month's rent in advance unless approved by the Venturers.

   5. Keep all books of account and other records of the Venture in accordance with the terms of this Agreement.

   6. Prepare and deliver to each of the Venturers periodic reports not less than quarterly of the state of the business and affairs of the Venture.

   7. Have an annual audit of the Venturer's books made by a firm of Certified Public Accountants of nationally recognized standing approved by the Venturers, and furnish each Venturer with a copy of such annual audit, including a balance sheet, a statement of the capital accounts of the Venture, and a statement of income, together with the certificate of said accountants covering the results of such audit as soon as reasonably practicable after the close of the Venture's fiscal year but in no event later than the date required by the Venture's lenders or mortgagees. In addition, within 75 days of the end of each fiscal year, the Manager shall have such accountants prepare and deliver to each Venturer a report setting forth in sufficient detail all such information and data with respect to business transactions affected by or involving the Venture during such fiscal year as shall enable the Venture and such Venturer to prepare its state, federal, and local income tax returns in accordance with the laws, rules, and regulations then prevailing. The Manager shall have such accountants also prepare federal, state, and local tax returns required of the Venture and shall file the same after approval by the Venturers. The Manager shall also furnish to each Venturer such other reports on the Venture's operations and condition as may be reasonably requested by either Venturer.

Joint Venture Agreements

8. Retain or employ and coordinate the services of all employees, supervisors, architects, engineers, accountants, attorneys, and other persons necessary or appropriate to carry out the business of the Venture, provided, however, that Manager shall not enter into any agreement with any such person which would require the Venture to pay more than $20,000 per year to any such person unless such agreement has been approved by the Venturers specifically or if such payment is specifically itemized in the budget by prior approval of the budget, and further provided that the Manager will not engage the services of any architects, engineers, accountants, or attorneys unless and until approved by the Venturers, and after such parties or any other parties or organizations performing personal services have been so engaged, Manager shall give the Venturers notice thereof, and at any time thereafter Manager shall discharge and terminate the services of any one or more of such parties upon receipt of a request therefor from any Venturer sent to Manager and the other Venturer. Manager shall report in writing to the Venturers at least quarterly all payments to any person for services in connection with the Venture, regardless of the amount of such compensation.

9. To the extent that funds of the Venture are available therefor, pay all debts and other obligations of the Venture, including amounts due under permanent financing of the Improvements and other loans to the Venture previously approved by the Venturers and costs of construction, operation, and maintenance of the Property and Improvements.

10. Maintain all funds of the Venture held by Manager in account and in a bank or banks approved by Company.

11. When approved by the Venturers pursuant to this Agreement, make distributions periodically to the Venturers in accordance with the provisions of this Agreement.

12. Operate, maintain, repair, and otherwise manage the Improvements, including the performance of such functions as the collection of rent, providing of utility, cleaning, repair and maintenance services to be furnished to the Venture or by the Venture, as landlord, under the respective leases involved, all in accordance with and as limited by this Agreement.

13. During the term of this Agreement, Manager shall promptly comply with all present and future laws, ordinances, orders, rules, regulations, and requirements of all federal, state, and municipal governments, courts, departments, commissions, boards and officers, the Constitution of the United States of America, any national or local board of Fire Underwriters, or any other body exercising functions similar to those

of any of the foregoing which may be applicable to the Property and Improvements and the operation and management thereof (including, without limitation, laws, ordinances, orders, rules, regulations, and requirements prohibiting restraints on trade, or discrimination whether on the basis of race, creed, color, national origin, or otherwise).

14. Perform other normal business functions and otherwise operate and manage the business and affairs of the Venture in accordance with and as limited by this Agreement.

15. Perform other obligations provided elsewhere in this Agreement to be performed by the Manager.

b. Any provision hereof to the contrary notwithstanding, except for expenditures made and obligations incurred previously approved by the Venturers or in direct pursuance of a budget approved by the Venturers or otherwise not required by the Venturers, Manager shall not have any authority to make expenditures or incur obligations on behalf of the Venture. Manager shall not expend more than the fair and reasonable market value at the time and place of delivery or performance for any goods purchased or services engaged on behalf of the Venture.

c. No part of Manager's central office overhead or Manager's (as distinguished from Venture's) general or administrative expense shall be deemed to be an expense of the Venture.

d. Any provision hereof to the contrary notwithstanding, all contracts, agreements, leases, or other arrangements for the furnishing to the Venture of goods, services, or space shall be terminable by the Venture on 60 days' notice unless a waiver of such right to terminate on such notice is approved by the Venturers.

Section 2.04 *Budgets*

Not less often than one time each fiscal year, Manager shall prepare and submit to the Venturers for their consideration a budget setting forth the estimated receipts and expenditures (capital, operating, and other) of the Venture for the period covered by the budget. When approved by the Venturers, Manager shall implement the budget and shall be authorized subject to the requirements of Section 2.01(12), without the need for further approval by the Venturers, to make the expenditures and incur the obligations provided for in the budget.

Section 2.05 *Compensation of venturers*

a. Except as may be expressly provided for herein or hereafter approved by the Venturers, no payment will be made by the Venture to

Joint Venture Agreements

any Venturer for the services of such Venturer or any member stockholder, director, or employee of any Venturer.

b. Each of the Venturers shall be reimbursed by the Venture for the reasonable out-of-pocket expenses incurred by such Venturer subsequent to the date hereof on behalf of the Venture in connection with the business and affairs of the Venture.

Section 2.06 *Contracts with related parties*

The Manager shall not enter into any contract, agreement, lease, or other arrangement for the furnishing to or by the Venture of goods, services, or space with any party or entity related to or affiliated with any Venturer or with respect to which any Venturer or party or entity related to or affiliated with any Venturer has any direct or indirect ownership or control unless such contract, agreement, or arrangement has been approved by the Venturers. By way of illustration and not as a limitation on the scope of the phrase "related or affiliated with," for the purposes of this Section 2.06, if the following persons or entities have any interest in persons or entities who are supplying or who will supply goods or services to the Venture, the supplying person or entity shall be deemed to be related to or affiliated with a Venturer:

Any corporation, partnership, association, or other entity (hereinafter in this Section referred to as "Entity") owned in whole or in part by _____; any holder of more than 10 percent of the issued and outstanding shares of or holder of more than a 10 percent interest in any Entity owned in whole or in part by _____; any Entity in which any officer, director, employee, partner, or shareholder (or a member of the family of any such officer, director, employee, partner, or shareholder) of any Entity owned by _____ has a direct or indirect interest in such Entity, which interest includes but is not limited to a partnership, employee, agent, or stockholder interest or any other form of interest.

ARTICLE III
INSURANCE

Section 3.01 *Minimum insurance requirements*

a. The Venture shall carry and maintain in force the following insurance, the premium for which shall be a cost and expense in connection with the operation of the Venture:

i. Workers' Compensation Insurance (including Employers' Liability Insurance for an amount not less than _____) covering all employees of the Venture employed in, on, or about the property of the Venture to provide statutory benefits as required by the laws of the State of _____.

ii. Comprehensive General Liability Insurance (including protective liability coverage on operations of independent contractors engaged in construction and also blanket contractual liability insurance) on an occurrence basis for the benefit of the Venturers as named insureds against claims for personal injury liability, including without limitation bodily injury, death, or property damage liability with limits of not less than _____ in the event of personal injury to one person and not less than _____ in the event of personal injury to any number of persons in any one occurrence, and with a limit of not less than _____ for property damage; such insurance shall also include coverage against liability for bodily injuries or property damage arising out of the use by or on behalf of the Venturers of any owned, nonowned, or hired automotive equipment for limits not less than those specified above.

iii. All Risks Builders Risk Insurance, including coverage against collapse, written on a completed value basis in an amount not less than the total value of the Improvements under construction (less the value of the Improvements that are uninsurable under the policy—site preparation, grading, paving, parking lots, etc.—excepting, however, foundations and other undersurface installations subject to collapse or damage by other insured perils) including, if applicable, the coverages available under the so-called Installation Floater, all in form and amount as may from time to time be required by any mortgagee of any project under construction, and fire and extended coverage insurance on the completed Improvements in an amount not less than 100 percent of the actual replacement cost of such Improvements (exclusive of excavation and foundation costs and costs of underground tanks, conduits, pilings, and other similar underground lines) without deduction for physical depreciation thereof, or for such larger amounts and against such additional perils as may from time to time be required by any mortgagee of such Improvements; such insurance on the completed Improvements shall contain the Replacement Cost Endorsement.

iv. Crime insurance in connection with all operations of the Venture and the business and affairs arising out of or in connection with the Property and Improvements and assets of the Venture.

v. Such other insurance, including but not limited to insurance on rental income as may be requested by Company.

b. All such aforesaid policies of insurance shall name all Venturers as named insureds, as their respective interests may appear. All such insurance shall be effected under policies issued by insurers and shall be in forms and for amounts approved by Company.

c. Within 30 days of the execution of the Agreement, the Company and Developer shall each select an insurance broker, and such insurance brokers shall independently and within 30 days of their selection develop an insurance program and obtain a premium quotation thereon. The Venturers shall agree in advance about which insurance companies will be approached by the brokers so that the brokers shall not approach the same insurance companies. The Venturers agree that the insurance broker who provides the more desirable insurance program from a coverage, service, and cost standpoint will be utilized to provide the insurance. In the event that the insurance proposals of the brokers are not considered to differ substantially in coverage, service, or cost, then the insurance broker selected by Developer shall be used.

ARTICLE IV
ACCOUNTING AND DISTRIBUTION

Section 4.01 *Interest, income, profits, and distributions*

a. The income, profits, and other distributions of the Venture shall be received by the Venturers in the percentages (hereinafter referred to as the "distribution percentage interest") set forth opposite each of their names below, to wit:

Developer __%
Company __%

Depreciation, net cash flow as hereinafter defined, and amortization, as such terms are used for the purposes of the Internal Revenue Code, shall be allocated to Company and Developer in their respective distribution percentage interests.

b. At such time as Company shall have received in distributions a sum equal to Company's capital contribution as that term is defined in that certain letter agreement dated _____, between Company and Developer together with any additional company capital contribution made by the Company subsequent thereto, the distribution percentage interests set forth above shall be amended as follows:

Developer 50%
Company 50%

Section 4.02 *Tax status, allocations, and reports*

a. Any provision hereof to the contrary notwithstanding, solely for U.S. federal income tax purposes, each of the Venturers hereby recognizes that the Venture will be subject to all provisions of Subchapter K of Chapter 1 of Subtitle A of the U.S. Internal Revenue Code of 1954; provided, however, that the filing of U.S. Partnership Returns of Income shall not be construed to extend the purposes of the Venture or expand the obligations or liabilities of the Venturers. At the request of Company, the Venture shall file an election under Section 754 of the U.S. Internal Revenue Code of 1954.

b. Manager shall prepare or cause to be prepared all tax returns and statements, if any, which must be filed on behalf of the Venture regarding this transaction with any taxing authority, and shall submit such returns and statements to all of the Venturers for their approval before filing and, when approved by the Venturers, make timely filing thereof.

c. Subject to the succeeding provisions of this Section for accounting and federal and state income tax purposes, except as herein otherwise specifically provided, all income, deductions, credits, gains, and losses of the transaction shall be allocated to the Venturers in proportion to their respective distribution percentage interests. Any item stipulated to be an expense of the Venture under the terms of this Agreement or that would be so treated in accordance with generally accepted accounting principles shall be treated as the expense of the Venture for all purposes hereunder, whether or not such item is deductible for purposes of computing net income for federal income tax purposes. The interest payable or distributable to any Venturer shall be considered an expense when paid in determining allocable income or loss of the transaction and shall be income allocable to the Venturer receiving it.

Section 4.03 *Distributions to venturers*

Within 30 days of the close of each calendar quarter, the Manager shall distribute the net cash flow of the Venture for the preceding calendar quarter in accordance with the distribution percentage interests of the Venturers as set forth in Section 4.01 hereof. For the purposes of this Article, "net cash flow" shall mean a plus b minus the aggregate of c and d as follows:

a. The gross income from the Venture assets computed in accordance with sound cash basis accounting principles, including all income earned or received from all sources whatsoever as a direct or indirect result of the ownership or operation of the Joint Venture assets such as, but without

Joint Venture Agreements

limitation, (i) the gross amount of all cash payments received whether as rent, additional rent, fees, charges, or otherwise, (ii) sundry income, (iii) concession income, (iv) interest on deposits, (v) the net amount of any refund of imposition of taxes applicable to any period of this Agreement, (vi) the proceeds from the sale of any property, including securities, notes, or other obligations received in lieu of or in addition to such cash payments, (vii) the proceeds of any sale of personal property or fixtures now or hereafter located on the Property and Improvements, and (viii) the amount of any other consideration, tangible or intangible, received in relation to or in connection with the Property and Improvements or any appurtenance thereto (but not including proceeds of insurance received and used or to be used for restoration of the Property and Improvements in the event of damage or destruction thereof, or proceeds of any sale, assignment, transfer, or mortgage as permitted herein of the whole or any part of the interest of a party hereto) received by the Venture, any of the Venturers, the Manager, or any other person on behalf of the Venture or by any associates, subsidies, agents, officers, directors, or employees of any of the Venturers or the Manager or by any corporation, partnership, organization, or individual in which the Venturers or the Manager or their associates, directors, officers, agents, or employees have any interest, direct or indirect, attributable in any degree to the ownership, leasing, management, operation, use, or servicing of the Property and Improvements or other assets of the Venture.

b. The amount of (i) any unused portion of any capital contributions of the Venturers; (ii) any proceeds received from the mortgaging of the Property and Improvements, the refinancing (to the extent that the proceeds exceed the amount of the mortgage or deed of trust being refinanced) of any mortgage or deed of trust on the Property and Improvements, or the sale of the Property and Improvements or any part thereof; and (iii) any payments received as a result of any other transactions involving the ownership, operation, or maintenance of the Property and Improvements that do not come within a above.

c. In accordance with sound cash-basis accounting principles consistently applied, insurance charges, real estate taxes, assessments, reasonable legal expenses, water, fuel, electricity, repairs and maintenance, supplies, decorating, normal fees paid to Certified Public Accountants, reasonable management expenses, and any other items that are normally considered operating expenses (excluding, however, any income or franchise tax imposed by federal, state, or local governments on either of the Venturers in their individual capacity, plus the aggregate amount of principal and interest paid under mortgages or deeds of trust on the Property and Improvements and under loans incurred in connection with the Property and Improvements as well as the cost of capital acquisition, alterations, or improvements, to the extent of payments made or provided for during the fiscal year (except that in the event and to the extent that capital acquisitions, alterations, or improvements are paid for out of borrowed funds, the amount paid or provided during the fiscal year for interest and amortization on mortgages or deeds of trust or loans made for such purpose shall be deducted from net cash flow in lieu of deducting the cost of such capital alterations and Improvements).

d. A reasonable reserve for budgeted tenant's work and for interest and amortization on mortgages or deeds of trust and loans, real estate taxes, assessments, water charges, sewer rents, insurance, commissions, and other expenses generally treated on an accrual basis.

In computing net cash flow, no deduction shall be made for depreciation or amortization as such terms are used for the purposes of the Internal Revenue Code, it being agreed that depreciation and amortization shall be allocated to each Venturer in proportion to its distribution percentage interest.

Section 4.04 *Accounting*

a. The fiscal year of the Venture shall be the calendar year.

b. The books of account of the Venture shall be kept and maintained at all times at the place or places approved by the Venturers. The books of account shall be maintained on an accrual basis in accordance with generally accepted accounting principles, consistently applied, and shall show all items of income and expense.

c The Manager shall prepare and furnish to each of the Venturers promptly after the close of each calendar quarter an unaudited statement, certified by Manager to be true and correct to the best of his or her knowledge and belief, showing the receipts and disbursements for the Venture for the preceding quarter, the balance in each Venturer's capital account, the unpaid balance under all obligations of the Venture, and all other information reasonably requested by any Venturer. The Manager shall cause to be prepared and furnished to each Venturer promptly after the close of each fiscal year a balance sheet of the Venture dated as of the end of the fiscal year, a related statement of income or loss for the Venture for such fiscal year, and the same information for the fiscal year as is required to be included in the aforesaid quarterly reports, all of which shall be certified in the customary manner by a firm of independent Certified Public Accountants approved by the Venturers.

d. Each Venturer shall have the right at all reasonable times during usual business hours to audit, examine, and make copies of or extracts from the books of account of the Venture. Such right may be exercised through any agent or employee of such Venturer designated by him or her or by an indpendent Certified Public Accountant designated by such Venturer. Each Venturer shall bear all expenses incurred in any examination made for such Venturer's account.

Section 4.05 *Bank accounts*

Funds of the Venture shall be deposited in an account or accounts of a type and form and in a name and a bank or banks approved by Company. Withdrawals from bank accounts shall be made by parties approved by the Venturers.

ARTICLE V
TERM AND TERMINATION

Section 5.01 *Term*

The Venture shall commence on the date hereof and shall continue until terminated and liquidated in accordance with the provisions hereof.

Section 5.02 *Voluntary termination*

Subject to the provisions of this Article, any Venturer shall have the right to withdraw from the Venture at any time and thereby cause the Venture to be terminated as hereinafter provided, by giving the Manager and all Venturers notice thereof and by delivering to all Venturers the offer required pursuant to Section 5.07(a). The Venturer giving such notice shall be referred to herein as the "Withdrawing Venturer."

Section 5.03 *Automatic termination*

a. If any of the following events shall occur, namely:

1. If any Venturer shall file a voluntary petition in bankruptcy or shall be adjudicated a bankrupt or insolvent or shall file any petition or answer seeking any reorganization, arrangement, composition, readjustment, liquidation, dissolution, or similar relief for itself under the present or any future federal bankruptcy act or any other present or future applicable federal, state, or other statute or law relative to bankruptcy, insolvency, or other relief for debtors or shall seek or consent to or acquiesce in the appointment of any trustee, receiver, conservator, or liquidator of

said Venturer or of all or any substantial part of said Venturer's properties or said Venturer's interest in the Venture (the term "acquiesce" as used in this Article includes but is not limited to the failure to file a petition or motion to vacate or discharge any order, judgment, or decree within 10 days of such order, judgment, or decree).

2. If a court of competent jurisdiction shall enter an order, judgment, or decree approving a petition filed against any Venturer seeking any reorganization, arrangement, composition, readjustment, liquidation, dissolution, or similar relief under the present or any future federal bankruptcy act or any other present or future applicable federal, state, or other statute or law relating to bankruptcy, insolvency, or other relief for debtors, and said Venturer shall acquiesce in the entry of such order, judgment, or decree or such order, judgment, or decree shall remain unvacated and unstayed for an aggregate of 60 days (whether or not consecutive) from the date of entry thereof, or any trustee, receiver, conservator, or liquidator of said Venturer or of all or any substantial part of said Venturer's property or said Venturer's interest in the Venture shall be appointed without the consent or acquiescence of said Venturer and such appointment shall remain unvacated and unstayed for an aggregate of 60 days (whether or not consecutive).

3. Any Venturer shall admit in writing its inability to pay its debts as they mature.

4. If any Venturer shall give notice to any governmental body of insolvency or pending insolvency or suspension or pending suspension of operations.

5. If any Venturer shall make an assignment for the benefit of creditors or take any other similar action for the protection or benefit of creditors.

Then, and in any such event, the Venture shall terminate automatically, and such Venturer shall be deemed, as of the date of occurrence of the respective event, to be the Withdrawing Venturer.

b. The Venture shall terminate automatically upon the dissolution or termination of any corporation or partnership that is or shall hereafter become a Venturer except where there is a transfer pursuant to Section 5.02 hereof and subsequent dissolution of such corporation or partnership. The corporation or partnership that is a Venturer that so dissolves or terminates shall be the Withdrawing Venturer.

Section 5.04 *Termination for default*

a. If any Venturer fails to perform any of its respective obligations hereunder, the other Venturer (herein called the "Nondefaulting Venturer") shall have the right to give the defaulting Venturer (herein called the "Defaulting Venturer") a notice of default. The notice of default shall set forth the nature of the default.

b. If, within the 30-day period following receipt of the notice of default, the Defaulting Venturer in good faith commences to cure such default and thereafter prosecutes to completion with diligence and continuity the curing thereof and cures such default within a reasonable time, it shall be deemed that the notice of default was not given and the Defaulting Venturer shall lose no rights hereunder. If, within such 30-day period, the Defaulting Venturer does not commence in good faith the curing of such default, does not thereafter prosecute to completion with diligence and continuity the curing thereof, the Nondefaulting Venturer hereunder shall have the right to terminate this Venture by giving the Defaulting Venturer and all other Venturers written notice thereof. If the Joint Venture is so terminated, the Defaulting Venturer shall be deemed to be the Withdrawing Venturer.

c. The foregoing subparagraph of this Section 5.04 shall not apply to any default with respect to the payment of any sums of money by or to any Venturer, which sums of money shall be paid within 15 days of receipt of a notice of default with respect thereto. If such sums are not so paid within such 15-day period, the Nondefaulting Venturer shall have the right to terminate this Venture by giving the Defaulting Venturer notice thereof, whereupon the Defaulting Venturer shall be deemed the Withdrawing Venturer.

Section 5.05 *Community of interests*

a. If Company or any assignee of the interest of Company is the Withdrawing Venturer, it shall be deemed that Company and all such assignors are the Withdrawing Venturers, and the entire distribution percentage interest of Company shall be deemed to be the interest of the Withdrawing Venturer for the purposes of Sections 5.06, 5.07, and 5.08 hereof. In such case Developer and its respective assignees shall be deemed the Nonwithdrawing Venturer and the entire distribution percentage interest of such parties shall be deemed to be the interest of the Nonwithdrawing Venturer for the purposes of Sections 5.06, 5.07, and 5.08 hereof.

b. If Developer or any assignee of the interest of Developer is the Withdrawing Venturer, it shall be deemed that Developer and all such assignees are the Withdrawing Venturer, and the entire distribution percentage interest of such parties is the interest of the Withdrawing Venturer for the purposes of Sections 5.06, 5.07, and 5.08 hereof. In such case, Company and the assignees of Company's interests shall be deemed the

Nonwithdrawing Venturer, and the entire distribution percentage interest of such parties deemed to be the interest of the Nonwithdrawing Venturer for the purposes of Sections 5.06, 5.07, and 5.08 hereof.

Section 5.06 *Remedies of nonwithdrawing venturer*

a. In the event of a termination of the Venture pursuant to Section 5.02 hereof, the Nonwithdrawing Venturer shall elect to institute the buy–sell procedures set forth in subsections 5.07(b), (c), and (d) hereof.

b. In the event of termination of the Venture pursuant to Sections 5.03 or 5.04 hereof, the Nonwithdrawing Venturer, at its election, may do either of the following:

1. Institute the buy–sell procedure set forth in Section 5.07 hereof.

2. Purchase the entire interest in the Venture of the Withdrawing Venturer pursuant to the appraisal procedure set forth in Section 5.08 hereof.

c. The rights of the Nonwithdrawing Venturer under this Article shall not be the exclusive remedies of the Nonwithdrawing Venture but shall be in addition to all other rights and remedies, if any, available to the Nonwithdrawing Venturer at law or in equity.

Section 5.07 *Buy–sell procedures*

a. If, upon termination of this Agreement pursuant to Section 5.03 or Section 5.04 hereof, the Nonwithdrawing Venturer elects to proceed under this Section 5.07, or if the Agreement is terminated pursuant to Section 5.02 hereof, such Venturer shall give notice thereof to the Withdrawing Venturer within 30 days of such termination. Within 30 days of receipt of such notice, the Withdrawing Venturer shall deliver to the Nonwithdrawing Venturer an offer in writing, stating the cash purchase price at which the Withdrawing Venturer is willing to purchase the Property and Improvements. Such price shall be the Withdrawing Venturer appraisal of the amount by which the value of the Property and Improvements is in excess of the aggregate unpaid principal amount of the mortgages, deeds of trust, or other liens subject to which the Property and Improvements shall be conveyed. Manager shall furnish, or, where appropriate, make available to the Withdrawing Venturer, or use his or her best efforts to obtain from third parties for the Withdrawing Venturer such certificates, documents, and information as the Withdrawing Venturer may reasonably request in order to enable the Withdrawing Venturer to prepare the offer. Upon failure of the Withdrawing Venturer to deliver to the Nonwithdrawing Venturer the offer within such 30-day period, the Nonwithdrawing Ven-

Joint Venture Agreements

turer may elect to proceed pursuant to Section 5.06(b)(2) hereof by giving notice of such election to the Withdrawing Venturer.

b. Upon receipt of the offer given and subject to the provisions of subparagraph c hereof and delivered pursuant to Section 5.07(a) hereof:

1. The Nonwithdrawing Venture shall purchase the Property and Improvements for cash at a price equal to the amount of the offer.
2. Or the Partnership shall sell to the Withdrawing Venturer and the Withdrawing Venturer shall purchase the Property and Improvements for cash at a price equal to the amount of the offer.

The Nonwithdrawing Venturer shall give written notice of such election to the Withdrawing Venturer within 30 days of receipt of the offer. Failure of the Nonwithdrawing Venturer to give the Withdrawing Venturer notice that the Nonwithdrawing Venturer has elected under subsection 1 above shall be conclusively deemed to be an election under 2 above.

c. The closing of a purchase pursuant hereto shall be held at a mutually acceptable place in _____ on a mutually acceptable date not more than 90 days after receipt of the offer by the Nonwithdrawing Venturer. The Venture shall convey by bargain and sale deed to the purchasing party the Property and Improvements free and clear of all claims, encumbrances, and liens except the mortgages, deeds of trust, or other liens listed in the offer as being the mortgages, deeds of trust, or other liens subject to which the Property and Improvements are being sold. The purchasing party shall pay the purchase price therefor in cash or by a good certified check after the parties have made the normal and customary real estate closing adjustments in the locality in which the Property is located.

d. If either the Withdrawing Venturer or the Nonwithdrawing Venturer elects, pursuant to Section 5.07(b) hereof, to purchase the Property and Improvements but thereafter does not conclude the purchase pursuant hereto, then such party ("Defaulter") shall be deemed to be in default pursuant hereto, and the other party ("Nondefaulter"), in addition to its other rights and remedies, may (i) continue this Agreement, (ii) purchase the Property and Improvements of the defaulter at the purchase price stated in the offer, or (iii) purchase the Property and Improvements pursuant to Section 5.08.

Section 5.08 *Appraisal procedure*

a. In the event of an election by the Nonwithdrawing Venturer pursuant to Section 5.06(b)(2) hereof to proceed under this section or in the event Section 5.07(d) becomes operative and the Nondefaulter thereafter elects to proceed under this Section 5.08, to purchase the Property and Improvements at the appraised value thereof, such party shall give the Withdrawing Venturer or Defaulter notice thereof within 30 days of such election, and, in such notice, shall designate the first appraiser ("First Appraiser").

b. Within 15 days of the notice referred to in Section 5.08(a) hereof, the Withdrawing Venturer or Defaulter shall give notice to the Nonwithdrawing Venturer designating the second appraiser ("Second Appraiser"). If the Second Appraiser is not so designated within or by the time above specified, then the appointment of the Second Appraiser shall be made in the same manner as is hereinafter provided for the appointment of a Third Appraiser in the event that the First and Second Appraisers are unable to agree upon the Third Appraiser. The First and Second Appraisers so designated or appointed shall meet within 10 days after the Second Appraiser is appointed, and if, within 30 days after the Second Appraiser is appointed, the First and Second Appraisers do not agree upon appraised value, as more fully set forth in Section 5.08(c) hereof, they shall themselves appoint a Third Appraiser, who shall be a competent and impartial person; and in the event of their being unable to agree upon such appointment within 15 days of the time aforesaid, the Third Appraiser shall be selected by the parties themselves if they can agree thereon within a further period of 15 days. If the parties do not so agree, then either party, on behalf of both, may request such appointment by _____.

In the event of the failure, refusal, or inability of any appraiser to act, a new appraiser shall be appointed instead, which appointment shall be made in the same manner as hereinbefore provided for the appointment of such appraiser so failing, refusing, or being unable to act. Each party shall pay the fees and expenses of the one of the two original appraisers appointed by such party, or in whose stead, as above provided, such appraiser was appointed, and the fees and expenses of the Third Appraiser, and all other expenses, if any, shall be borne equally by both parties. Any appraiser designated to serve in accordance with the provisions of this Agreement shall be disinterested and shall be qualified to appraise real estate in _____ of the type covered by this Agreement, shall be a member of the American Institute of Real Estate Appraisers (or any successor association or body of comparable standing if such Institute is not then in existence) and shall have been actively engaged in the appraisal of real estate in _____, for a period of not less than five years immediately preceding his or her appointment.

c. The appraisers shall determine the appraised value of the Property and Improvements, which shall be the amount by which (i) the fair market value at the time such appraisal is made of the Property and Improvements is in excess of (ii) the aggregate unpaid principal amount of the mortgages, deeds of trust, and other liens affecting the Property and Improvements as of the date of appraisal. A decision joined in by two of the three appraisers shall be the decision of the appraisers. After reaching a decision, the appraisers shall give written notice thereof to the Venturers.

d. The Nonwithdrawing Venturer shall purchase the Property and Improvements for a cash price equal to the appraised value. The closing of such purchase shall occur at a mutually acceptable time within 90 days after notice of the decision of the appraisers has been delivered to the Venturers, and otherwise shall be conducted in accordance with Section 5.07(c) hereof.

e. If the appraisers fail to reach a decision within 90 days of the appointment of the Third Appraiser, the Nonwithdrawing Venturer, in addition to its other rights and remedies, may (i) elect to extend the time within which the appraisers must reach a decision by a period of not less than 30 nor more than 60 days, or (ii) withdraw its election to purchase the Property and Improvements pursuant to this Section 5.08, and continue this Agreement or institute the buy–sell procedure set forth in Section 5.07 by giving the Withdrawing Venturer notice thereof within 30 days of the end of such 90-day period. If the appraisers fail to reach a decision within any such extended period of time, there shall be no further extensions, and the appraisal procedure shall terminate. Upon such termination the Nonwithdrawing Venturer shall make the elections set forth in ii above.

Section 5.09 *Liquidation procedures*

a. After the closing of the purchase pursuant to Sections 5.07 and 5.08 hereof, the purchasing party shall, by a legally enforceable agreement, assume the payment of any indebtedness under any lien on the Property and Improvements set forth in the Offer to the extent that the Venturers are personally liable for payment of such indebtedness.

b. Upon transfer of title to the Property and Improvements, the Venture shall be deemed dissolved if it has not by the provisions of this Agreement been previously dissolved, and the Venturers shall proceed to wind up the business and affairs of the Venture, paying all just debts and obligations and distributing the assets in accordance with the Venturers' respective distribution percentage interests at the time of transfer of title to the Property and Improvements. Upon such distribution and winding up, this Agreement shall be deemed terminated, and the parties hereto shall be relieved of all obligations hereunder except for obligations, duties, or rights that have not been determined or ascertained as of the date of such termination. During the period beginning with the first election to proceed under this section and ending with the winding up of the Venture and termination of this Agreement, the business and affairs of the Venture shall be conducted by the Nonwithdrawing Venturer if dissolution occurs pursuant to Section 5.03 or 5.04 hereof and by the Venturers jointly if dissolution occurs pursuant to Section 5.02 hereof. During such period, the business and affairs of the Venture shall be conducted so as to maintain the continuous operation thereof and preserve the assets of the Venture.

c. If, at the time of the purchase by one party of the Property and Improvements, such Property and Improvements are subject to an encumbrance other than an encumbrance listed in the offer, the purchasing party shall discharge such encumbrance and reduce the amount of the purchase price by the amount of money required to discharge such encumbrance. If the purchase price is less than the amount of all the encumbrances on the Property and Improvements, the purchaser may, at its option, cancel the purchase or conclude the transaction on terms acceptable to the purchaser, the Venture, and the holder of the encumbrance or holders of the encumbrances. In the event that the purchase is canceled by the purchaser, the terms of this Agreement shall remain in effect and continue to be binding on the parties.

ARTICLE VI
SALE, ASSIGNMENT, TRANSFER, OR OTHER DISPOSITION

Section 6.01 *Prohibited transfers*

a. Except as provided in this Article, no Venturer may sell, transfer, assign, or otherwise dispose of or mortgage, hypothecate, or otherwise encumber or permit or suffer any encumbrance of all or any part of his or her interest in the Venture unless approved by the Venturers, and any attempt to so transfer or encumber any such interest shall be void.

b. Developer, any stockholder or member thereof, shall not sell, assign, transfer, or otherwise dispose of the capital stock of Developer or the partnership interest of Developer unless such sale, assignment, transfer, or other disposition is approved in advance and in writing by Company, and the issued and unissued shares of Developer's stock or Developer's partnership interest in the Agreement shall, in a legally effective manner, be made subject to this restriction.

c. Developer shall not consolidate with, merge into, or become a member of any other corporation, partnership, or other entity, or convey or transfer a substantial part of its properties or assets.

d. Developer shall promptly notify Company of any and all changes whatsoever in the ownership of its stock or of any interest in Developer or a partnership or other entity, legal or beneficial, or of any other act or transaction involving or resulting in any change in either ownership or interest or in the relative distribution thereof, or with respect to the identity of the parties in control of Developer or the degree thereof of which it or any of its officers or members have been notified or otherwise have knowledge or information.

e. Developer shall, at such time or times as Company may reasonably request, furnish Company with a complete statement, subscribed and sworn to by an officer of Developer duly authorized, setting forth all of the stockholders and members of Developer and the extent of their respective holdings, and, in the event that any other parties have a beneficial interest in such stock, their names and the extent of such interest, all as determined or indicated by the records of Developer, by specific inquiry made by said officer of all parties who, on the basis of such records, own 10 percent or more of the stock of or interest in Developer, and by such other knowledge or information as said officer shall have.

Section 6.02 *Permitted transfers—right of transferee*

a. Company shall have the right, without the consent of the other Venturer, to transfer all or any part of its interest in the Venture to an affiliated corporation, as hereinafter defined. For the purposes of this Section 6.02, an affiliated corporation shall be (i) any corporation that owns substantially all the stock of Company, and (ii) any corporation, the stock of which is all or substantially all owned by Company or Company's affiliated corporation.

b. The transferee of a part of an interest in the Venture shall become a Venturer unless the terms of the transfer expressly provide to the contrary; provided, however, that no such transferee shall have any right to participate in the management of the Venture independently of the Venturer making such transfer unless such participation is approved by the Venturers.

ARTICLE VII
GENERAL

Section 7.01 *Notices*

a. All notices, demands, or requests provided for or permitted to be given pursuant to this Agreement must be in writing. All notices, demands, and requests to be sent to Developer or any assignee of the interest of Developer hereunder pursuant hereto shall be deemed to have been properly given or served by depositing the same in the U.S. mail, addressed to Developer, postpaid and registered or certified with return receipt requested at the following address: _____

b. All notices, demands, or requests to be sent to Company or any assignee of the interest of Company hereunder pursuant hereto shall be deemed to have been properly given or served by depositing the same in the U.S. mail, addressed to Company, postpaid and registered or certified with return receipt requested at the following address: _____

c. All notices, demands, and requests shall be effective upon being deposited in the U.S. mail. However, the time period in which a response to any such notice, demand, or request must be given shall commence to run from the date of receipt on the return receipt of the notice, demand, or request by the addressee thereof. Rejection or other refusal to accept, or the inability to deliver because of changed address of which no notice was given, shall be deemed to be receipt of the notice, demand, or request sent.

d. By giving to the other parties at least 30 days' written notice thereof, the parties hereto and their respective successors and assigns shall have the right from time to time and at any time during the term of this Agreement to change their respective addresses, and each shall have the right to specify as its address any other address within the United States of America.

e. No transferee of any interest by any Venturer shall be entitled to receive a notice independent of the notice sent to the Venturer making such transfer. A notice sent or made to a Venturer shall be deemed to have been sent and made to all transferees, if any, of such Venturer.

Section 7.02 *Preferential right to purchase other lands*

If, during the term of this Venture, Developer or any party comprising Developer ("Acquiring Party") directly or indirectly acquires any interest in any one or more of the tracts or parcels of land, any part of which is located within the area of interest ("area of interest" as used herein shall mean any land situated within one mile outside any boundary of the Property), the Developer shall give notice thereof to Company and shall advise Company of all terms and conditions of such acquisition not later than 30 days after such acquisition has been consummated. Company shall have the right and option to acquire from the Acquiring Party an undivided interest equal to Company's distribution percentage interest in and to the interest so acquired by the Acquiring Party on the same terms and conditions as the terms and conditions of such acquisition. Such right and option may be exercised by giving notice thereof to the Acquiring Party and all other Venturers within 30 days of receipt of the aforesaid notice from the Acquiring Party. Failure by Company to give such notice shall constitute an election by Company not to exercise such right and option. If Company desires to exercise its preferential right and option to purchase and so notifies the Acquiring Party, Developer agrees to close the purchase of such interest before the expiration of 60 days after such election.

Section 7.03 *Governing law*

This agreement and the obligations of the Venturers hereunder shall be interpreted, construed, and enforced in accordance with the laws of the State of _____.

Section 7.04 *Fees and commissions*

a. The Venture shall pay the following fees and commissions:
_____ _____

b. Except for the commissions, fees, and expenses referred to in Section 7.04(a) hereof, Developer hereby represents and warrants to Company that there are no claims for brokerage or other commissions or finder's or other similar fees in connection with the transactions covered by this Agreement insofar as such claims shall be based on arrangements or agreements made by or on its behalf, and Developer hereby agrees to indemnify and hold harmless the Company from and against all liabilities, costs, damages, and expenses from any such claims.

Section 7.5 *Entire agreement*

This Agreement contains the entire agreement between the parties hereto relative to the formation of a Venture to develop the Property and Improvements. No variations, modifications, or changes herein or hereof shall be binding upon any party hereto unless set forth in a document duly executed by or on behalf of such party.

Section 7.06 *Waiver*

No consent or waiver, express or implied, by any Venturer to or of any breach or default by the other in the performance by the other of its obligations hereunder shall be deemed or construed to be a consent or waiver to or of any other breach or default in the performance by such other party of the same or any other obligations of such Venturer hereunder. Failure on the part of any Venturer to complain of any act or failure to act of any of the other Venturers or to declare any of the other Venturers in default, irrespective of how long such failure continues, shall not constitute a waiver of such Venturer of its rights hereunder.

Section 7.07 *Severability*

If any provision of this Agreement or the application thereof to any person or circumstance shall be invalid or unenforceable to any extent, the remainder of this Agreement and the application of such provisions to other persons or circumstances shall not be affected thereby and shall be enforced to the greatest extent permitted by law.

Section 7.08 *Status reports*

Recognizing that each party hereto may find it necessary from time to time to establish to third parties, such as accountants, banks, mortgagees, and the like, the then current status of performance hereunder, each party agrees, upon the written request of any other made from time to time, to furnish promptly a written statement (in recordable form, if requested) on the status of any matter pertaining to this Agreement to the best of the knowledge and belief of the party making such statement.

Section 7.09 *Terminology*

All personal pronouns used in this Agreement, whether used in the masculine, feminine, or neuter gender, shall include all other genders; the singular shall include the plural, and vice versa. Titles of articles and sections are for convenience only and neither limit nor amplify the provisions of the Agreement itself; and all references herein to articles, sections, or subdivisions thereof shall refer to the corresponding article, section, or subdivision thereof of this Agreement unless specified reference is made to such articles, sections, or subdivisions of another document or instrument.

Section 7.10 *Indemnity of company*

Developer agrees to indemnify and hold Company harmless from any liability to any third person incurred by reason of any acts of commission or omission or of any negligence or tortious acts by Developer or any member thereof under and by reason of this Agreement unless Company shall have approved the same in writing or participated therein. This indemnity shall not be applicable with respect to the acts of Developer duly performed in accordance with the terms and provisions of this Agreement. Subject to 30 days' prior written notice to Developer, Company shall have the right, in its sole discretion, but without being required to

Joint Venture Agreements

do so, to adjust, settle, or compromise any claim, obligation, debt, demand, suit, or judgment against Company or Developer and, in such event, the Venture, as an operating expense hereunder, shall pay over, reimburse, and make good to Company all sums of money that Company shall pay or cause to be paid or become liable to pay under or by reason of this Agreement, including any and all charges and expenses of whatsoever kind and nature in connection therewith or in connection with any litigation, investigation, or other matters in connection with such payment or payments.

Section 7.11 *Binding agreement*

Subject to the restrictions on transfers and encumbrances set forth herein, this Agreement shall inure to the benefit of and be binding upon the undersigned Venturers and their respective heirs, executors, legal representatives, successors, and assigns. Whenever in this instrument a reference to any party or Venturer is made, such reference shall be deemed to include a reference to the heirs, executors, legal representatives, successors, and assigns of such party or Venturer.

Section 7.12 *Nondiscrimination*

The Manager and the Venturers will not discriminate against any employee or applicant for employment by the Joint Venture because of race, creed, color, or national origin. The Manager and the Venturers will take affirmative action to ensure that applicants are employed and employees are treated during employment without regard to their race, creed, color, or national origin. Such action shall include but not be limited to the following: employment, upgrading, demotion, or transfer; recruitment or recruitment advertising; layoff or termination; raise of pay or other form of compensation; and selection for training, including apprenticeship. The Manager and the Venturers agree to post in conspicuous places, available to employees and applicants for employment, notices setting forth the provisions of this nondiscrimination clause.

Section 7.13 *Labor*

In connection with undertaking the construction of any Improvement on the land or in making alterations, repairs, painting, or doing any maintenance or cleaning work in the Improvement or furnishing any materials for the Improvements Manager shall use only such contractors, labor, and materials as will cause no interruption in the construction, maintenance, operation, or repair work. If Company shall notify Manager at any time that any contractors, labor, or materials used by Manager in or about the Improvements have caused any interruption or difficulty in the maintenance, operation, or repair of the Improvements, Manager shall promptly discontinue the use of any such contractor, labor, or material.

Section 7.14 *Equitable remedies*

The rights and remedies of any of the Venturers hereunder shall not be mutually exclusive, that is, the exercise of one or more of the provisions hereof shall not preclude the exercise of any other provisions hereof. Each of the Venturers confirms that damages at law may be inadequate remedies for a breach or threatened breach of this Agreement and agrees that, in the event of a breach or threatened breach thereof, the respective rights and obligations hereunder shall be enforceably by specific performance, injunction, or other equitable remedy, but nothing herein contained is intended to nor shall it limit or affect any rights or rights at law or by statute or otherwise of any party aggrieved as against the other for a breach or threatened breach of any provision hereof, it being the intention of this paragraph to make clear the agreement of the Venturers that the respective rights and obligations of the Venturers hereunder shall be enforceable in equity as well as at law or otherwise.

In witness whereof, this Agreement is executed effective as of the date first set forth above.

By_____

Developer

By_____

Company

Index

A

Accelerated versus Straight Line Depreciation, 82
Accounting Problems: Joint Venture, 92
Accrual Method: Tax Benefits, 71, 73
Admission of New Limited Partners: Tax Impact, 79
Agreement of General Partnership: Form, 186
Agreement of General Partnership: Form: Discussion, 186
Agreement of Joint Venture: Form, 233
Agreement of Joint Venture Favoring Developer: Form, 236
Agreement of Joint Venture Favoring Investor: Form, 254
Agreement of Limited Partnership: Form, 167
Anti-Churning Rules, 83
Appreciation, Effect on Return, 60

B

Broker-Dealer Sell Sheet: Form:
    Commissions, 146
    Contract of Sale, Summary, 148
    Credit Rating of Tenants, 145
    Description of Operating Leases, 144
    Description of Parties, 146
    Description of Underlying Senior Mortgage, 149
    Highlights, 140
    Income and Expense Projections, 154

Broker-Dealer Sell Sheet (cont.)
    Income and Expense Projections, Including Percentage Rents, 162
    Investment Summary Projections: 50% Tax Bracket, 156
    Key Sales Considerations, 144
    Legal Opinion, 145
    MAI Appraisal, 146
    Managing General Partner, 145
    Operating Leases, Description, 149
    Partnership Accountants, 146
    Prohibition against Circulation, 141
    Projected Cash Flow, 152
    Projected Cash Flow and Benefits, 158, 160
    Projections: Assumptions, 150
    Projection of Reinvestment Returns, 166
    Property Description, 143
    Structuring the Transaction, 147
    Suitability Standards, 142
    Syndicator Leaseback Arrangement, 149
    Syndicator Leaseback Summary, 147
    Tax Benefits, 145
    Tax Benefits Summary, 143
    Wraparound Mortgage, Discussion, 148
    Write-Off Summary, 145
Building versus Land: Depreciation, 68

C

Cash Distribution Problem: Joint Venture, 94
Cash Flow: Impact on Return, 59
Cash versus Accrual Accounting, 73

Index

Centralization of Management: Tax Problems, 31, 35
Checklist: Joint Venture, 229
Checklist: Syndication, 109
Component Depreciation, 82
Computer Calculations, 56
Construction Period: Deducting Taxes and Interest, 84
Continuity: Tax Problems, 31, 35
Contributions of Partners: Joint Venture, 93
Corporation Taxes: Eliminating Them, 27
Corporation versus Partnership, 29

D

Deposits on Contract, 4
Depreciation Changes: ERTA, 81, 82
Depreciation: Component, 82
Depreciation and Leverage, 65, 66
Depreciation: Recapture of Prior to 1981 Deductions, 80
Depreciation Rules·
  ACRS, 80
  Anti-Churning Rules, 83
  Post 1981 (ERTA), 80
  Use of Straight Line, 80
Discounted Cash Flow, Computation of, 61
Disclosing Facts: Joint Venture, 93
Disclosure: SEC, 99
Dissenters: General Partnership, 39
Dummies or Nominees, 48, 49

E

Encyclopedia of Forms, 107
Expertise: Real Estate, 3

F

Forms: Simplifying the Maze, xii
"Free Lease": Syndication Technique, 6
"Free Piece": Subordination of Equity, 18
"Free Piece": as a Syndication Technique, 16

G

General Partner: Rights and Duties, 94
General Partnership:
  Dissenters, 39
  Investors' Voting Rights, 37
  Liability Problems, 38
  Management Problems, 38
  Mortgage Refinancing, 37
  Mortgage and Sales Problems, 37

General Partnership Agreement:
  Form, 186
  Agency (Form), 187
  Arbitration Clause (Form), 189
  Centralized Management, 36
  Consent on Sale (Form), 187, 188
  Discussion of Technique, 36
  Discussion (Form), 186
  Escrow of Quitclaim Deed (Form), 188
  Removal of Agent (Form), 188
  Transferability of Interests (Form), 188
General Partnership versus Limited Partnership, 39
Guide 5 (SEC): Form:
  Compensation of General Partner, 193
  Compensation to Syndicator, 215
  Completed Programs; Summary of Results, 219
  Conflicts of Interest, 194
  Deductibility of Expenses, 204
  Depreciation Recapture, 203
  Description of Real Estate Investment, 201
  Description of Units, 207
  Federal Taxes, 202
  Fiduciary Responsibility, 195
  Financial Reports to Partners, 206
  IRS Rulings, 211
  Investment Objectives, 201
  Management Disclosures, 200
  Narrative Summary, 199
  Plan of Distribution, 208
  Preparation of Cover Page, 190
  Preparation of Limited Partnership Registration, 190
  Prior Performance, 214
  Prior Performance of General Partner, 198
  Prior Program's Operating Results, 217
  Real Estate Investments, Description, 201
  Redemption and Repurchase, 207
  Risk Factors, 196
  Sale of Partnership Interest, 204
  Sale of Partnership Property, 205
  Sales or Other Disposition of Prior Properties, 220
  SEC Regulations, 190
  Suitability Standards, 191
  Summary of Partnership Agreement, 206
  Summary of Promotional and Sales Material, 208
  Tax Liability in Later Years, 204
  Tax Returns, 205
  Termination of Partnership, 205
  Track Record, 214
  Track Record of General Partner, 198
  Undertakings and Guarantees, 210

Index

Guide 5 (SEC) (*cont.*)
  Use of Proceeds, 192
  Use of Proceeds Section, Summary, 212

I

Installment Payments, 67
Interest versus Mortgage Amortization, 68
Internal Rate of Return: Computation of, 61
Intrastate Exemption: SEC, 100
Investment Interest Rules, 84
Investment Interest: Tax Trap, 83
Investor Installments, 67
Investor Sophistication, 102
Investor Suitability Standards: Form:
  Discussion, 137
  Representation, Purchase for own Account, 138
  Net Worth, Lack of Liquidity, Income, and Tax Bracket, 138
Investors' Voting Rights: General Partnership, 37

J

Joint Venture:
  Accounting Problems, 92
  Cash Distribution Problems, 94
  Checklist, 229
  Contributions, 93
  Disclosure, 93
  Management Problems, 95
  Organization, 91
  Partnership Changes, 95
  Rights and Duties of General Partner, 94
  Sales Parameters, 97
  Short Form, 90
  Tax Problems, 91
  Term, 92
  Withdrawals, 93
Joint Venturing: Getting Started, 25
Joint Ventures, x, 89
Joint Ventures: Locating Prospects, 89
Joint Venture Agreement, Discussion, 92
  Form, 233
Joint Venture Agreement Favoring Developer:
  Form, 236
  Amendments, 253
  Arbitration, 252
  Capital, 237
  Capital Contributions and Loans, 239
  Cash Distributions, 241
  Character of Business, 237
  Counterpart Execution, 253
  Discussion, 233

Joint Venture Agreement Favoring Developer (*cont.*)
  Dissolution of Partnership, 247
  Duties of General Partners, 238
  Exculpatory Clause, General Partner, 245
  Form of Vehicle, 236
  General Partner's Right to Hire, 244
  General Partner's Rights and Powers, 243
  Limitations on Limited Partners, 245
  Limited Partner's Transferability, 245
  Management, 242
  Name of Entity, 237
  Personal Liability, 250
  Power of Attorney, 252
  Tax Aspects, 242
  Term, 237
Joint Venture Agreement Favoring Investor.
  Form, 254
  Accounting, 268
  Accounting and Distribution, 265
  Appraisal Procedure, 273
  Automatic Termination, 269
  Bank Accounts, 269
  Books of Account, 269
  Budgets, 262
  Buy and Sell Procedures, 272
  Compensation of Venturers, 262
  Contracts with Related Parties, 263
  Developer's Indemnity, 280
  Entire Agreement, 279
  Equitable Remedies, 282
  Fees and Commissions, 279
  Governing Law, 279
  Improvement and Capital Budgets, 258
  Insurance Requirements, 263
  Interest Income, Profits, and Allocations, 265
  "Major Decisions," 257
  Manager's Duties, 259
  Manager's Right to Employ, 261
  Management, 257
  Nondiscrimination, 281
  Notices to Parties, 277
  Partnership Formation, 255
  Permitted Transfers, 277
  Preferential Right to Purchase Other Properties, 278
  Prohibited Transfers, 276
  Replacement of Manager, 259
  Sale or Assignment, 276
  Scope of Venture, 256
  Severability, 280
  Term of Agreement, 269
  Termination on Default, 270
  Trade Name Certificate, 256
  Transfer or Other Disposition, 276

Joint Venture Agreement Favoring Investor (*cont.*)
  Unaudited Statements, 268
  Voluntary Termination, 269
  Waiver, 279

L

Land versus Building, 68
Lease:
  Buyout, 10
  Refinancing, 10
  versus Piece, 18
Leaseback:
  Delaying Rent, 12
  Syndicator's Option to Purchase, 12
  Valuation, 13
  When Does Rent Start, 11
Leverage and Depreciation, 65, 66
Leveraging: Effect on Returns, 57
Liability Problem: General Partnership, 38
Limited Liability: Tax Problems 37
Limited Partners:
  Admission of New Ones, 79
  Ratification, 96
Limited Partnership Agreement: Form, 167
  Accounting Matters, 181
  Admission of Additional Limited Partners, 176
  Advances by Partners, 180
  Applicable Law, 185
  Arbitration, 183
  Assignability of Limited Partner's Interest, 180
  Assignment of General Partner's Interest, 179
  Bank Accounts, 182
  Capital Contributions, 168
  Capital Contributions, 174
  Continuity, 35
  Contributions in Cash of Property by General Partner, 176
  Discussion of Form, 167
  Distribution of Net Proceeds of Borrowings, 171
  Distribution of Proceeds on Sale, 172
  Gains in Earnings Account, 171
  General Partner, 176
  General Partner's Bankruptcy, 179
  Interest on Capital Contributions, 181
  Limited Partners' Control, 180
  Limited Partner's Death, 180
  Limited Partner: Withdrawal, 180
  Net Profit Allocations, 169
  Oral Modification, 184
  Partners' Distributions and Allocations, 168

Limited Partnership Agreement (*cont.*)
  Power of Attorney, 184
  Purpose Clause, 168
  Self-Dealing, 177, 178
  Term of Agreement, 168
  Termination on Dissolution, 182
  Transferability, 35
  Unit Value Determination, 170
Limited Partnership Agreements: Discussion, 34
Limited Partnership versus General Partnership, 39

M

Management Problems:
  General Partnership, 38
  Joint Venture, 95
Mortgage Amortization, 68
  Impact on Return, 60
Mortgage Refinancing, 11
  General Partnership, 37
Mortgage and Sales Problems: General Partnership, 37
Mortgage: Wraparound, 69, 70

N

Net Lease "Trap," 85
Nominees or Dummies, 48, 49

O

Offeree Questionnaire: Form, 125
  Assumption of Economic Risks, 127
  Representations re Education Experience and Tax Bracket, 128
  Representations re Income, 129
  Representations re Investment Experience, 129
  Representations re Net Worth, 129
  Representations re Prior Investments, 130
Offerees: Number, 101

P

Partnership Changes: Joint Venture, 95
Partnership versus Corporation, 29
Personal Liability of Partners: Tax Trap, 78
Private Offering: Sample Table of Contents (Form), 223
Private Offering Guidelines, 103, 104
Private Offering Tests, 102
Private Placement Exemption, 101
Profit on Syndication, 14, 15
Prospectus. Contents 104

Index

Purchaser Representative Questionnaire: Form. 132
   Disclosures as to Representative's Compensation, 135
   Representations as to Knowledge of Private Placement Memorandum, 135
   Representative's Length of Acquaintance with Purchaser, 134
   Representation as to Nonconflicting Position, 135
   Representations as to Representative's Knowledge, Experience and Occupation, 133

R

Real Estate Investment Trusts, 49
   Equity versus Mortgage, 52
   Tax Elections, 51
Regulation D Guidelines, 103, 104
Regulation D Offering: Form:
   Investor Suitability, 137
   Prospect Questionnaire, 125
   Purchaser Representative Questionnaire, 132
   Sample Table of Contents, 223
REIT, 49
Returns on Investment, 55
   Calculations, 56, 62
   Leveraging, 57
   Real Estate versus Other Investments, 62

S

Safe Harbor Rules: Partnerships, 39
Sale of Partnership Interest, 79
Sales Literature: Broker-Dealer Summary, 141
SEC:
   Disclosure, 99
   Intrastate Exemption, 100
   Number of Offerees, 101
SEC Regulations: Guide 5: Form, 190
Section 754 Election, 78
"Sell Sheet": Broker-Dealer: Form, 140
Selling Syndication Units, 24
Smaller Transactions, 4
Subchapter S Corporations, 46
Subscription Agreement: Form, 112
   Assignability, 123
   Appointment of Attorney-in-Fact, 121
   Availability of Documents, 120
   Indemnification, 120
   Limited Partnership Form, 113
   Non-Public Offering, 119

Subscription Agreement (cont.)
   Nontransferability, 122
   Subscriber's Representations, 115
   Termination, 122
Syndicate Vehicles:
   Joint Ventures, 43
   Tenancies in Common, 43
   Thin Corporations, 44
   Trusts, 43, 44
Syndicator:
   As an Investor, 16
   Up Front Profit, 14, 15
Syndicator's Penalties, 86
Syndication:
   Amount to be Raised, 14
   Checklist, 109
   Getting Started, 25
   Kinds of Real Estate for Syndication, 23
   Public versus Private Offerings, 22
   Summary, 21
   Taking Apart Actual Deals, 22
   Tax Traps: Avoiding Them, 33
   Why Do It, x
Syndication Vehicles:
   Types of, 32
   Which Type, 53

T

Tax Angles, 63
Tax Basis:
   Individual Partner's, 78
   Practical Tips, 77
Tax Know-How, 65
Tax Loss Deals: Vehicle, 28
Tax Problems:
   Continuity, 31, 35
   Limited Liability, 31
   Transferability, 30, 35
Tax Savings: Impact on Return, 59
Tax Shelter: Value, 64
Tax Shelter Penalties, 86
   Fines, 87
   Third Parties, 87
Tax Structuring, 75
Tax Trap:
   The Association, 29
   Corporate, 29, 45
   Mortgage Basis, 76
   Personal Liability, 78
Techniques of Syndicating, 5
   Lease: Escape for Syndicator, 9
   Frauds, 8

Techniques of Syndicating (*cont.*)
   "Free" Lease, 6
   "Free Piece" of the Deal, 16
   Return to Investors, 7
   Syndicator's Liability on Lease, 7
Thin Corporations, 45
Time Value of Money, 57
Transferability: Tax Problems, 30, 35

V

Vehicle: Business Requirements, 28

W

Withdrawal of Partners: Joint Venture, 93
Wraparound Mortgage, 19, 69, 70